IMAGES
of America

FUN PIER
1957 TO ADVENTURE PIER

On the Cover: Three iconic rides are pictured here in the summer of 1967. At that time, Fun Pier was under the sharp management of Joseph L. Barnes—always a consummate professional—and his family. The Fun Pier monorail was in top shape, providing a view of the beautiful Wildwood Beaches and ocean. (Courtesy Ellen Fried.)

IMAGES
of America

FUN PIER
1957 TO ADVENTURE PIER

Scott Hand and Diane Pooler

ARCADIA
PUBLISHING

ISBN 978-0-7385-7693-0

Published by Arcadia Publishing
Charleston, South Carolina

Printed in the United States of America

Library of Congress Control Number: 2011942700

For all general information, please contact Arcadia Publishing:
Telephone 843-853-2070
Fax 843-853-0044
E-mail sales@arcadiapublishing.com
For customer service and orders:
Toll-Free 1-888-313-2665

Visit us on the Internet at www.arcadiapublishing.com

We would like to dedicate this book to the late Joseph L. Barnes, founder of Fun Pier. Had it not been for Barnes, there may never have been a Fun Pier in Wildwood, New Jersey. Also, to the Barnes family and the former Fun Pier Gang for all their support during the production of this book.

Contents

FOREWORD

My father, Joseph L. Barnes Sr., was a clever, well-respected man in the amusement field. He had been renting Fun Pier for 10 years when he learned that Robert M. Dare, the pier's owner, sold it to the Konidas family and Wyoming Properties. They went to court, and the judge ruled in my father's favor. The Konidas family sold the pier to my father within weeks.

Despite political opposition at the time, Joseph Barnes organized other New Jersey businessmen in support of the game-of-chance industry. Through his entrepreneurial skills, Joseph was able to strategically place games of chance so as to entice visitors from cities such as Baltimore and Philadelphia. This proved to be the embryonic beginning of the Fun Pier empire.

Later, Bill Howard, who some called a "real carnie," set up additional games of chance while importing off-season carnival rides from around the country each summer season, as well as establishing a Kiddieland—a collection of rides geared toward small children—and other amusements owned by Joseph, a partner of ours named Ed Mullin Jr., my brother Pete, and me.

Some time around 1972, Tennessee native J.D. Floyd proposed that he rent pier space for his amusements. This served to improve the overall quality of the pier, as J.D. Floyd always had the most popular rides.

At the end of the summer of 1976, my father entered into an agreement of sale with Bill Howard, but the fires of 1984 left both the pier and my father ready for a change. Dad explained to Bill Howard that they had to do something, and the decision followed to sell the pier to Morey's.

That era, from the earliest efforts until the pier was ultimately sold, was a wonderful time to be a part of the amusement industry in Wildwood. The work was often hard, the sun was often hot, and nights often ran into days. However, those memories continue to enrich my life, and it is my hope that this book will enrich yours.

—Jay Barnes

Acknowledgments

As this book goes to print, it will be more than a quarter-century since Fun Pier drifted into history. This amusement pier was very much a unique entertainment center, with many colorful characters and attractions. The majority of photographs used in this book come courtesy of former Fun Pier employees, known affectionately as the "Fun Pier Gang." While we could never write or say enough about their help and support, we felt it was necessary to highlight a few. We would like to begin by saying thank you to those who helped start this project and motivated us to soldier on.

We sincerely appreciate the support, direction, and enthusiasm of Arthur "Artie" Fiala and his family, especially his daughters Debbie Fiala-Davis, Cyndi Fiala-Taylor, and Patti Fiala. Debbie's extensive photograph collection, along with Artie's great memories, helped make us feel like we were there with them the whole time on Fun Pier.

Without the help, cooperation, and support of the former Fun Pier Gang, this book would not have been possible, including Jay Barnes, Jack Seddon, Wayne Seddon, Larry Mosher, Angelo Quisito, Stephen "Trooper" Armstrong, Lee Durland, Gary Ross, Albert Butler, Ron Mathis, Jeff Laird, Mike Bailey, Peter and Kathy Savard, Sheila Rubin, Jim Pietrowski, Bob Brewster, and Martin Morley.

We would also like to thank Kirk Hastings, president of the Wildwood Crest Historical Society, who also worked for Fun Pier; David and Theresa Williams, also of the Wildwood Crest Historical Society; Anne Vinci, president of the Wildwood Historical Society; Jim Abbate of the National Amusement Park Historical Association; Ellen Fried for her help and photographs from her late father Herb Fried's collection; Steve Oxenrider; Paul Dare; Jim DeMusz; Carl DeMusz; Bob Lee; Sonny Evans; Lindsey Young, formerly of Morey's Piers; and Richard Ramagosa.

Scott Hand would like to thank his mother, Sally Hand; grandmother Lorraine Hand; aunt Pat; aunt Anna Harris, who was a great Wildwood historian; the Delli-Paoli family; and especially Abby Henry of Arcadia Publishing.

Diane Pooler would like to thank her parents, Audrey and Michael Pooler, but most of all her grandmother Lillian Kay, who took her to the Wildwood Boardwalk every year.

INTRODUCTION

When dreams come true, it is usually because someone had a vision and found a way to make it happen either by hard work and determination or by happenstance. Sometimes it takes a little bit of both.

—Robert C. Brewster

It was 1957, America was living the real "Happy Days," and only bright skies and sunny days lay ahead. It was a golden age. People were watching Westerns on television, and the phenomenon called Elvis had the music world "all shook up." In 1957, Hunt's Pier, Marine Pier, Playland, and Casino Arcade were up and running. Local businessman Joe Barnes, along with a couple of partners, decided to extend the now very successful boardwalk, which then stopped at the original Wildwood Convention Hall that he was already renting as an entertainment venue, and extend it into Wildwood Crest, where there was still room for economic development and expansion. Wildwood Beach extends from North Wildwood to Wildwood Crest and is 7.4 miles long, though it is referred to and is well known as the "five-mile island." Most people believed that the extended boardwalk would be good for the local economy, while others alleged it would destroy the tranquil and serene environment of the Crest. Regardless, Wildwood was quickly becoming the summer destination of choice for families up and down the East Coast, thanks to the new Garden State Parkway.

Bob Brewster first arrived on the scene in 1968, when he spent two weeks camping with family and friends at the Wildwood campgrounds and fell in love with the place that was soon becoming a mecca for Canadian tourists, especially those from Quebec. The next year, Brewster arrived in Wildwood in early June. It was the East Coast's "Summer of Love," though most did not know it yet. It would also be the summer of a lot of other incredible firsts, including the first moon landing and Woodstock. The Manson murders and the Stonewall riots occurred as Timothy Leary and his friends were "tripping" across America. The Who released *Tommy*—the first rock opera—the last original episode of *Star Trek* aired on NBC, Joe Namath briefly retired from the NFL, the war raged on in Vietnam, and the Beatles' "Get Back" was at the top of the pop charts. When Brewster was 19 years old and his whole life was in front of him, he had no way of knowing that he was living in a very pivotal moment in the history of mankind. That was the reality of 1969.

That summer, Bob Brewster worked for a couple of weeks on Hunt's Pier and spent a couple more on Morey's before ending up at the place that he would call home for the next five years. Fun Pier! Where you could have your cake and eat it too! Brewster ended up working for Bill and Helen Howard at the bushel basket game at the front of the pier for the first four summers, then he was banished to the back of the newly extended Fun Pier, working the Break a Plate game during his last full summer on the pier in 1973. There are so many fond memories of those formative years, not just for Bob, but also for a whole generation and a nation. The world was changing. Attitudes and mores were shifting rapidly. There was a generational shift going on, and most people never saw it coming.

What he remembers the most about his time spent on Fun Pier was the people . . . very special people, including "Papa" Joe Barnes, who he remembers smiling all the time. Recently, Brewster found out that Barnes had finally gained sole possession of Fun Pier in 1969, explaining that wide, eternal grin he always wore on his face. Then there was "Big" Pete and "Little" Jay Barnes, along with "Shorty" Franchville and, of course, Peggy and Eddie Franchville and eventually "Little" Pete Franchville. There was never any shortage of laughter and family drama on the pier, because that is what they all felt like—one big dysfunctional family— and Bob Brewster means that in the nicest sense of the word. It is hard to explain it, but the best analogy that he can think of is that people worked on other piers or along the boardwalk while people lived on Fun Pier and considered it home. Brewster remembers opening the bushel basket game every weekday at noon as he listened to Paul Harvey and Howard Cosell expounding their wisdom on WABC as it was piped through the pier's public address system. He remembers frantic Saturdays where he opened two hours earlier and usually closed well past midnight. It was like being invaded with a tidal wave of people every weekend.

The Sky Tower and the monorail were the two rides that appealed to Bob the most, for various different reasons. Escaping the frenzy on the pier for a few precious moments and being able to look down upon it and then out at the usually friendly ocean was an experience that never failed to excite him and also cleanse him with a wave of peace and serenity at the same time. Oh, those hazy, crazy, lazy Wildwood days and nights. They will always live forever in the hearts and souls of those who lived it.

One

Where the Fun Began

In 1924, the Holly Beach Realty Company purchased a sizeable parcel of land on the Atlantic Ocean in the small summer resort city of Wildwood, New Jersey, from the Goldstein family with plans to build a privately owned convention hall at the location. The City of Wildwood became a tenant of the property but struggled financially during the Depression and defaulted on the lease.

By 1957, after years of leasing out Convention Hall Pier to various vendors, Holly Beach Realty entered into a long-term lease with Joseph Barnes, a man who had gained respect in the amusement business at Willow Grove Park, just outside Philadelphia, Pennsylvania. Over the next several years, Barnes enlisted amusement designer Alan Hawes to install unique rides on what was by then known as Fun Pier. Three of Hawes's rides became iconic of the pier: the Ski Ride, the monorail, and Sky Tower. These one-of-a-kind attractions on the Wildwood Boardwalk made Joe Barnes and Alan Hawes very wealthy men. The construction of the monorail ride signaled the end for the Convention Hall building, however, as it was decided that the structure would be in the way and should be demolished to make room for the track supports. Hawes's company, Universal Design, Ltd., also installed a "dark ride" on Fun Pier known initially as Batcave, then renamed Tiki Train, and while in this incarnation, it too became iconic of Fun Pier, known especially for a huge gorilla at the front of the ride, a figure that remained on the pier for years through its many changes. By 1969, the dark ride was renamed Devil's Inn.

On December 21, 1966, Holly Beach Realty attempted to sell Fun Pier to Wyoming Properties. When news of this reached Joe Barnes, he challenged the sale with a lawsuit. He had been solely responsible for the pier's rapid growth and major development during the previous 10 years, and in the end, the court sided with Barnes and granted him the right to purchase Fun Pier early in 1969.

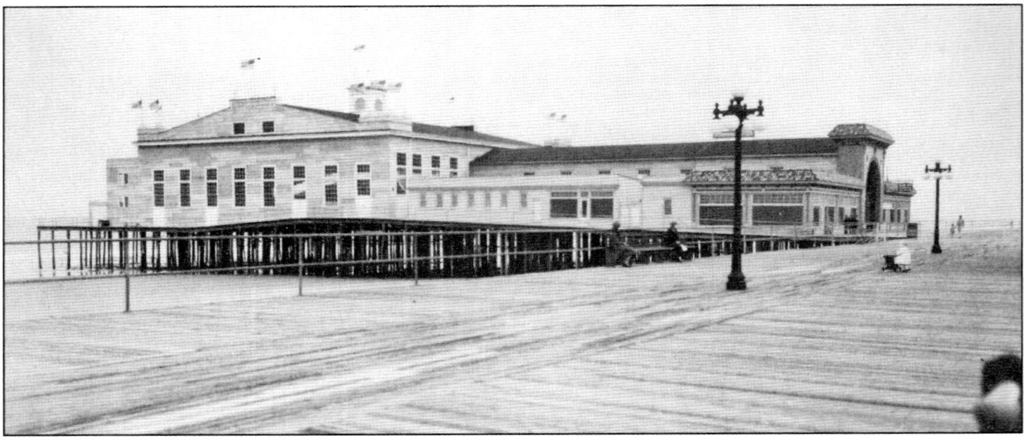

C.J. Scully & Son were awarded the contract to build Convention Hall. The $500,000 project is pictured here shortly after its completion, around August 1, 1927. Early advertisements boasted an auditorium that seated 5,000 people. The facility would host popular bands of the era, with performances every afternoon and evening during the summer season. On July 4, 1947, the wooden platform on the pier collapsed, injuring several people and leading to a lawsuit against the pier's owner, the Holly Beach Realty Company. The building was later used to promote sporting events, such as wrestling. In 1957, Joe Barnes acquired a long-term lease on the property, and Fun Pier was born. (Courtesy Wildwood Historical Society.)

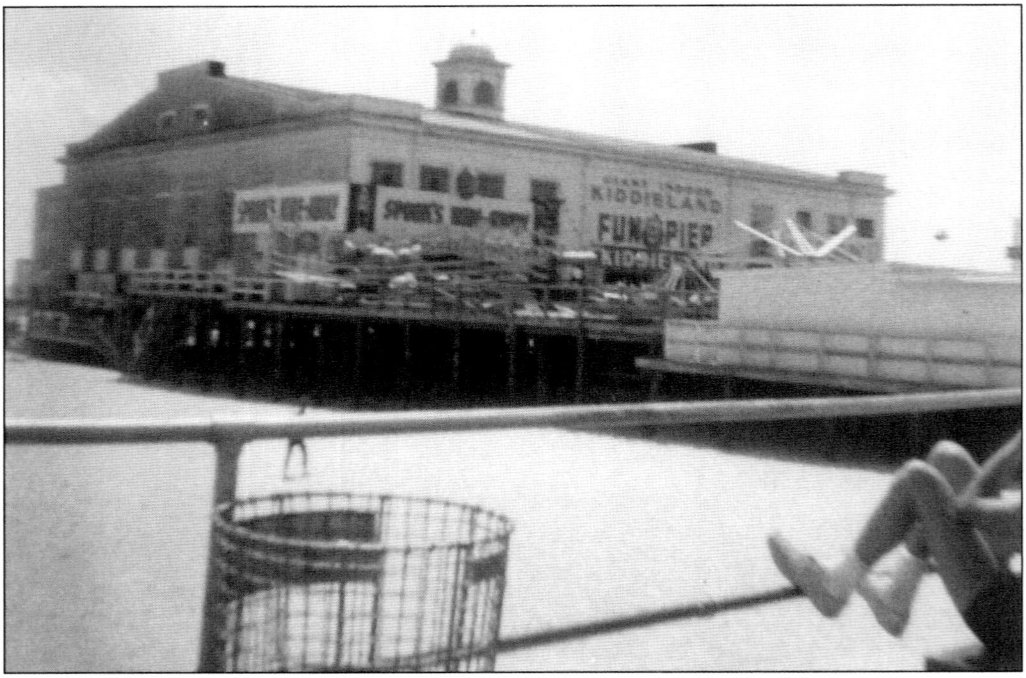

Joe Barnes started Fun Pier by introducing a series of children's rides and called the new amusement center Kiddieland. Joe Barnes had many connections in the carnival industry, and through those connections, he was able to get the popular rides for his new amusement pier. In addition, Barnes built a new dark ride, Spook's Hide-Away, which was enclosed in the original Wildwood Convention Hall. The building also served as housing for the pier's employees. During its first few years, Fun Pier also featured rides such as a Wild Mouse roller coaster, a Ferris wheel, and a miniature golf course. (Courtesy Steve Oxenrider.)

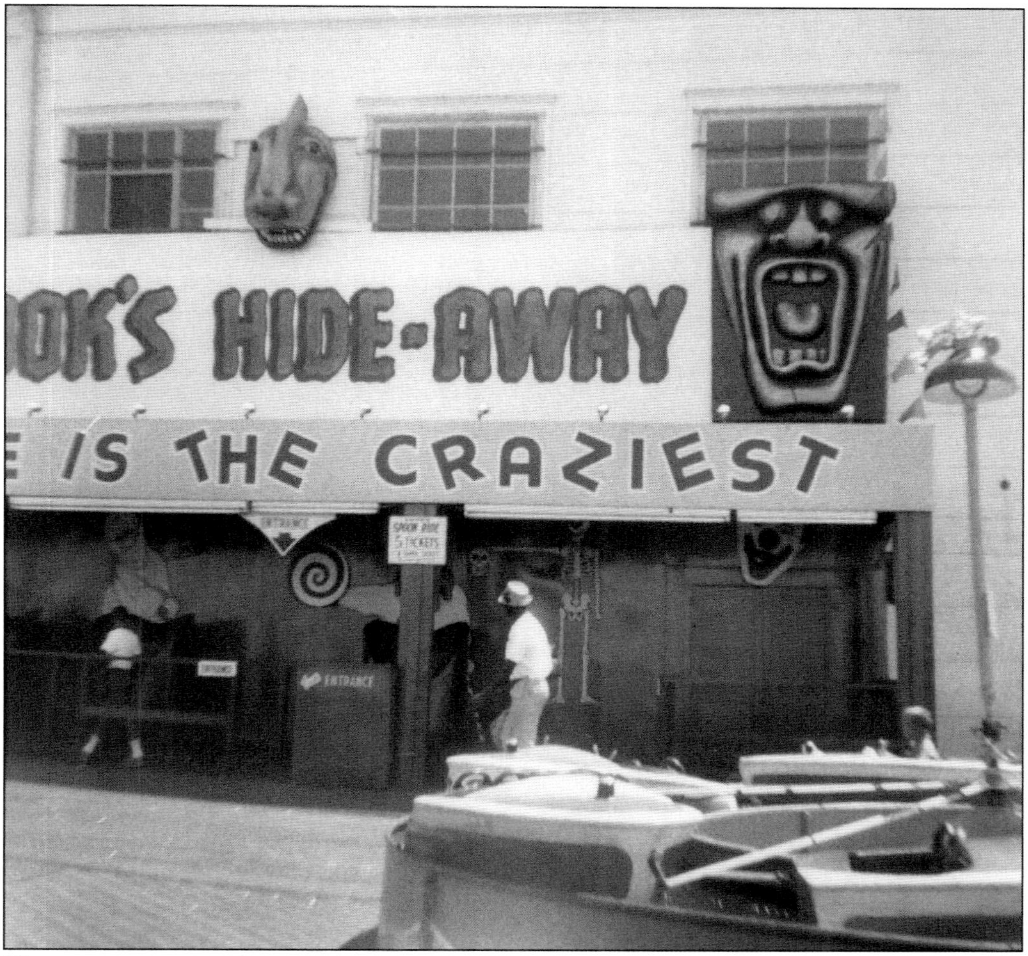

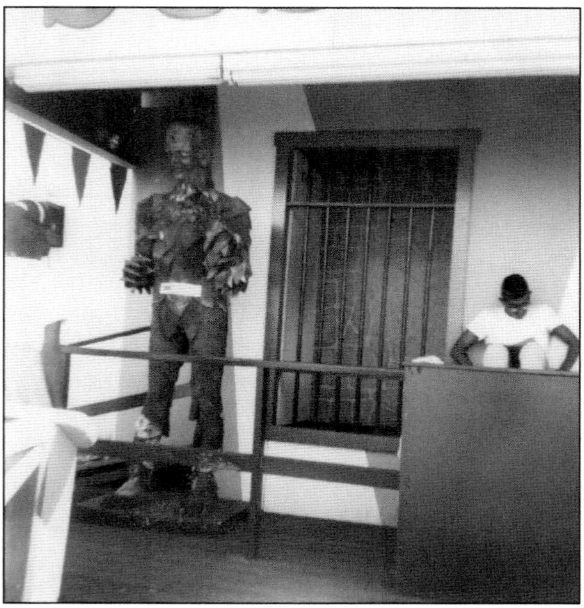

These are some rare photographs of the Spook's Hide-Away loading station. The cars for the ride were known as pretzel cars and were among the first cars to pivot, swinging the rider left to right into a certain scene inside the ride. Frankenstein seems to have been popular with the managers of the pier. This dark ride was known as a horror fun house. The patrons would ride through the dark while encountering a few scenes accompanied by sounds. Spook's Hide-Away remained on Fun Pier until the construction of the monorail. As the monorail was meant to take its passengers out over the ocean, Spook's Hide-Away had to be demolished to make that accommodation. (Both, courtesy Steve Oxenrider.)

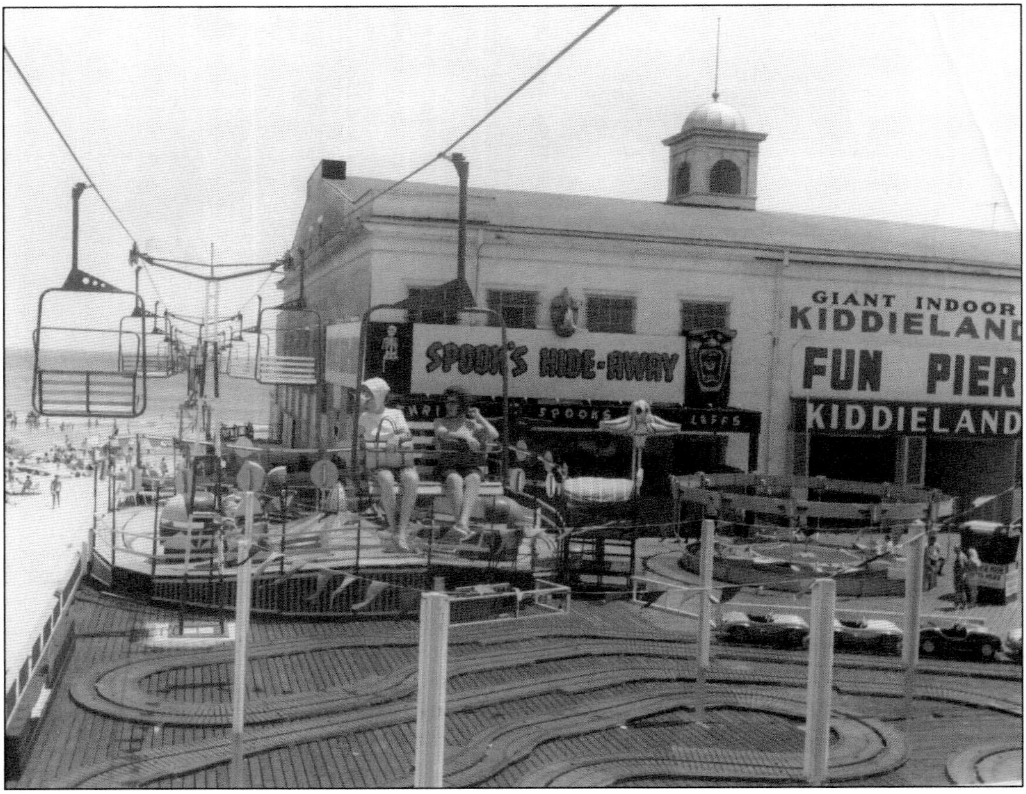

Patrons enjoy a ride on the ski lift, which overlooks the many attractions on the pier. The Spook's Hide-Away dark ride and the Fun Pier Kiddieland utilized one of the original Wildwood Convention Hall buildings. The first set of chairs for the Ski Ride had wooden planks, while in later years, the chairs were made of fiberglass. (Courtesy Wildwood Historical Society.)

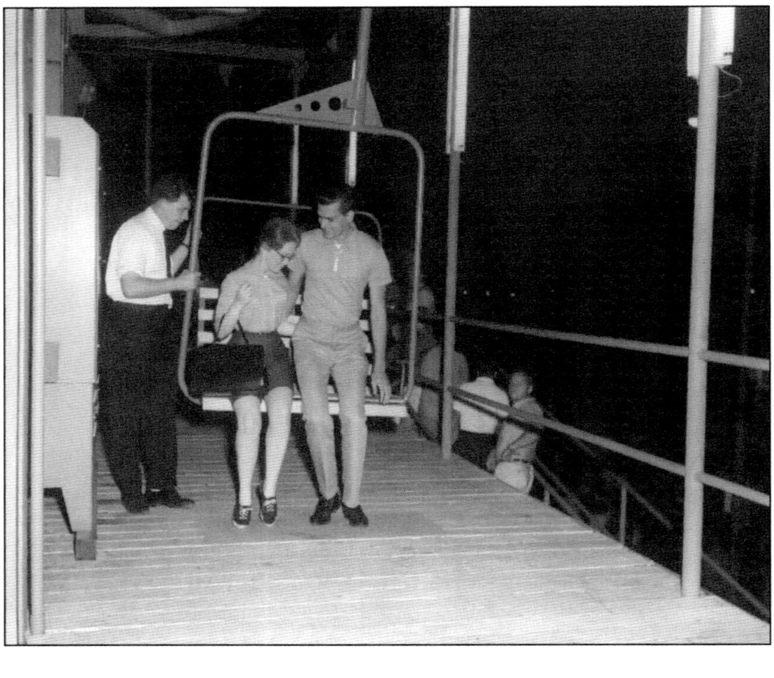

Pictured here is the loading station for the Ski Ride, which was popular all the way to the end of its term on Fun Pier. It was the first ride designed by the late Alan Hawes. Today, Morey's Piers offers patrons a much taller version of this ride, which now sits on the southern side of the pier. (Courtesy Wildwood Historical Society.)

During the early years, the Ski Ride would take its riders right over the ocean. Those who rode the Ski Ride could enjoy the beauty of Wildwood Beach and the atmosphere of Fun Pier. In later years, as the ocean moved farther out, the pier was extended. No longer would patrons be able to ride right over the ocean. (Courtesy Wildwood Historical Society.)

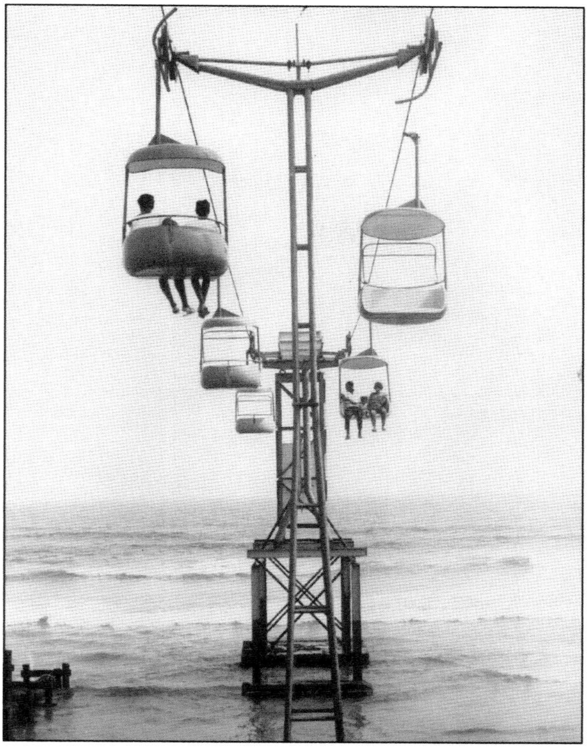

This is the Ski Ride in its early years of operation. Alan Hawes had been the master designer for many of the rides on Fun Pier. The Ski Ride was the first big attraction that made Fun Pier special. Joe Barnes and Alan Hawes became good friends and would continue to collaborate on new rides that would keep Fun Pier special. (Courtesy Wildwood Historical Society.)

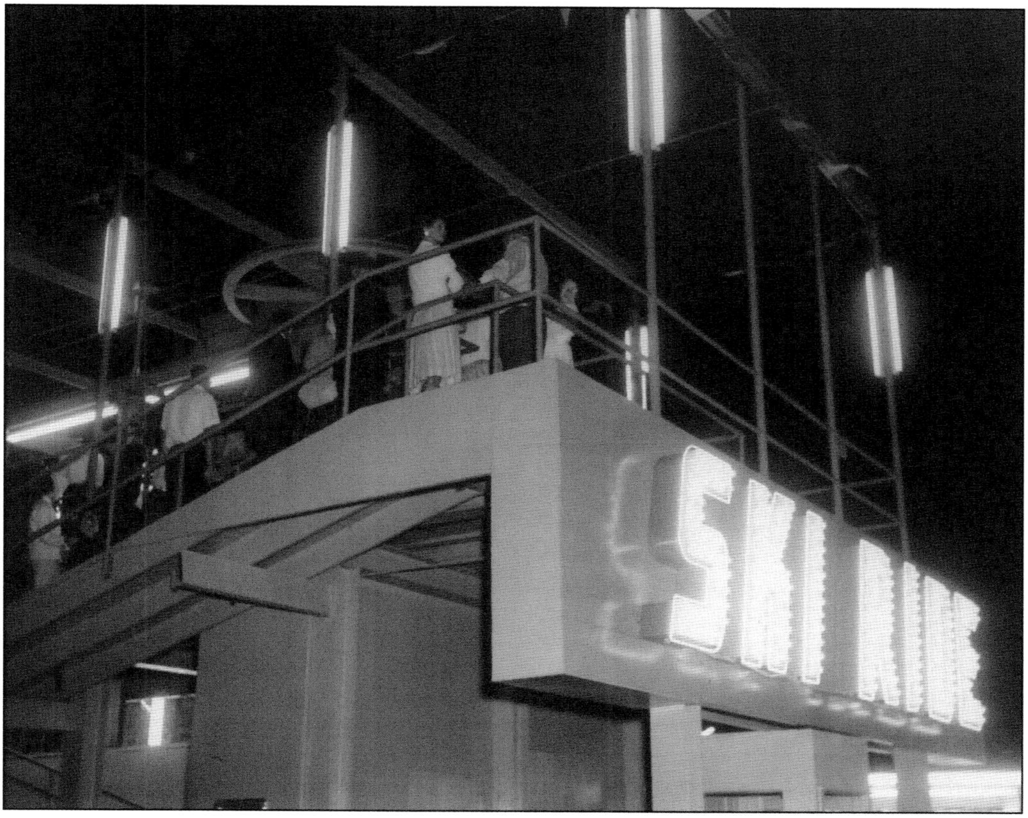

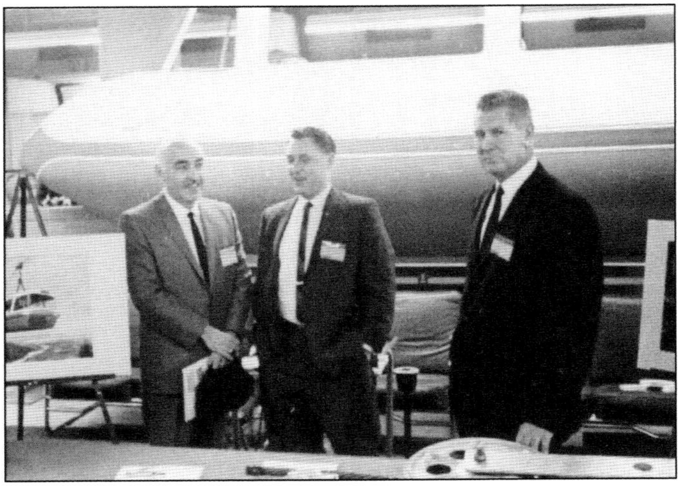

Joseph Barnes (left) and Alan Hawes (center) are pictured here inside Universal Design, Ltd., at the Cape May County Airport. Note the monorail in the background, undergoing final inspection. Hawes continued to operate Universal Design for many years. In fact, he set up a monorail at the Cape May County Airport as a promotion to sell monorails to other amusement parks. (Courtesy Scott Hand.)

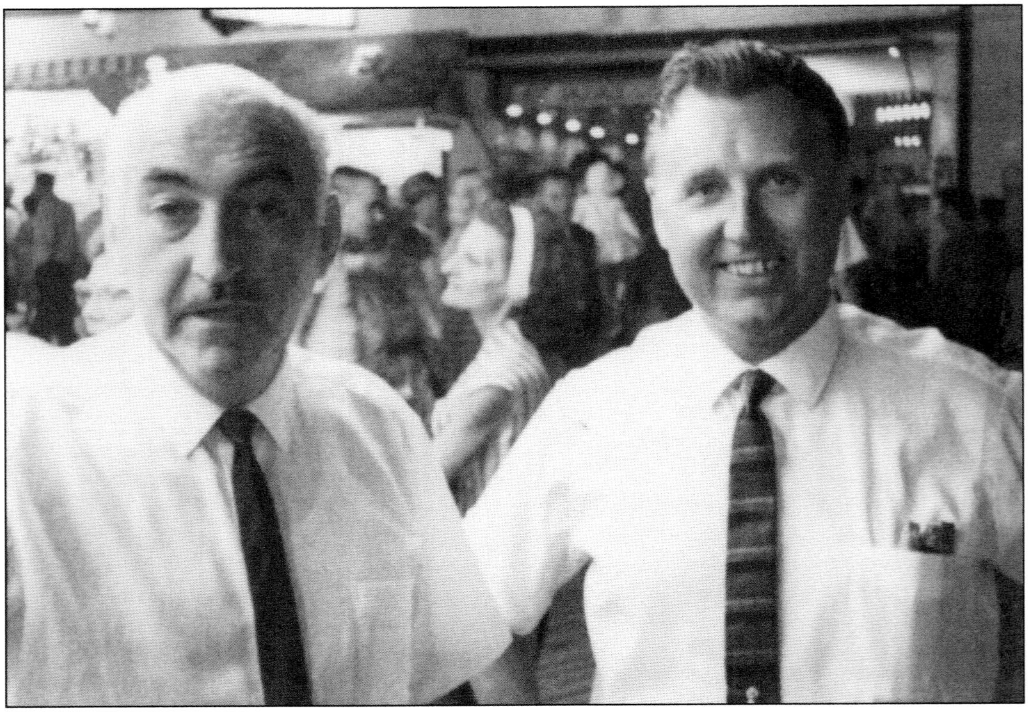

Joe Barnes (left) and Alan Hawes are pictured at a trade show. They were the best of friends: Hawes made millions by starting his enterprise on Barnes's Fun Pier, and Barnes made millions from Hawes's iconic attractions that drew the attention of many customers. (Courtesy Scott Hand.)

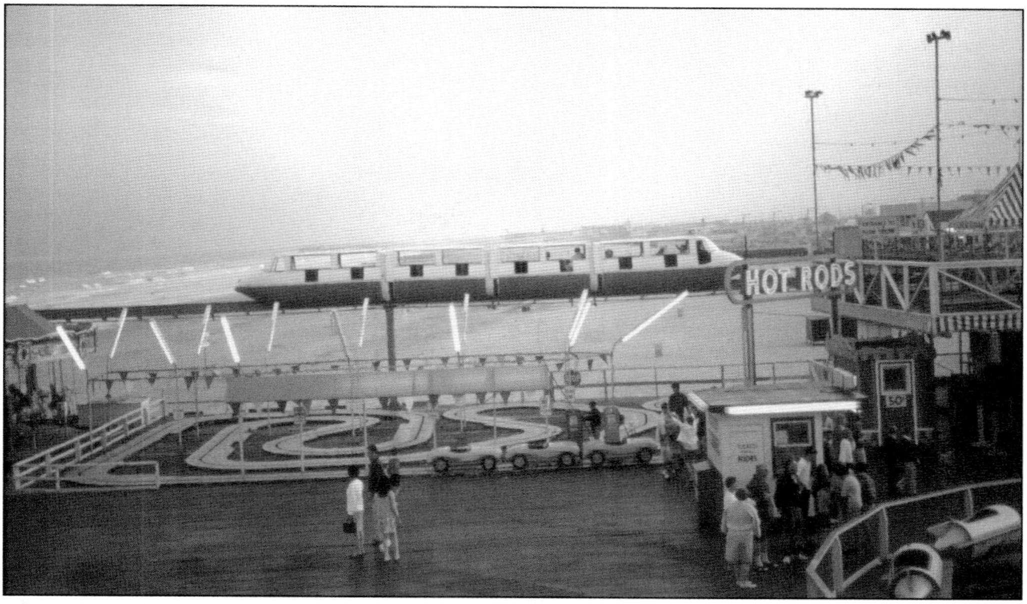

The monorail appears here in all its glory in the summer of 1967. Joe Barnes ran his pier differently than his competition. This proved a wise decision, as it gave Fun Pier a different image from the other piers. Many other carnies had games and rides on the pier, including Bill Howard and J.D. Floyd. The Old Pro Golf Course was a two-level golf course on the pier. The Rotojets were also a popular attraction during the 1960s, as Casino Arcade pier also had them. (Courtesy Ellen Fried.)

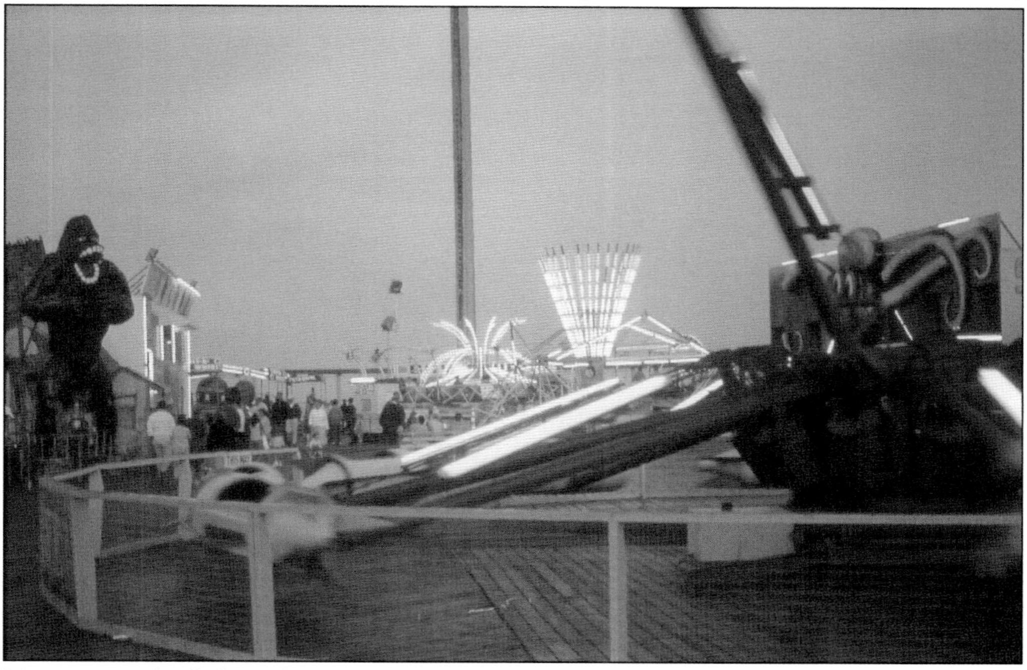

The rotojets take flight as the gorilla, also known as "King Kong," keeps a watchful eye on activities. At the time of this photograph, the dark ride was the Tiki Train. Note that the Funcade is next to the Tiki Train. The Funcade was the first incarnation of what would become the more elaborate Crazy House. The Scrambler, Tilt-A-Whirl, and a Trabant are also visible in the photograph. Note the Seascape dark ride on the right. (Courtesy Ellen Fried.)

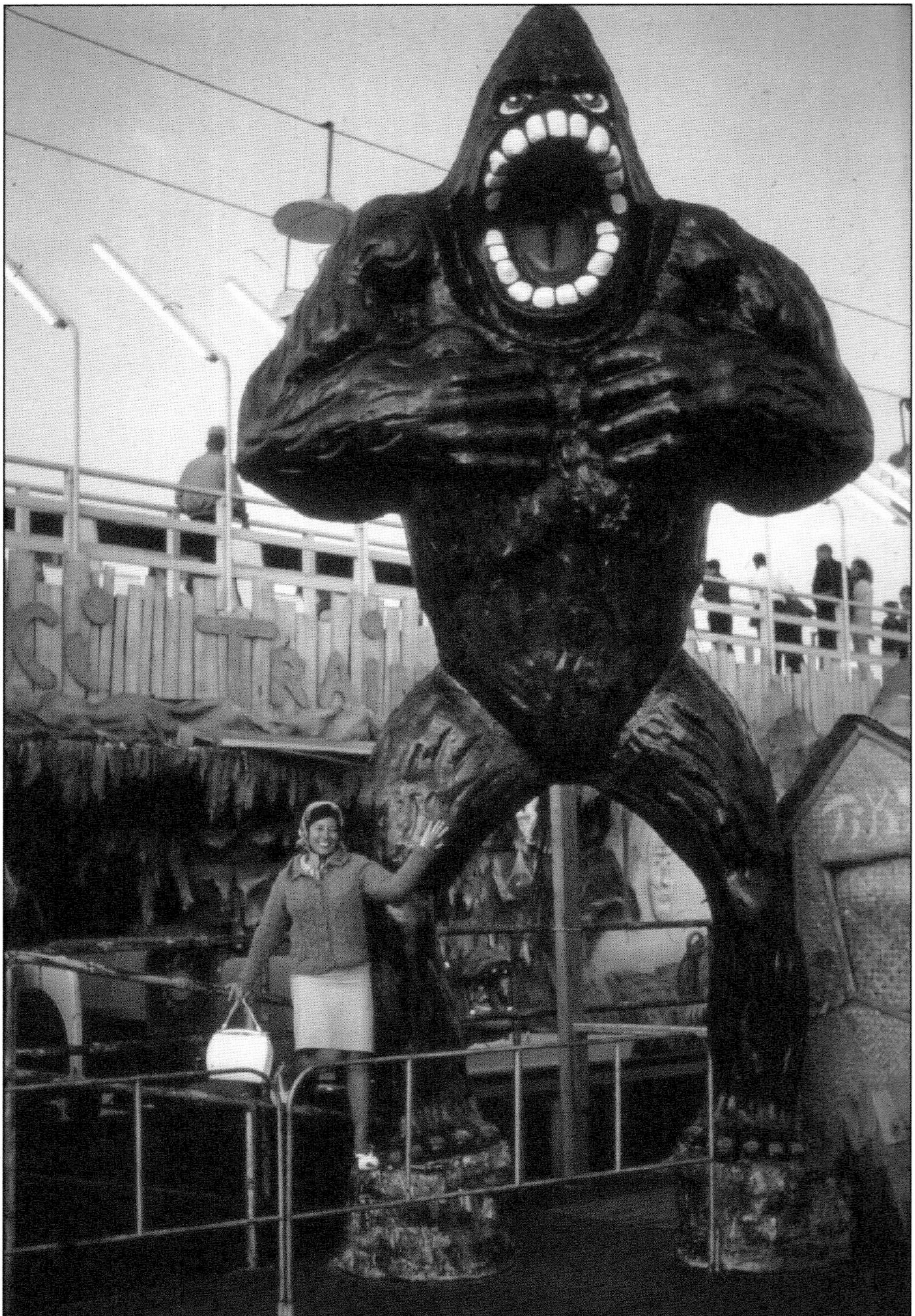

Barbara Fried poses with the 20-foot King Kong. Tiki Train is still remembered by those who worked the pier during the 1960s, but details of what was inside the ride are hazy. The original design for this dark ride was made by Universal Design, Ltd., the same company that designed and built the monorail, Sky Tower, and Ski Ride. During this period, King Kong was the pier mascot. Note the hippo prop with the face inside his mouth. (Courtesy Ellen Fried.)

Two

The 1970s and the Bill Howard Era

By 1970, additional vendors were becoming involved with Fun Pier. Some had been around since the 1960s, such as Bill Howard and J.D. Floyd. Part of the carnival business for years, Floyd had acquired many nice amusement rides. Before the 1972 summer season, Barnes and Floyd entered into a deal whereby Barnes would lease Floyd's rides for Fun Pier, saving Barnes the expense of purchasing the latest rides himself. Floyd brought Glenn Bergathon to Fun Pier to act as manager of the rides.

As the summer of 1973 approached, the decision was made to redevelop Bill Howard's Seascape ride into Castle of Frankenstein. Not only would the facade need a complete face-lift, but all the underwater-themed props inside had to be replaced as well. Money was running out, so in place of props, the pier hired actors in costumes and makeup. When the decision was made to move the structure to the back of Fun Pier, the car track was damaged beyond repair. So, in late 1977, Sheila Rubin, along with her then-husband, Dennis "Easy" Gibson, reworked the ride into a walk-through attraction and renamed it Castle Frankenstein.

By 1975, the Devil's Inn was failing financially, so local idealist Freddy Mahana came on board, bringing along his lead artist Jim DeMusz, who started an elaborate retheming of Devil's Inn into Lost World, based on Mahana's title.

On November 15, 1976, Joe Barnes sold Fun Pier to Bill and Helen Howard. The management of J.D. Floyd left the pier, paving the way for the Howards to run the pier as they saw fit. Bill Howard made the decision to remove the monorail because its tracks sat low over the game roofs, and he wanted to house the games in more elaborate structures. Display artists Jack and Wayne Seddon arrived in 1979 and began their tenure at Fun Pier by converting an old building into a Jungleland dark ride, not to be confused with Hunt's Pier's Jungleland. As the 1970s came to an end, few knew that this would be the last full decade for Fun Pier as it had been known.

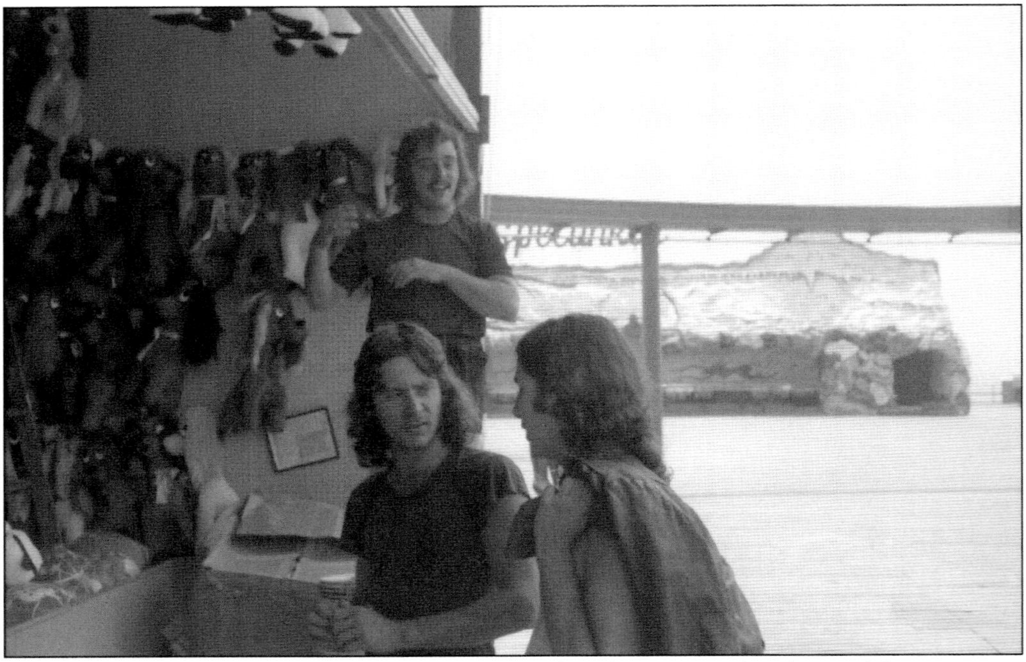

Bob Brewster (above the other men) works the Break a Plate game. The object of this game was to throw the balls at the plate and break them. The more plates a person broke, the bigger the prize. Note the monorail track and the Spelunker in the background. (Courtesy Larry Mosher.)

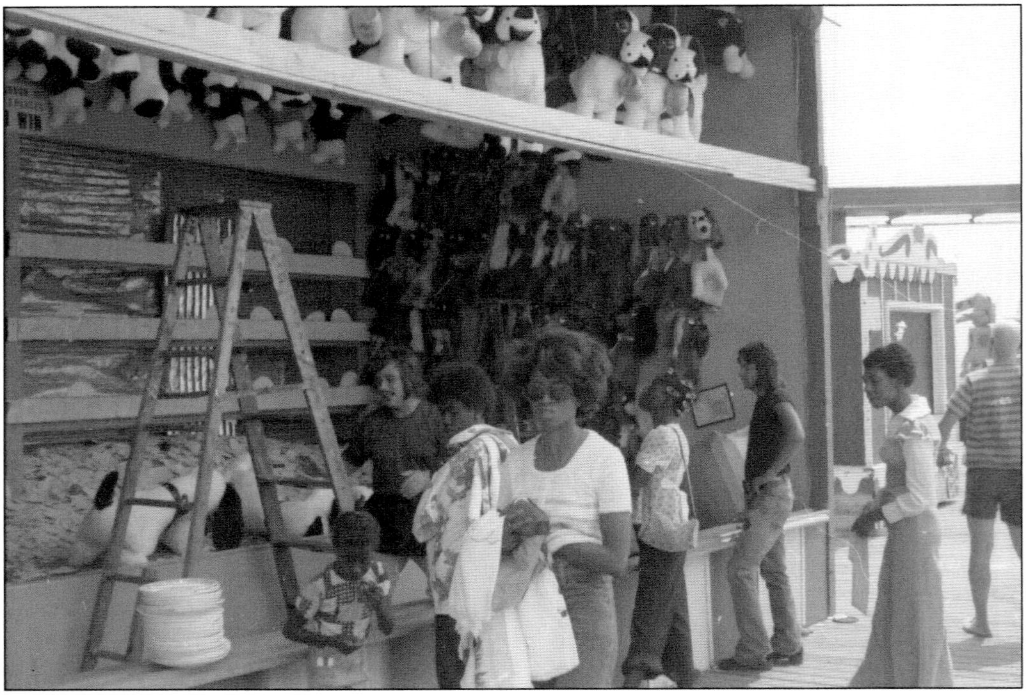

Bob Brewster uses a ladder to retrieve a high-hanging prize for a winning patron at the Break a Plate game. Note the partially broken plates. People love the challenge of these games of chance, and many times, employees would be paid to walk down the boardwalk with an exceptionally large stuffed animal to attract attention to the game. (Courtesy Larry Mosher.)

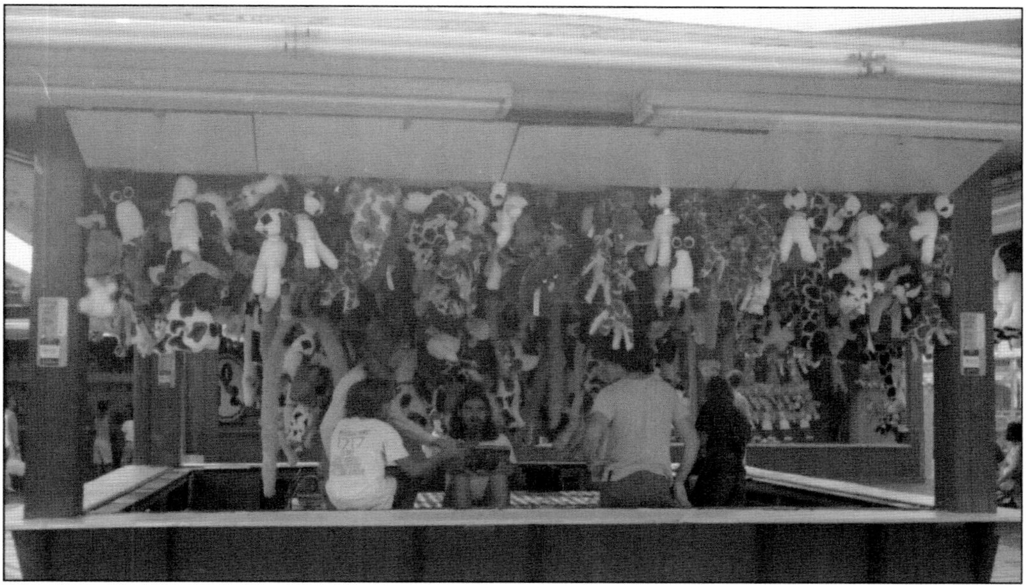

Erroll Rubin (center, with goatee) operated the Dime Pitch for many years on Fun Pier. In this game, a patron had to land the dime inside one of the circles. The smaller the circle, the bigger the prize. The Dime Pitch was located centrally at the front of the pier, and the prizes could be seen easily from the main boardwalk. People walking by would see prizes that grabbed their interest, enticing them to pitch a dime. (Courtesy Larry Mosher.)

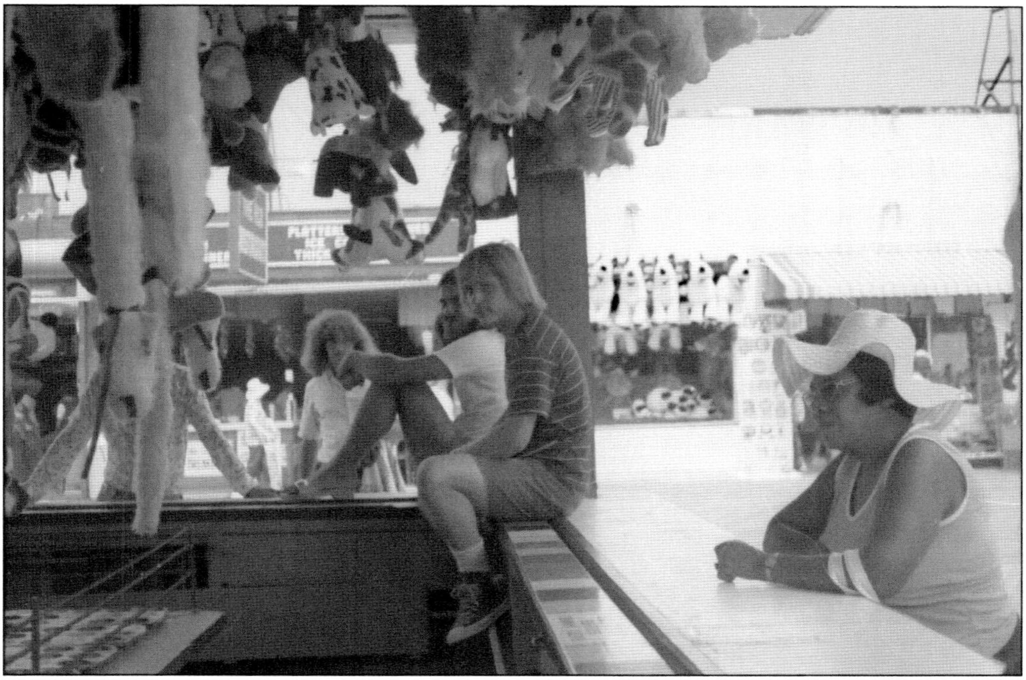

Erroll Rubin (center, with beard) and Ed Franchville (in striped shirt) stand at the Dime Pitch game in front of Fun Pier in 1973. The Dime Pitch was a highly profitable concession that lasted many years, mainly because a dime was not much to spend. It was a simple set up with simple rules. Customers would have a lot of fun trying to win the stuffed animals. Those dimes added up quickly. (Courtesy Larry Mosher.)

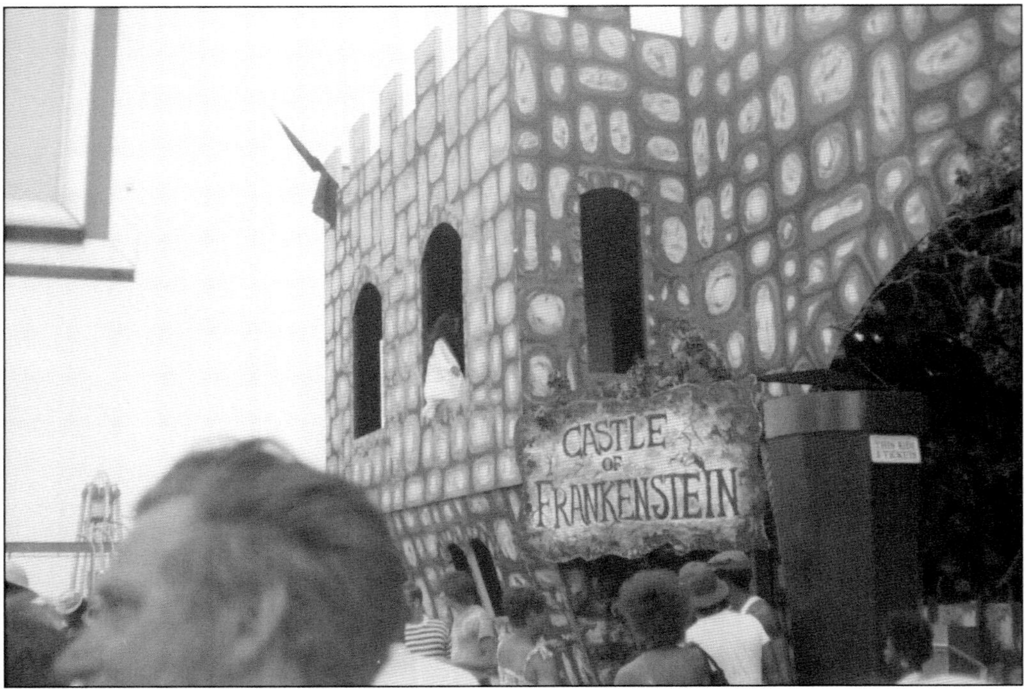

The first Castle of Frankenstein opened in 1973. Originally known as the Seascape dark ride, it closed in 1972 due to declining ticket sales. Frisco Follies was brought on to help come up with new ideas. They determined that it would be more beneficial to gut and revamp the attraction, rather than sell it. In its first years, the castle had few props inside. Helen Howard determined that actors would be needed to fill in the gaps and to create genuine fright. (Courtesy Larry Mosher.)

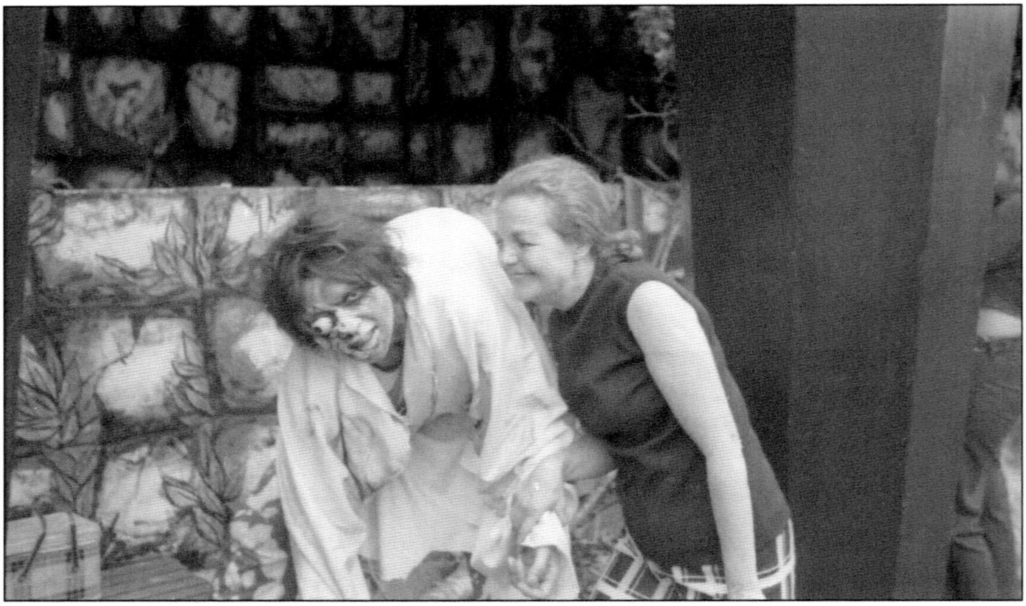

Helen Howard, wife of eventual pier owner Bill Howard, poses with one of the Castle of Frankenstein's actors portraying the infamous Hunchback of Notre Dame. As manager of the ride, she would hire similar actors to wander around outside to draw in customers. Note the sharp detail on the walls of the ride. (Courtesy Larry Mosher.)

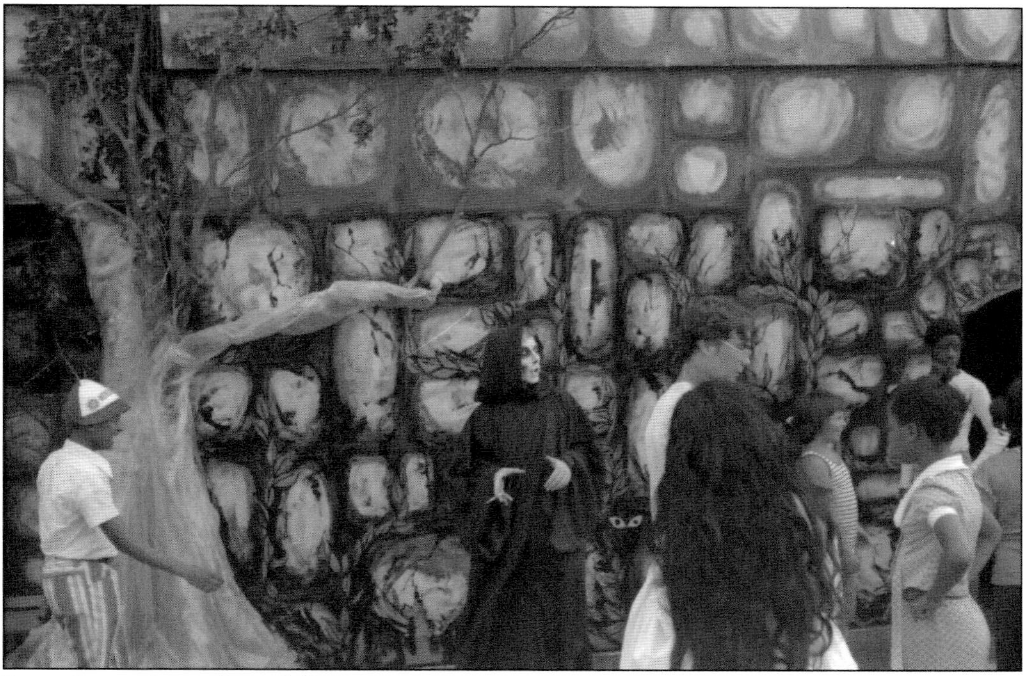

Jamie James (center), in full vampire costume and makeup, stands in front of the Castle of Frankenstein while on a break in 1973. Note the eyes looking out from the castle walls below his left arm. While the outside of the castle was not appealing, the actors working inside made sure to make the most of it. (Courtesy Larry Mosher.)

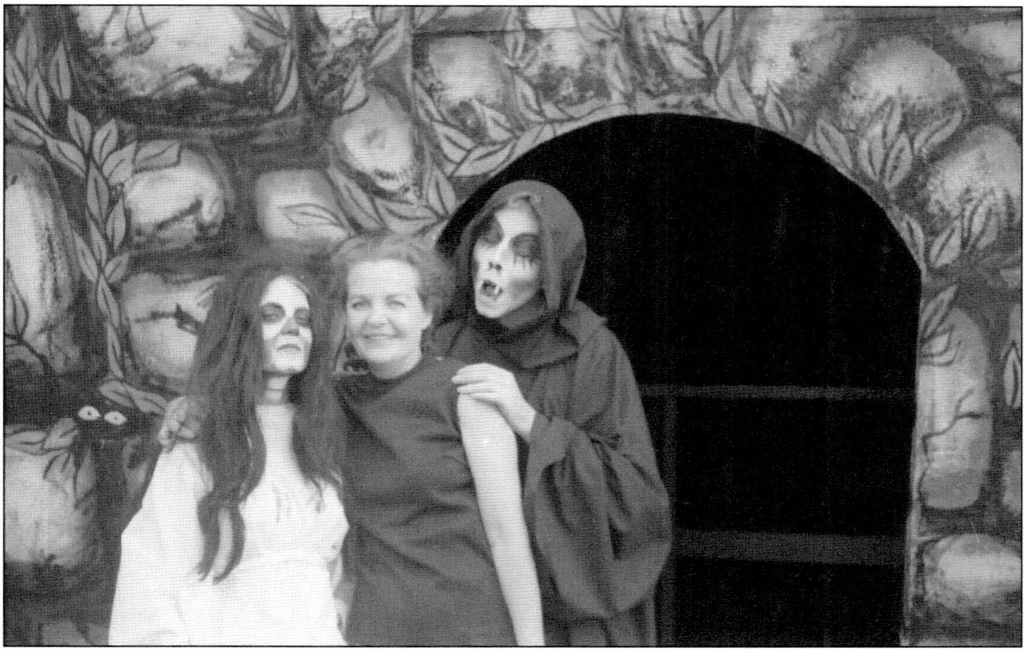

Helen Howard is about to receive a bite from vampire Jamie James in front of the Castle of Frankenstein. Howard's daughter Gerry is at left in ghoul makeup. At the time of this photograph, in 1973, Helen was manager of the cigarette game as well as the castle. Just three years later, Helen and her husband, Bill, would own Fun Pier. (Courtesy Larry Mosher.)

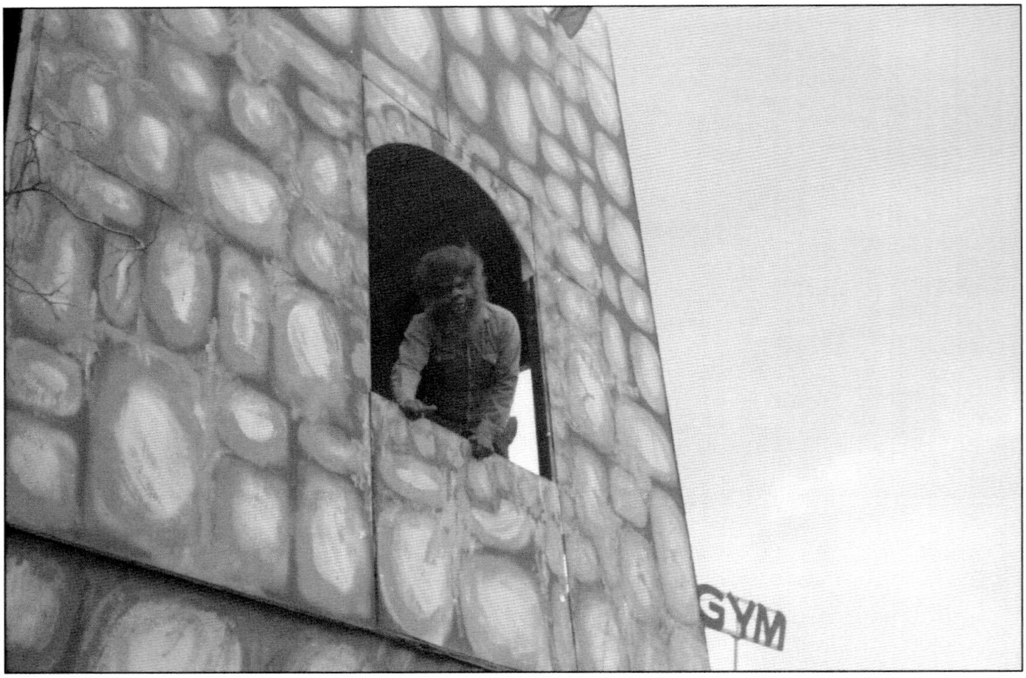

The Wolfman became the most popular attraction at the Castle of Frankenstein during the early 1970s. Mike Kelley, the actor who played the Wolfman, took the role to heart in such a way that he would even spring from the windows of the castle and land directly on the boardwalk below. He eventually broke an ankle performing this stunt, putting an end to the Wolfman's daring leaps. In place of this dangerous feat, he stood atop the castle and howled loudly at the moon, attracting massive crowds who would watch the Wolfman's antics on a nightly basis. (Courtesy Larry Mosher.)

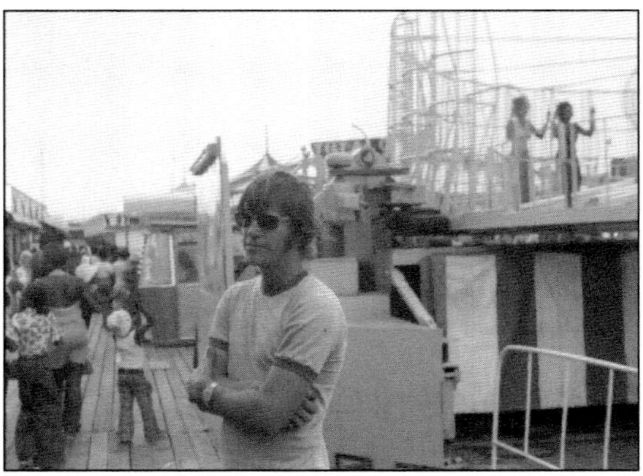

Art Fiala was the pier mechanic and later became pier manager. He is seen here in 1973 standing in front of the Castle of Frankenstein—a creation that he helped to build. He was known for his generosity and quick wit, and he and his family actually lived on Fun Pier for many summers. From 1973 to 1985, Fiala was involved with moving and repairing the rides and basically anything mechanical that needed to be done. He did much of the maintenance on the Sky Tower. (Courtesy Larry Mosher.)

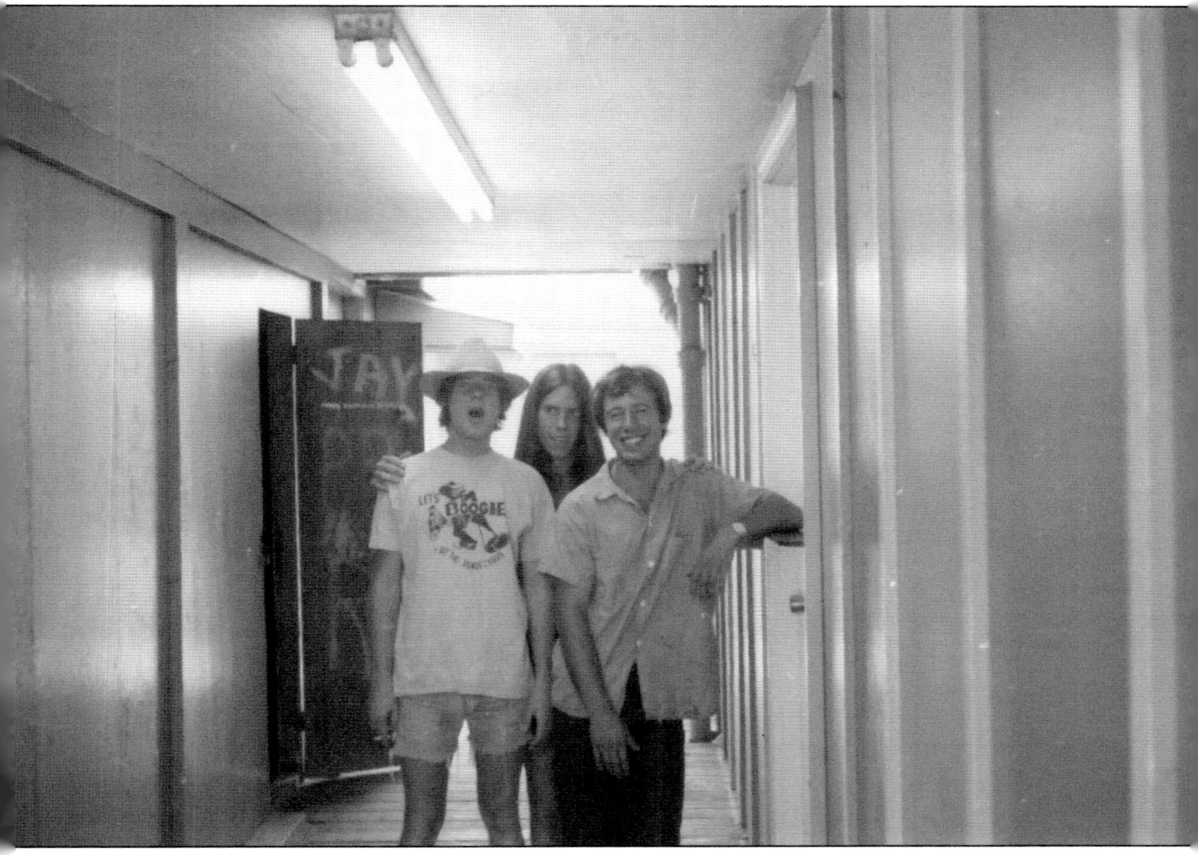

John Burke (left), Bruce ? (center), and Peter Savard stand in the hallway of the managers' offices on Fun Pier. Burke and Savard would stay and work on Fun Pier for many summers beginning in 1969, becoming regular fixtures on the pier. Savard became a master carpenter and one of Wildwood's premiere homebuilders. Burke became a world traveler and continued to work in the carnival business. In fact, John Burke, Peter Savard, and Bob Brewster joke that Burke travels so much, he can be found in all 50 states at any given time to this day! (Courtesy Larry Mosher.)

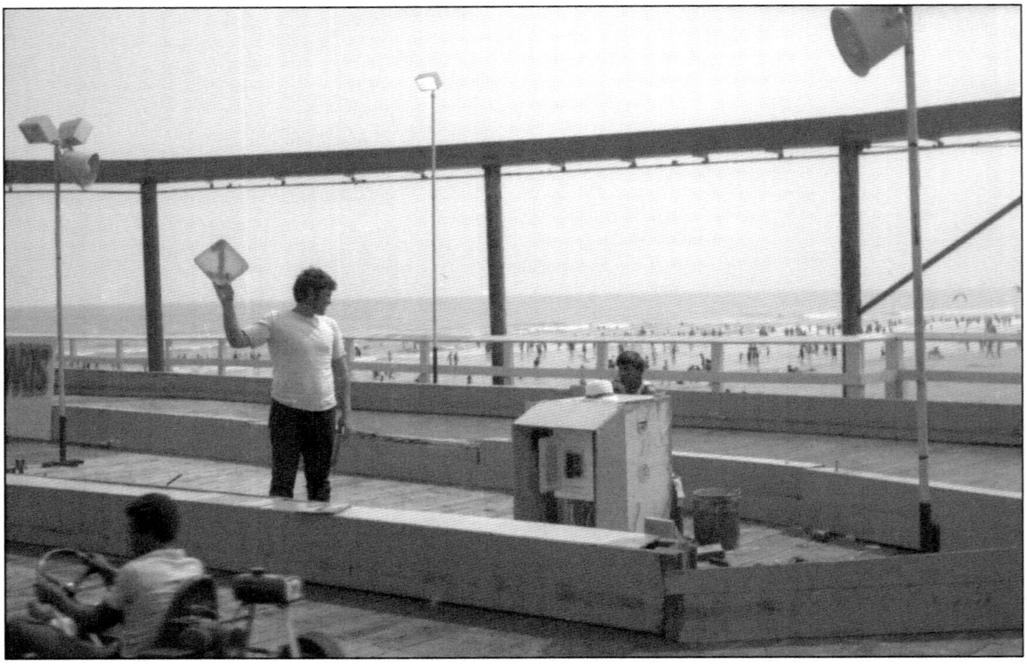

The Go Karts were a popular attraction on Fun Pier, as they were on almost every pier in Wildwood. These gas-powered cars were attractive to young patrons but could also be expensive to maintain. This 1973 photograph shows part of Fun Pier's monorail, which was still in operation at that time. (Courtesy Larry Mosher.)

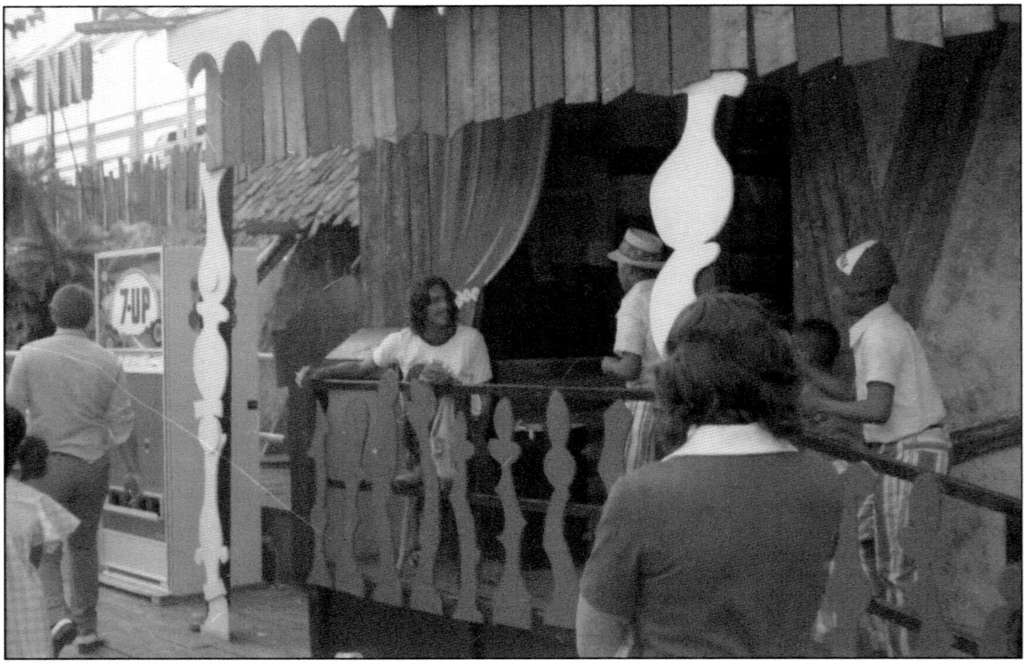

Display artist extraordinaire Bill Tracey was employed to give the Fun Pier Funcade a new name and a new facade. It was a two-story fun house with all the bells and whistles, such as moving floorboards and a spinning barrel. The Crazy House also had an apartment attached to the back. Note the mod 7-Up machine and the Devil's Inn dark ride to the left. (Courtesy Larry Mosher.)

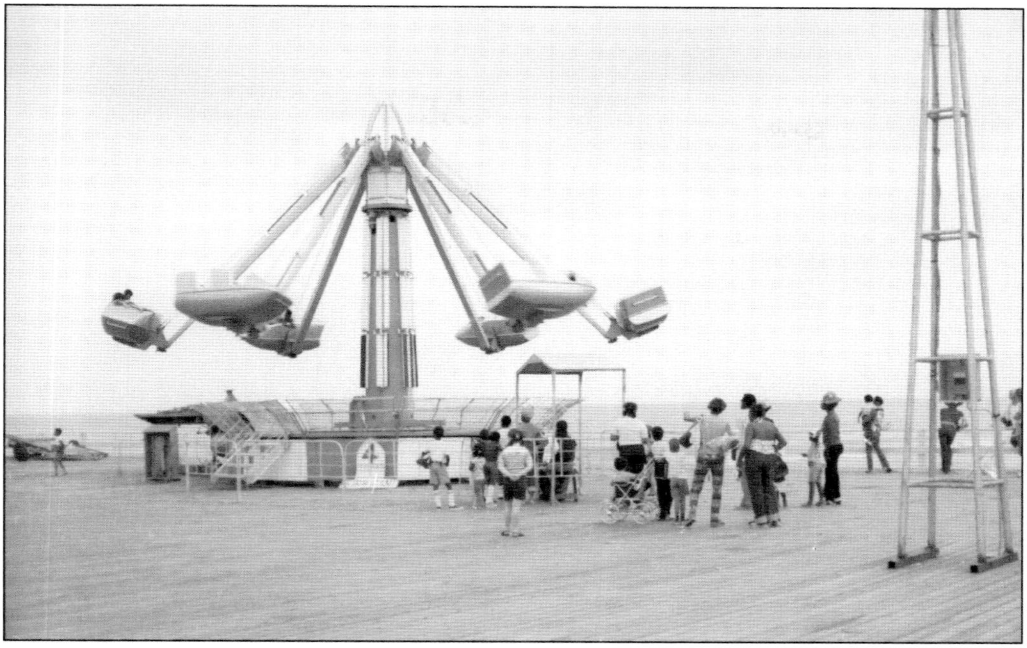

The Hurricane, located at the back right of the pier, was very popular at the time. This ride would start in the down position, and as the speed picked up, the arms of the ride would stretch out higher. This would give the rider the sensation of flying horizontally over the pier. (Courtesy Larry Mosher.)

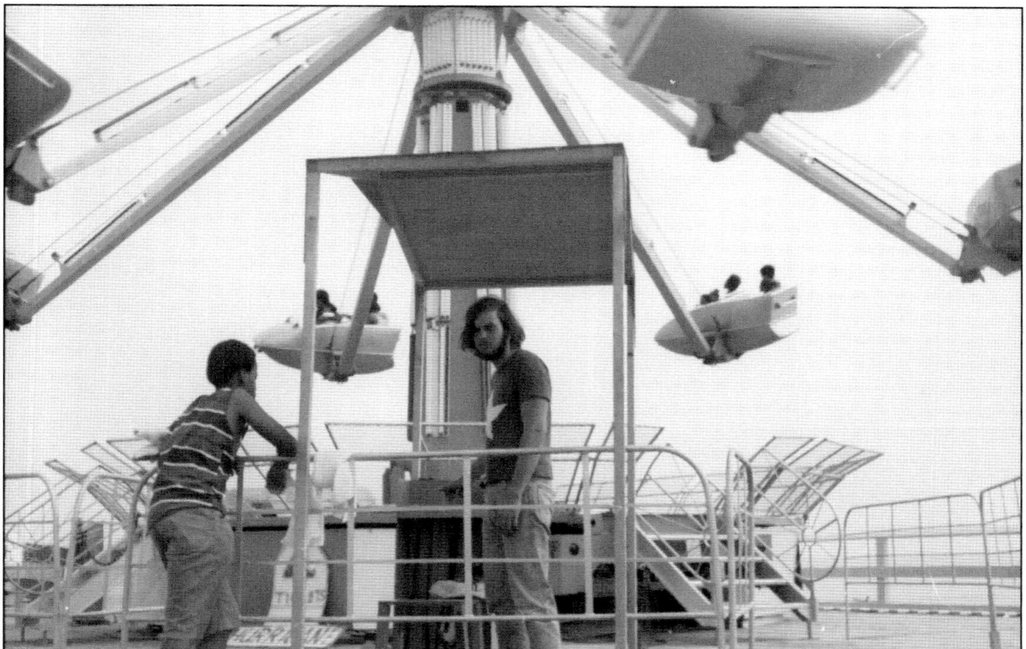

Larry Mosher operates the Hurricane. He spent three summers on Fun Pier in a variety of roles but mainly as a ride operator. The back end of Fun Pier always seemed to have trouble finding the right attractions. Spook's Hide-Away and the Castle Frankenstein seem to be the most remembered. (Courtesy Larry Mosher.)

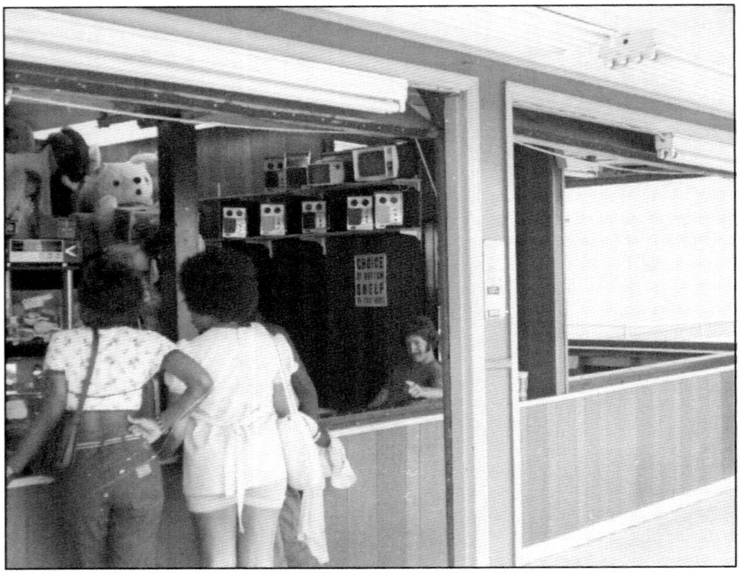

This is the Spin'em and Win'em game, a standard spinning-wheel game where patrons could win items such as televisions, radios, and Corningware. The Record Stand is on the right, another wheel game in which patrons could win brand new 33 1/3 record albums. The game owners did their best to have sought-after prizes that would attract customers. (Courtesy Larry Mosher.)

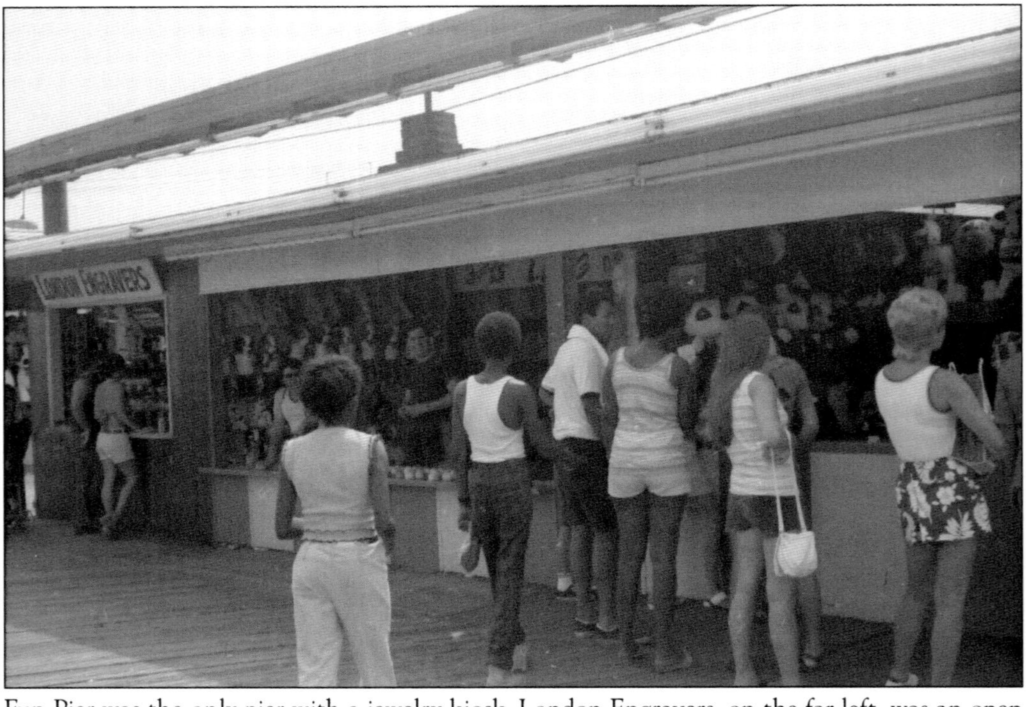

Fun Pier was the only pier with a jewelry kiosk. London Engravers, on the far left, was an open three-sided store that gave the pier a little touch of class. It was a novel concession at the time; engraving was not as common in 1973 as it is today. To the right, a customer throws balls at various animal heads. On the far right is the Beebee or Shoot-out-the-Star game. Note the monorail tracks directly above the games. This would later play a role in the fate of the legendary Fun Pier monorail. (Courtesy Larry Mosher.)

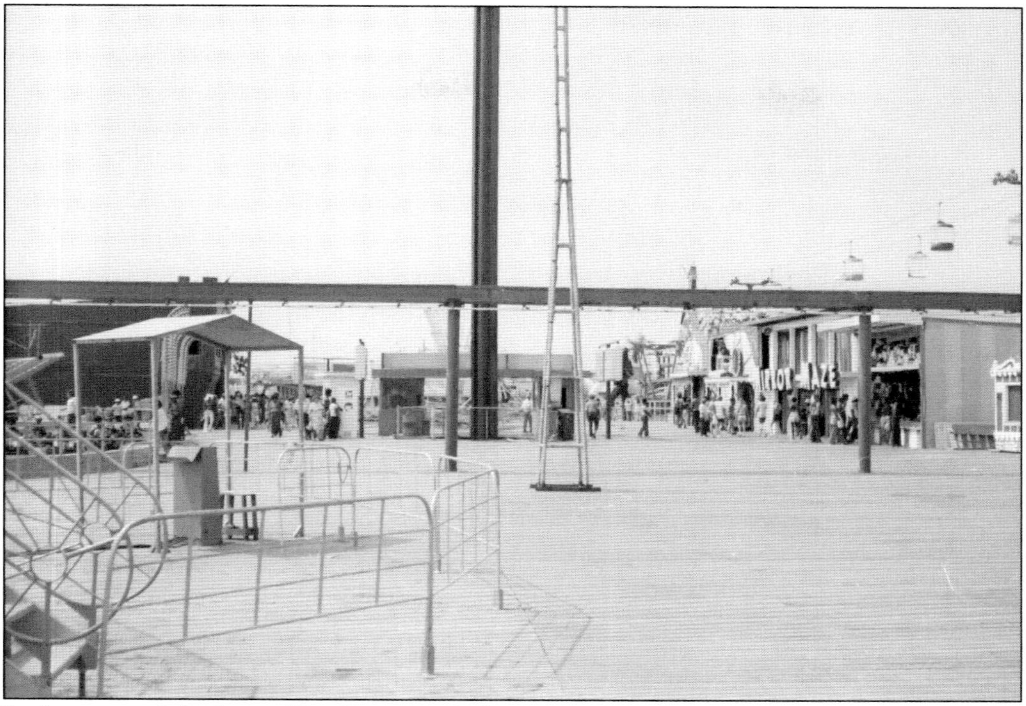

Looking toward the front of Fun Pier in 1973, the monorail cuts horizontally across the photograph, the Sky Tower pole is in the center, and Castle of Frankenstein is on the left. To the right of the Mirror Maze is the Break a Plate game, and to the maze's left are the Crazy House and Devil's Inn. (Courtesy Larry Mosher.)

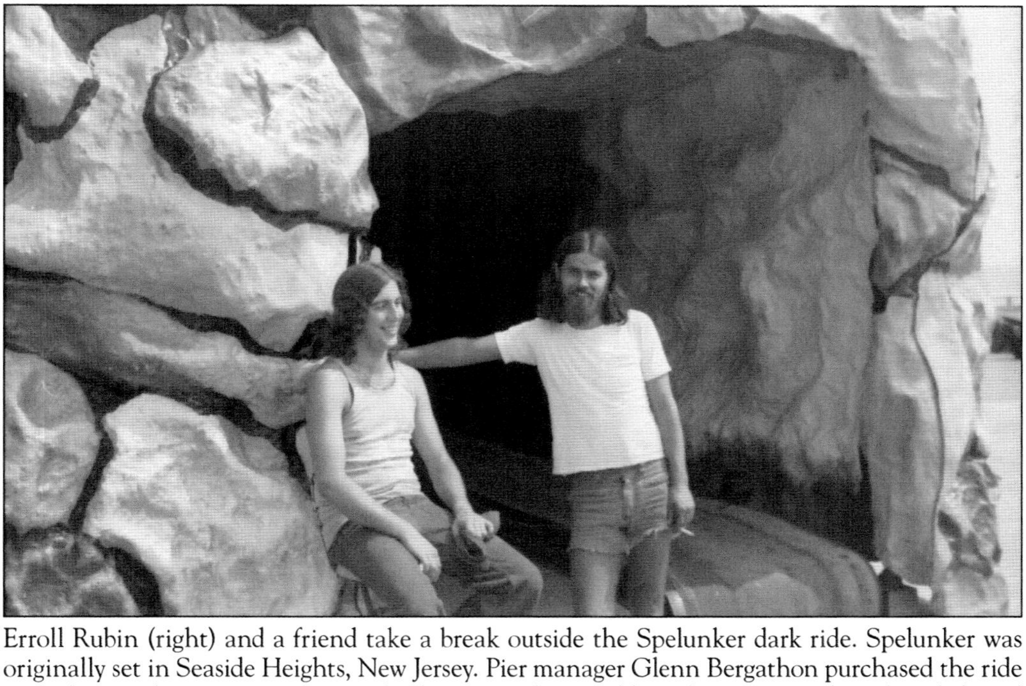

Erroll Rubin (right) and a friend take a break outside the Spelunker dark ride. Spelunker was originally set in Seaside Heights, New Jersey. Pier manager Glenn Bergathon purchased the ride and, along with Peter Savard, moved it from Seaside to Wildwood's Fun Pier. The ride only lasted one or two seasons. (Courtesy Larry Mosher.)

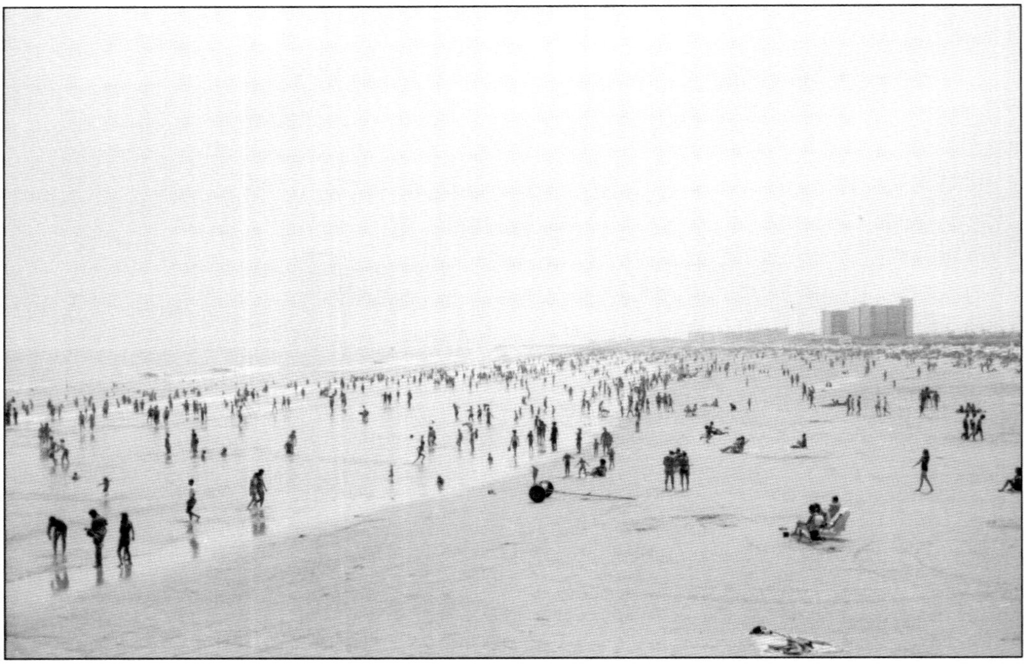

This photograph shows Wildwood Crest to the south during the height of the summer season. Wildwood is known for its beautiful golden-sand beaches, which are quite sizable compared to neighboring beaches. After a beautiful afternoon soaking up the summer sunshine, tourists would head to the amusement piers after dark. (Courtesy Larry Mosher.)

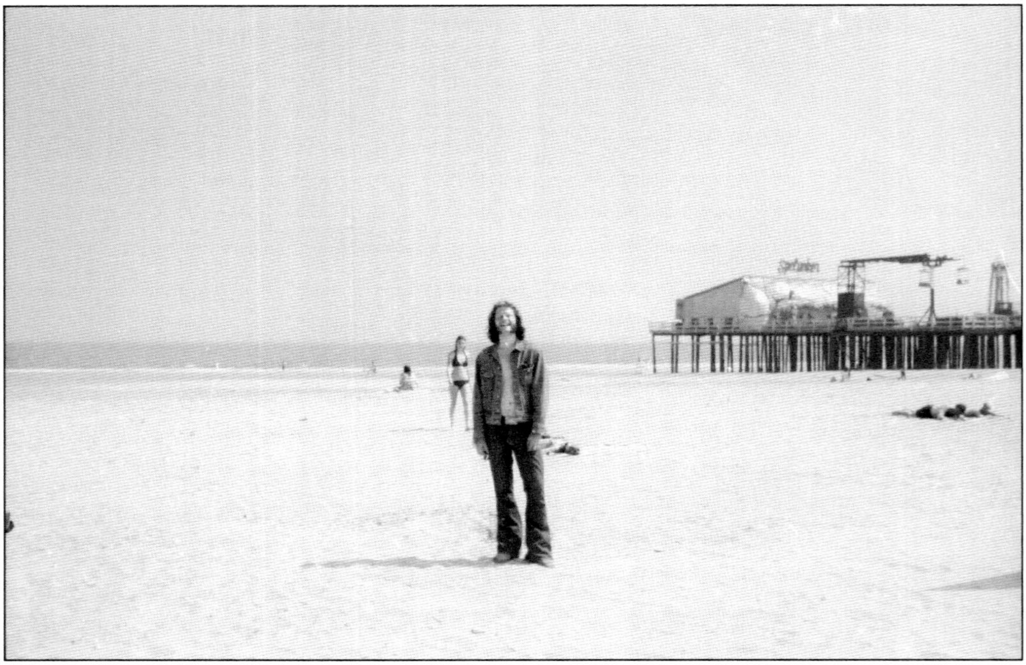

Phil Hearns from Montreal stands proud on the beach with Fun Pier to the right. Spelunker is at the back of the pier, with the Ski Ride just in front of it. Note that the pier has been extended. The Ski Ride originally took customers out over the ocean, but by 1973, the waterline had receded so far that even after the pier extension, riders only passed the Spelunker. (Courtesy Larry Mosher.)

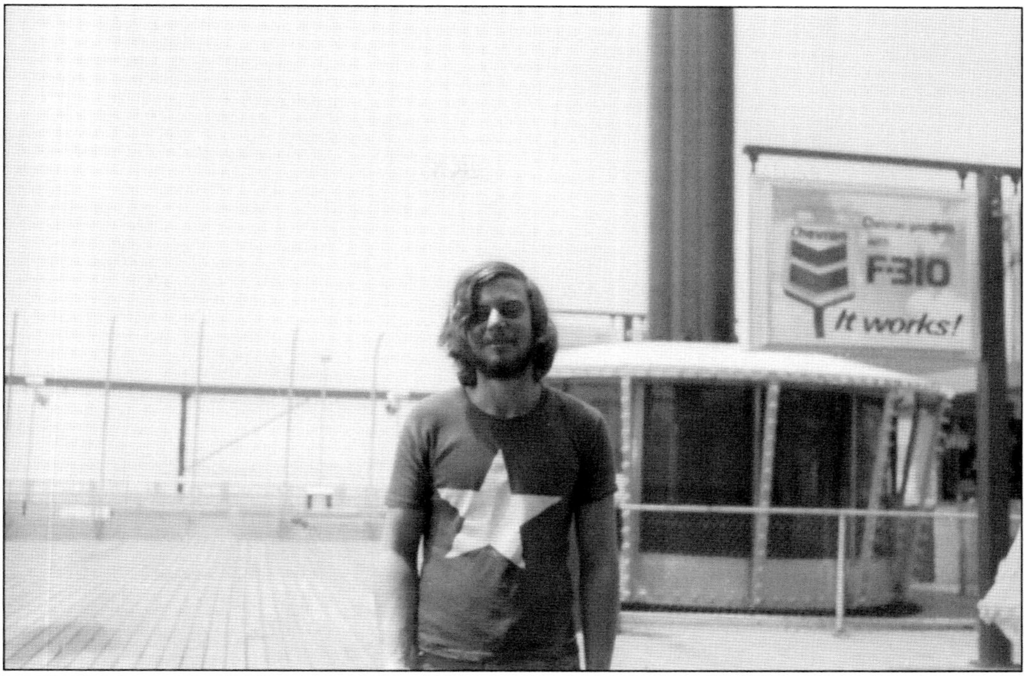

Larry Mosher poses at the base of the Sky Tower capsule. Note the Chevron gas sign in the background. Although corporate advertising is a common thing on the boardwalk today, in 1973, Fun Pier became the first amusement pier in Wildwood to accept advertising, netting Joe Barnes a promotional fee. (Courtesy Larry Mosher.)

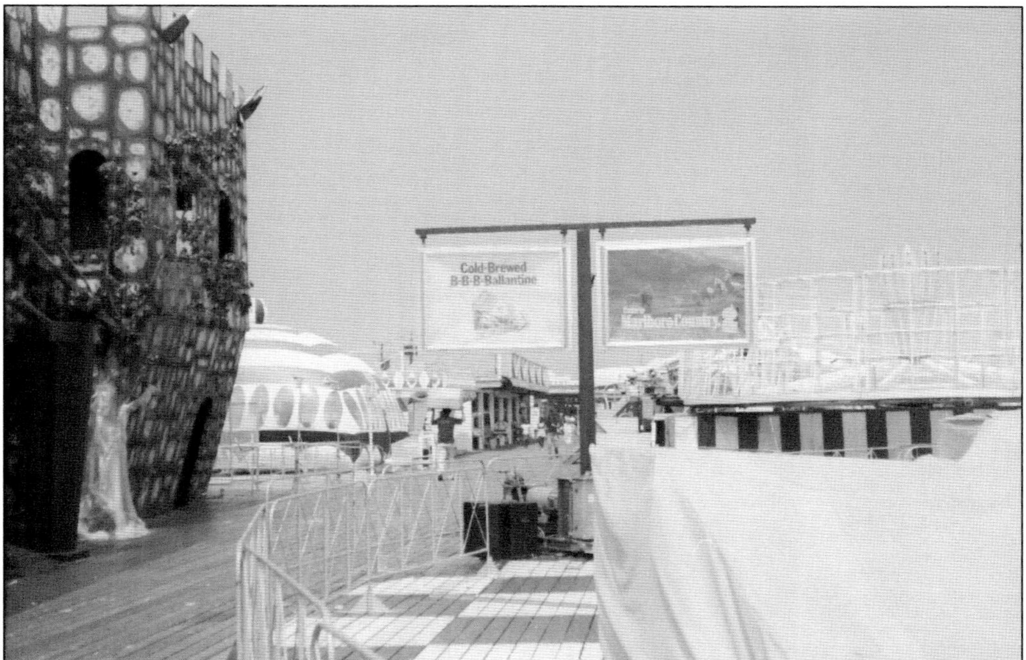

It is the start of the day on the front of the pier. Some rides still have not been uncovered, like the Scrambler in the foreground. On the left is the Castle of Frankenstein, and more corporate advertisements are dead center. (Courtesy Larry Mosher.)

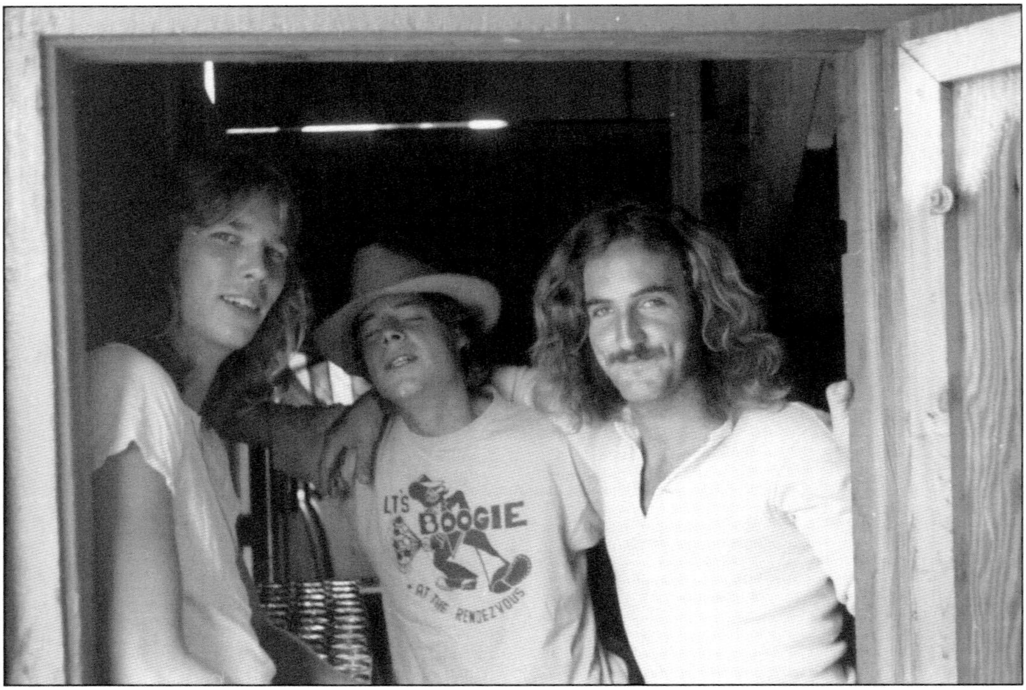

Pictured here in the 1970s are, from left to right, Drew ?, John Burke, and Andre Drerichard. Fun Pier employees hung out before and after work. The hairstyles and clothing are hallmarks of the time. (Courtesy Larry Mosher.)

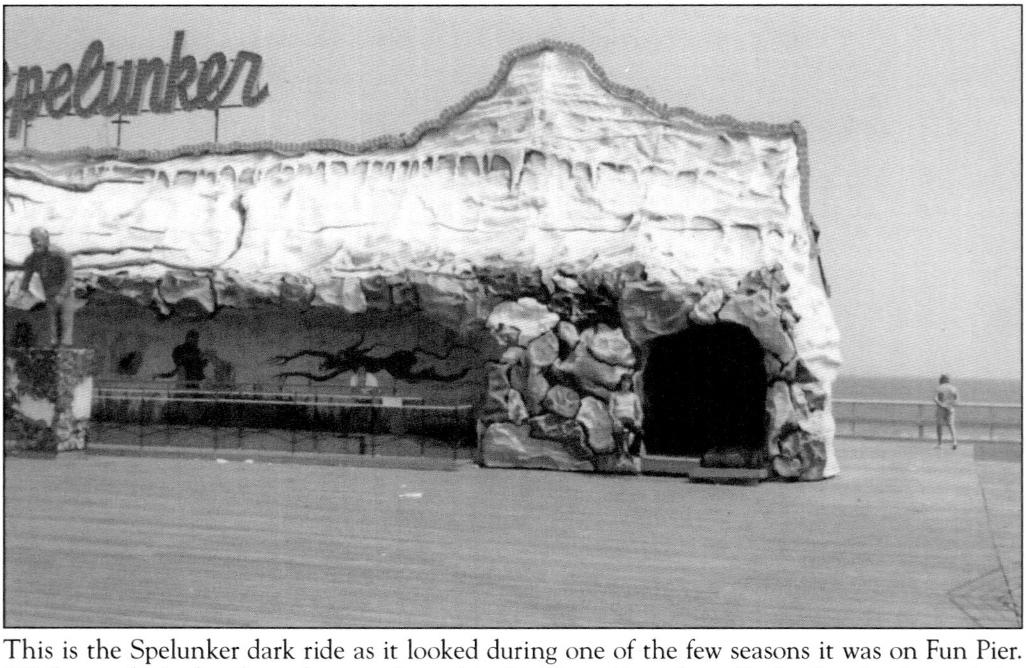

This is the Spelunker dark ride as it looked during one of the few seasons it was on Fun Pier. While very little details are known about this ride, Peter Savard recalls the day that he and pier manager Glenn Bergathon went up to Seaside Heights and purchased the ride. The facade was neat, but the inside just was not very special. In the end, if people liked the facade, they would pay to see what was inside. (Courtesy Larry Mosher.)

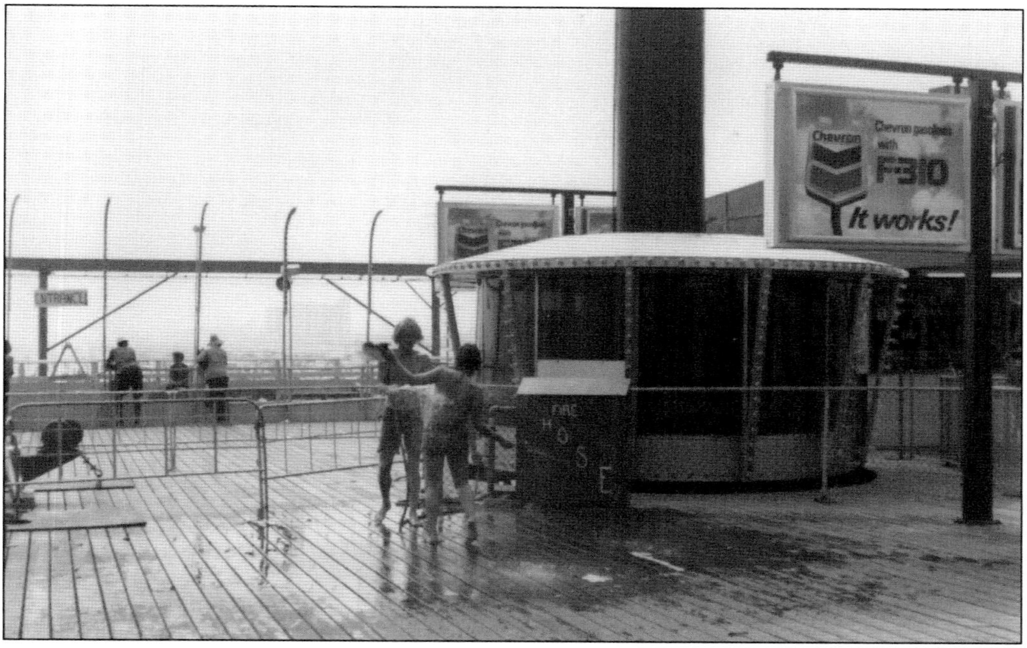

To cool off on a hot afternoon, Fun Pier employees use the fire hose. As most of the former employees will tell anyone, it really was a "fun" pier. The Sky Tower still looks to be in tiptop shape in this photograph, taken during the summer of 1973, when the rides were leased out to J.D. Floyd. (Courtesy Larry Mosher.)

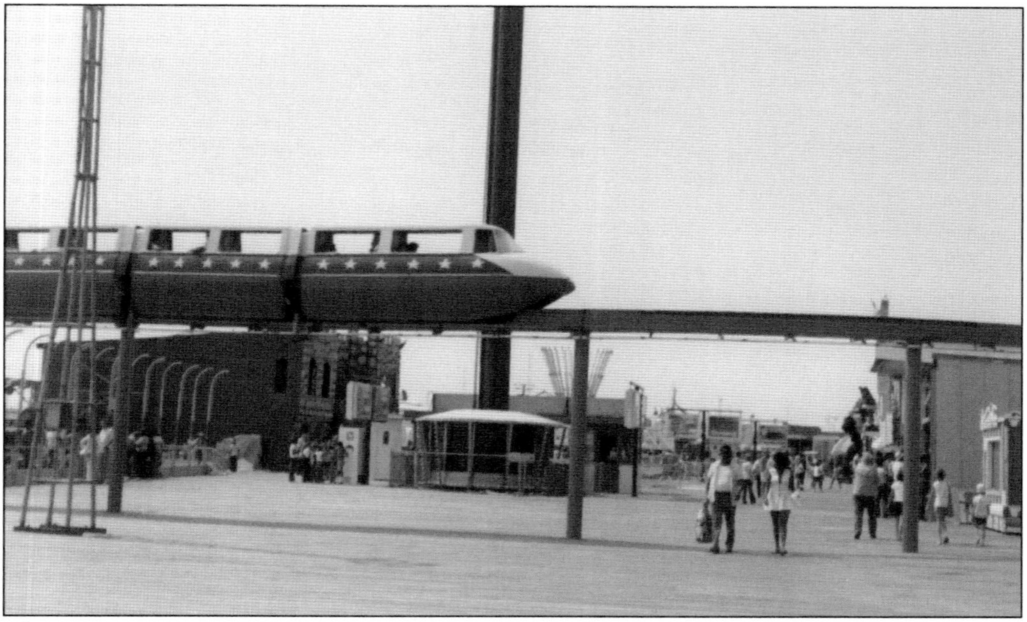

The Fun Pier monorail is red, white, and blue in this photograph. Even the stars symbolize the American heritage of Fun Pier. Perhaps this was done in preparation for the upcoming Bicentennial year celebrations. Both sides of the Fun Pier are full of eye-catching amusement rides; even the midsection of the pier seems busy in this photograph. Note that Castle of Frankenstein is on the left, Sky Tower is in the center, and the 20-foot King Kong is in front of what was then known as Devil's Inn. (Courtesy Larry Mosher.)

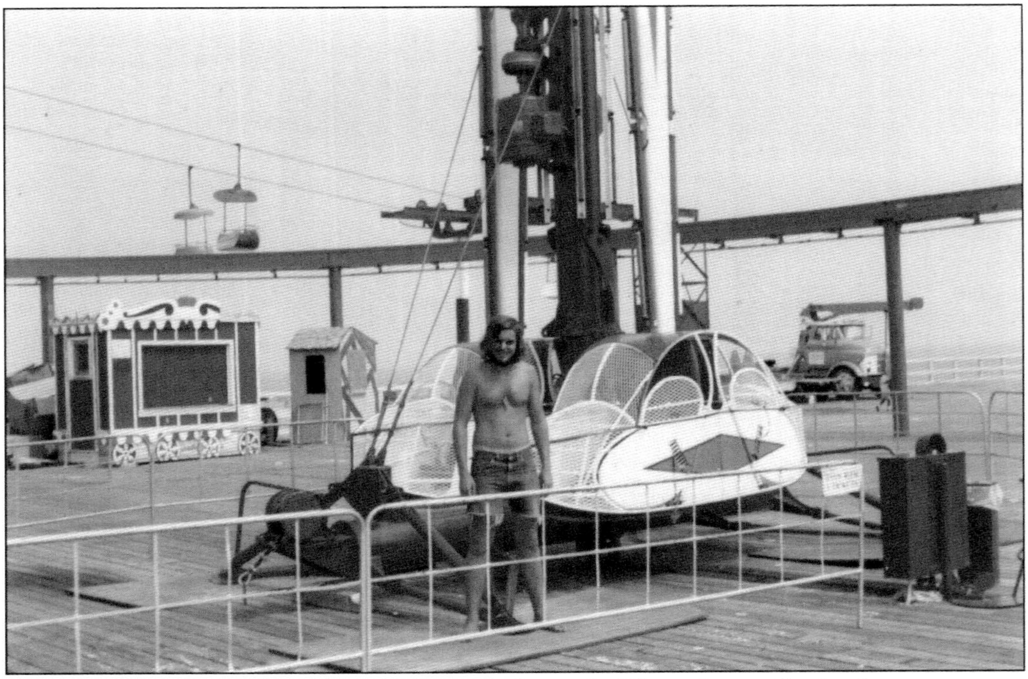

Larry Mosher operates the Salt and Pepper Shakers ride. This ride would take the customer up to high levels and shake them up. Mosher says this was a very popular ride on Fun Pier. Salt and Pepper Shakers would remain on Fun Pier for many years to follow. It looks like some sort of construction was going on at the back of the pier, as evidenced by the large truck with the crane attached. (Courtesy Larry Mosher.)

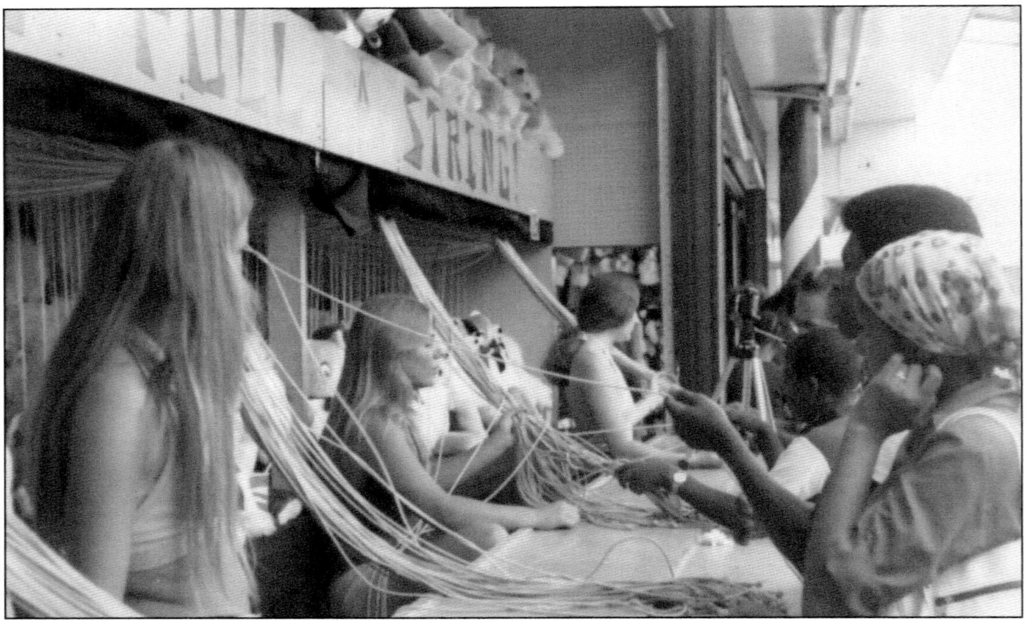

The String game was a big attraction in the 1970s. The rules were simple, the prizes were enticing, and the pretty girls working the game attracted the attention of many men. Each girl working the game held a bundle of strings, and only one was a winner. The prize was a stuffed animal. (Courtesy Larry Mosher.)

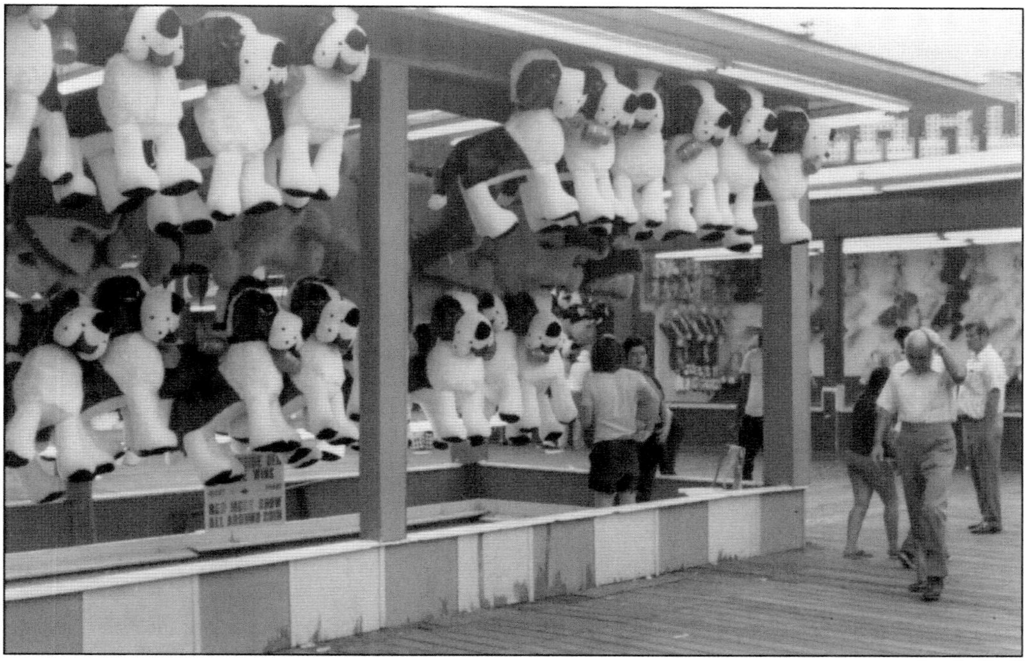

Joe Barnes, walking with his hand on his head, was always on Fun Pier overseeing the games. Barnes is fondly remembered for calling most young men "son" and for being a very compassionate and family-oriented gentleman. Barnes was friends with fellow amusement pier owners, including Gilbert Ramagosa, owner of Sportland Pier and Casino Arcade on the Wildwood Boardwalk; the Hunt family, owners of Hunt's Pier, also on the Wildwood Boardwalk; and Helen Coombs-Kelley, co-owner of Wildwood's Marine Pier & Playland. (Courtesy Larry Mosher.)

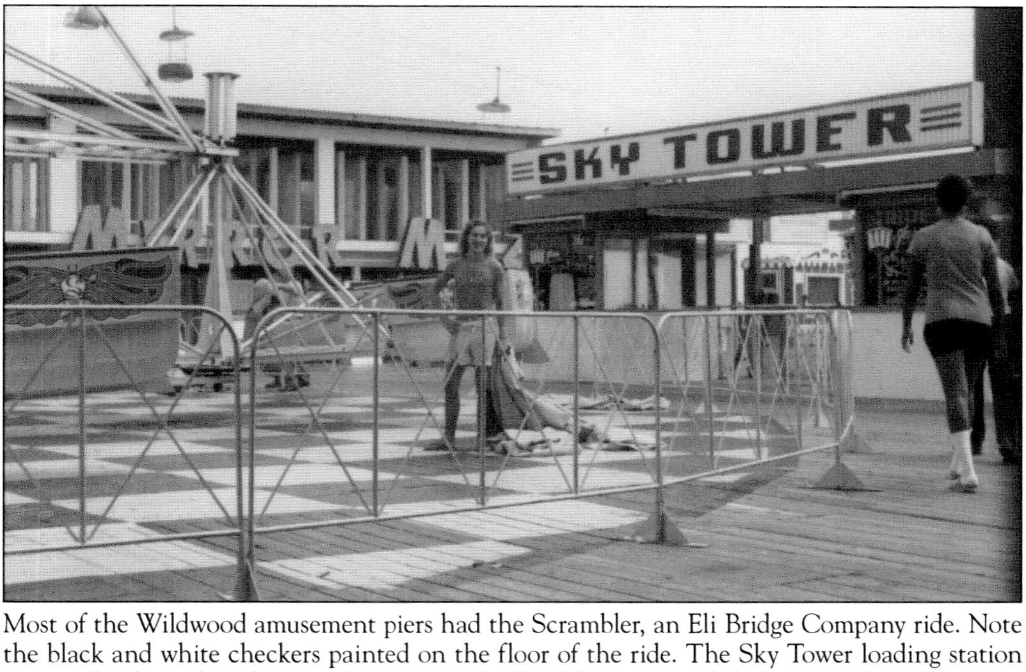

Most of the Wildwood amusement piers had the Scrambler, an Eli Bridge Company ride. Note the black and white checkers painted on the floor of the ride. The Sky Tower loading station is seen clearly in this photograph, as are both Ski Ride chairs and the Mirror Maze. (Courtesy Larry Mosher.)

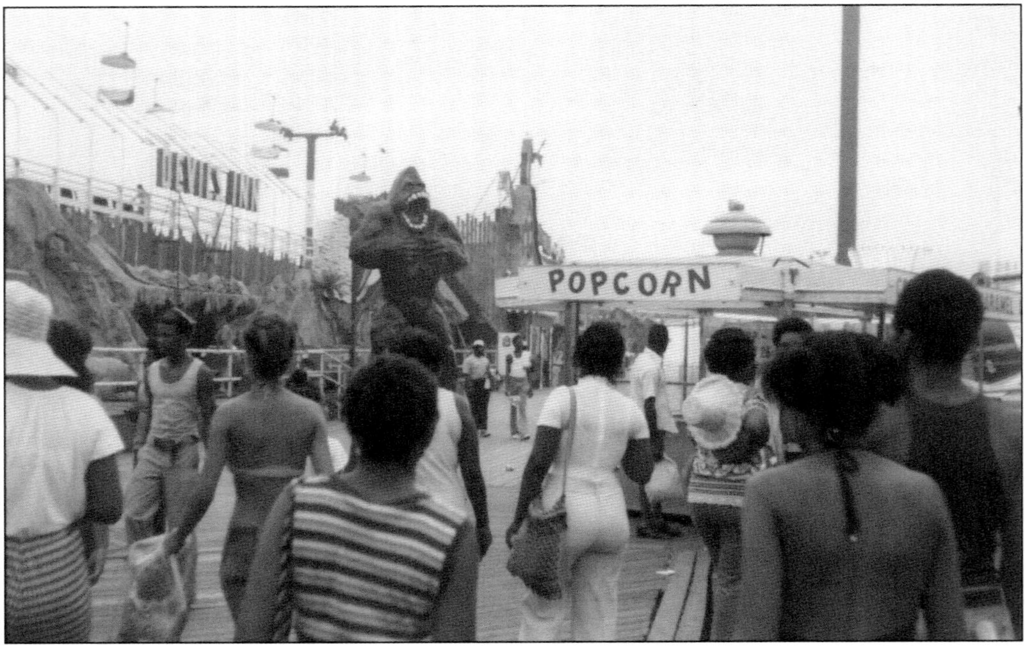

Here is the Devil's Inn dark ride as it looked during the summer of 1973. King Kong was a staple of the ride in all of its incarnations. At the time this photograph, Devil's Inn was about to undergo its final renaming as Lost World. Fun Pier always had a carnival atmosphere, with concessions such as popcorn, cotton candy, and fountain sodas. (Courtesy Larry Mosher.)

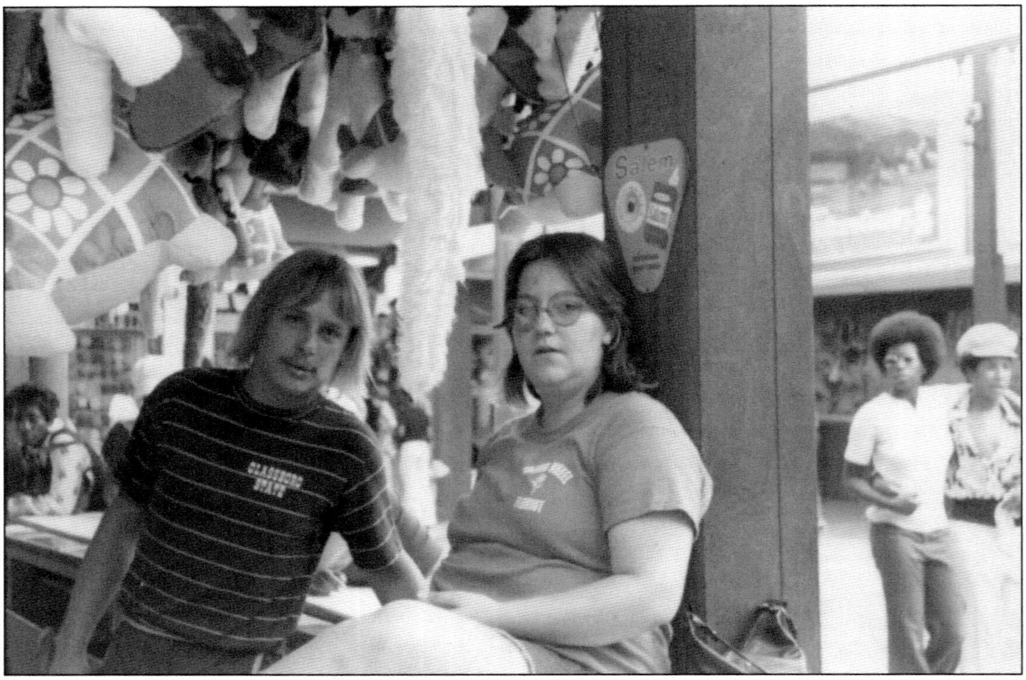

Ed Franchville and Peggy Barnes-Franchville work one of the games on Fun Pier. Peggy was the only daughter of Joe Barnes. This photograph confirms Fun Pier was a family-operated pier. Joe Barnes's sons, Jay and Peter, and his daughter, Peggy, worked the games on the front of the pier. Franchville married Peggy, joining the family. (Courtesy Larry Mosher.)

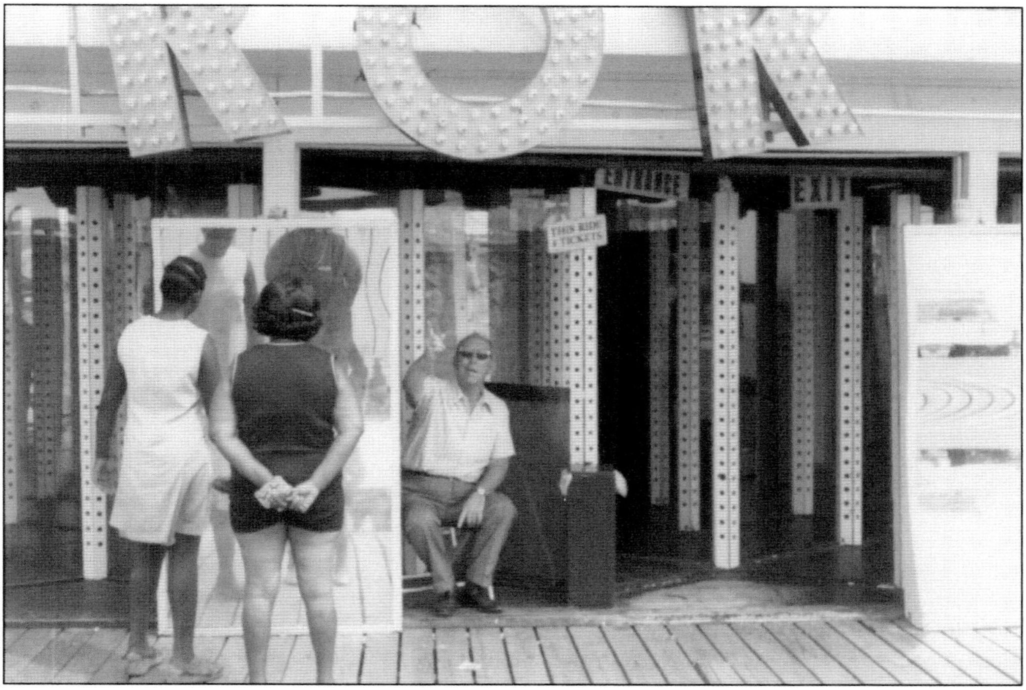

Mirror mazes have always been a lot of fun, and how fitting it was to have one right on Fun Pier. Eventually this attraction was scrapped, and only a section of it was incorporated into the Crazy House, located right next to the Mirror Maze building. (Courtesy Larry Mosher.)

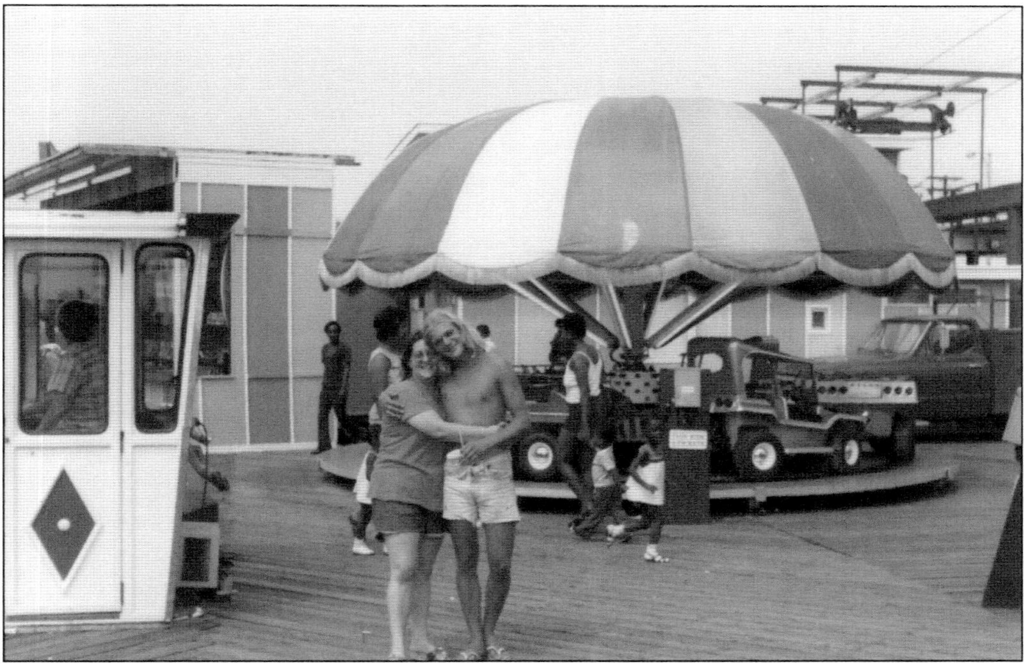

Peggy Barnes gives Leslile Brauld a big hug on Fun Pier. Fun Pier was under the management of J.D. Floyd from 1972 to 1976. During this time, Joe Barnes was looking toward early retirement. The four-year lease to J.D. Floyd represented his desire to leave the amusement-ride industry. (Courtesy Larry Mosher.)

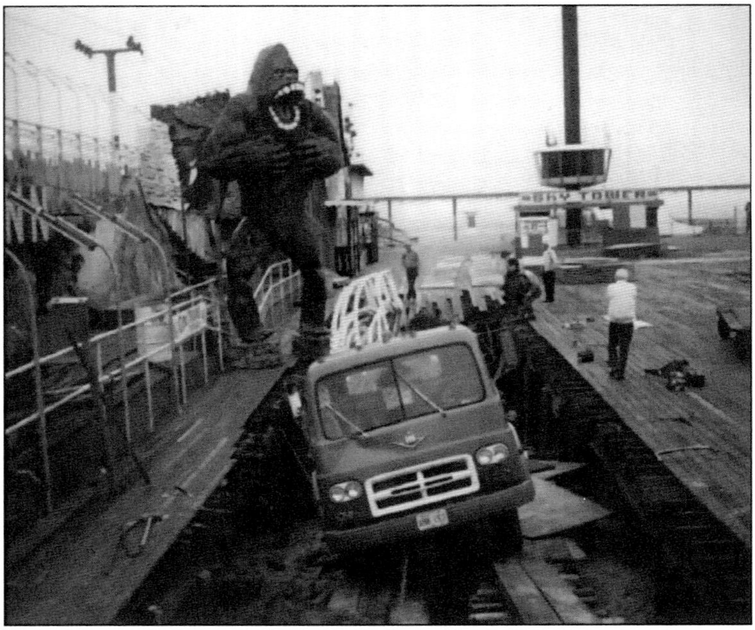

Fun Pier's original wooden planks and pilings were laid out in 1927. Throughout the years, many sections of the pier's wooden planks would need to be replaced. The best time to test the planks was during preseason, as large trucks would drive onto the pier. In this photograph, a truck carrying a piece of the Trabant crashed to the beach. Joe Barnes (right) is seen overlooking the wreck. (Courtesy Shawn Cunningham.)

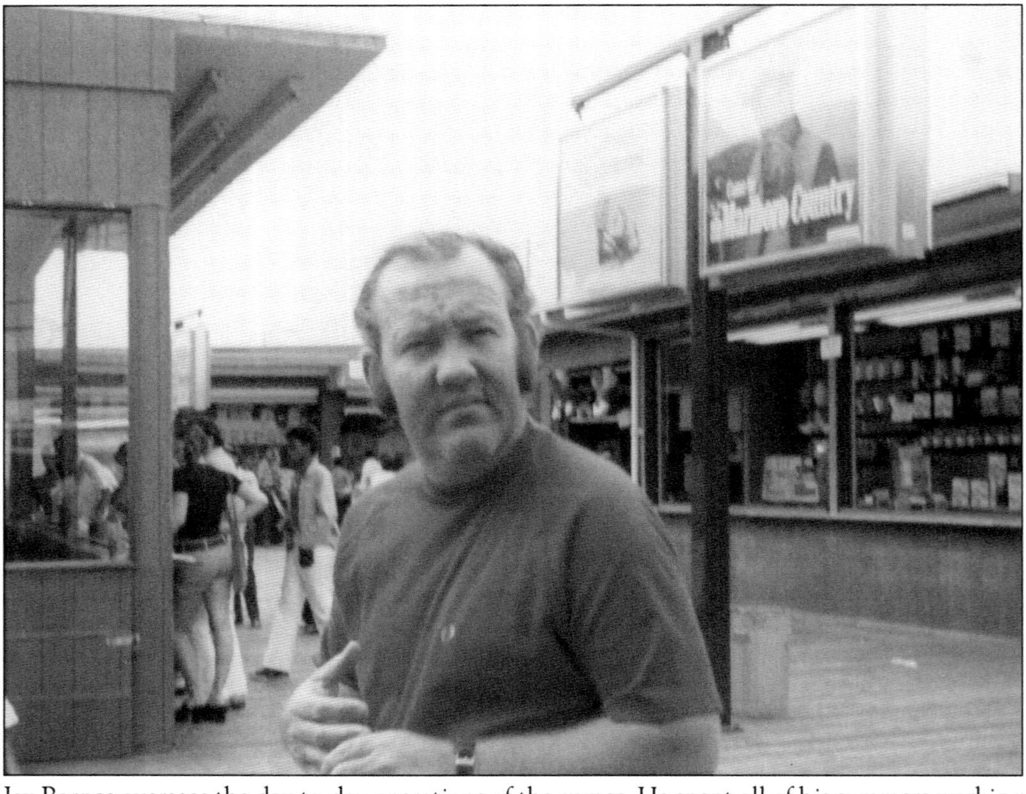

Jay Barnes oversees the day-to-day operations of the games. He spent all of his summers working for his father on Fun Pier and continued to work there even after his father sold the pier to Bill Howard. The Barnes family continued to be involved with the pier even after the sale to Morey Development. During that time, Barnes ran the Boat Tag game that stood in front of Wild Wheels for many years. (Courtesy Jay Barnes.)

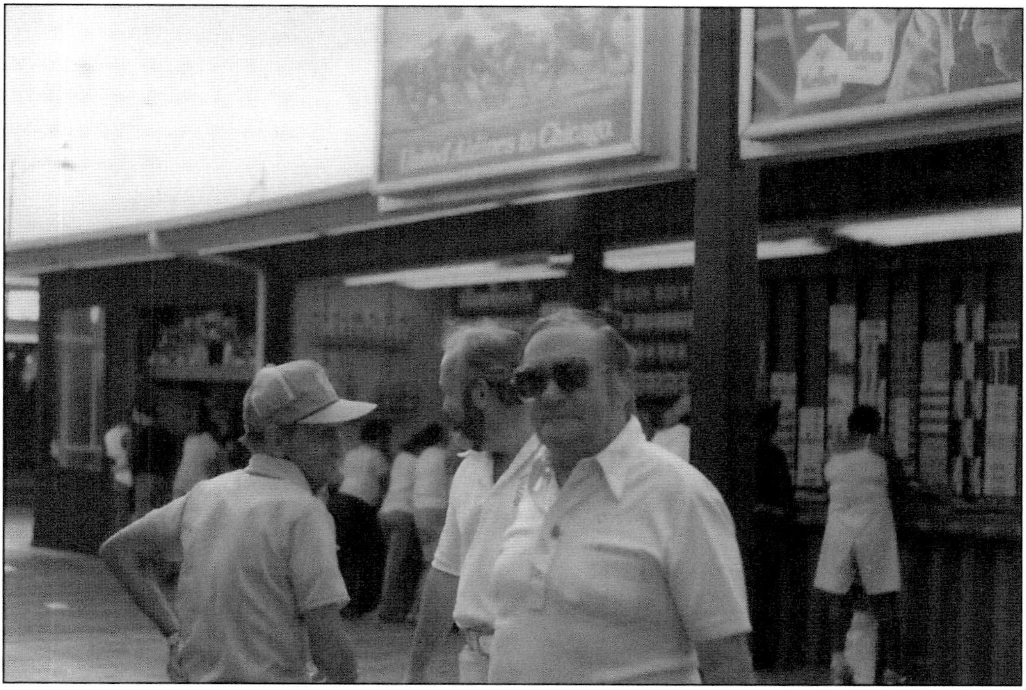

Shorty Franchville (left), Jay Barnes (center), and Warren Grubb are pictured on Fun Pier around 1973. Grubb operated game stands and owned a spiral slide that was on the pier during the 1960s. He was heavily involved in all Joe Barnes operations, whether they were on the Wildwood Boardwalk or at Willow Grove Amusement Park. Grubb got the name "Babe" during his time as a boxer. (Courtesy Jay Barnes.)

Pictured here are Warren Grubb, also known as "Uncle Babe" (left), and Fun Pier founder Joseph L. Barnes. Grubb was the original general manager for Fun Pier; he kept the books and organized everything for the next day. (Courtesy Jay Barnes.)

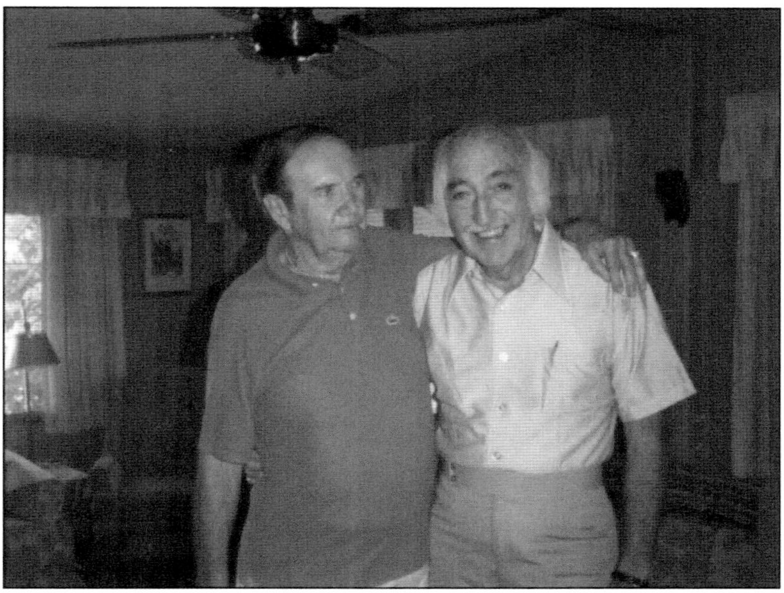

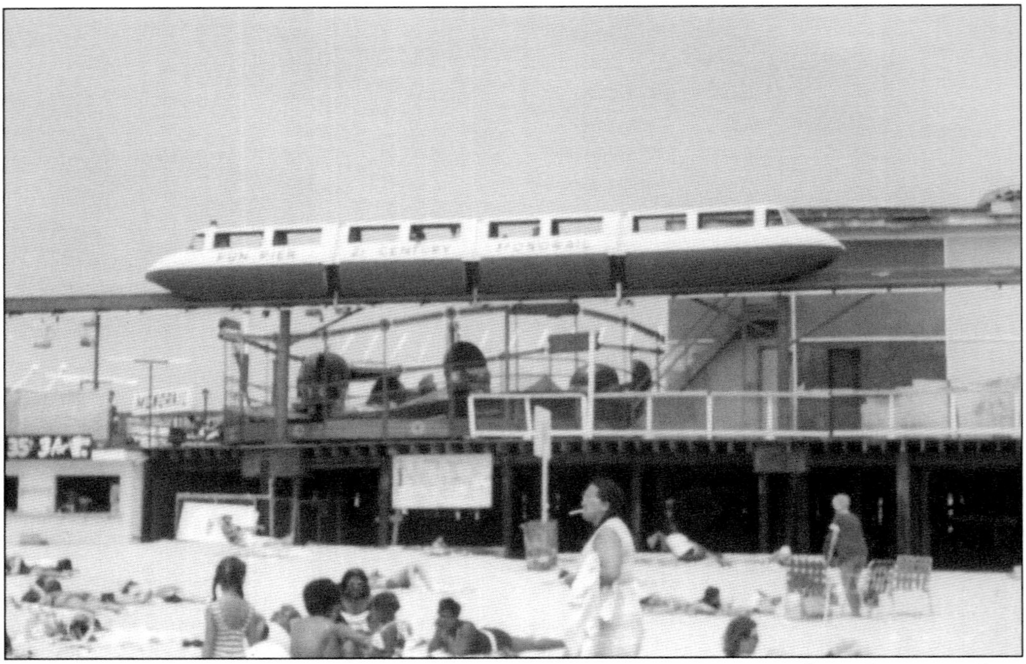

Fun Pier's 21st Century Monorail was still in full operation in 1972. It was the only monorail on the Wildwood Boardwalk, but maintenance issues and a desire to eliminate the tracks led Bill Howard to take it down after he acquired the pier from Joe Barnes. It is said that Barnes was unhappy with Howard's decision to get rid of the monorail. (Courtesy Diane Pooler.)

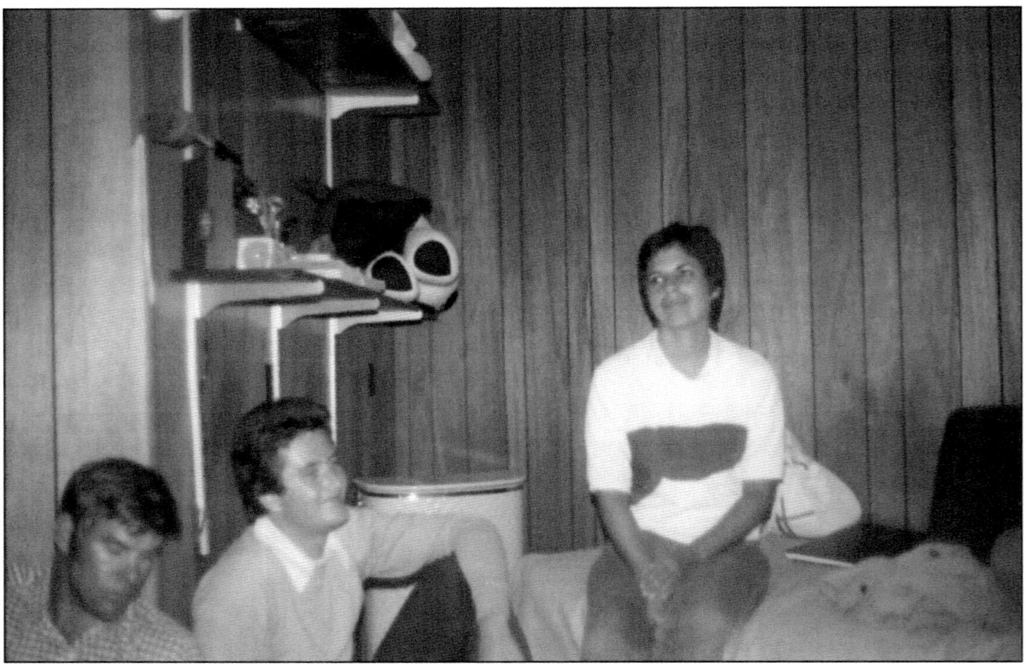

Art Fiala (left), Dennis Easy (center), and Sheila Rubin are inside the living quarters above the front office. Easy and Rubin were both from Canada and together redesigned the second incarnation of Castle Frankenstein in 1978. Working long hours, sometimes 16 hours a day and seven days a week, called for rest. (Courtesy Debbie Fiala-Davis.)

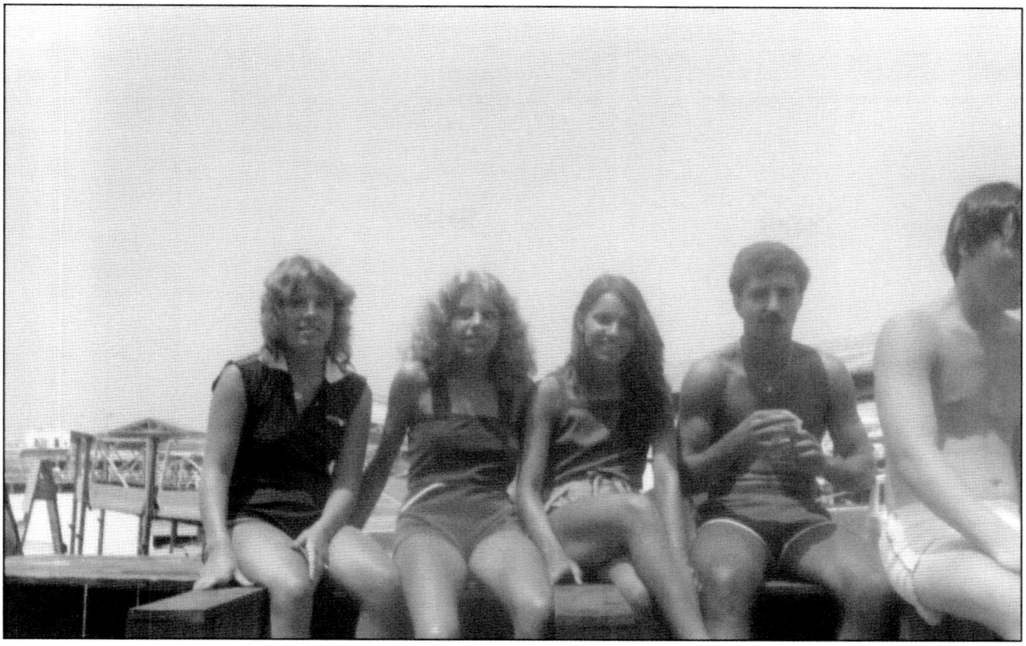

By 1979, pier mechanic Art Fiala had been promoted to pier manager. His daughter Debbie Fiala-Davis, pictured above on the left, had begun working on Fun Pier, too. Virtually all of Fiala's family worked and lived on the pier. Debbie is pictured above with, from left to right, friends Maggie, Mary, and Danny at the foot of the Fun Slide. Debbie recalls that the yellow mats were the smallest and fastest of all the mats used on the waterslide, and when the undersides were coated with soap, watch out, as the mat would fly down the chute. Display artist Jack Seddon rode a soap-coated mat and thought he was going to fly right off the chute onto the boardwalk. (Both, courtesy Debbie Fiala-Davis.)

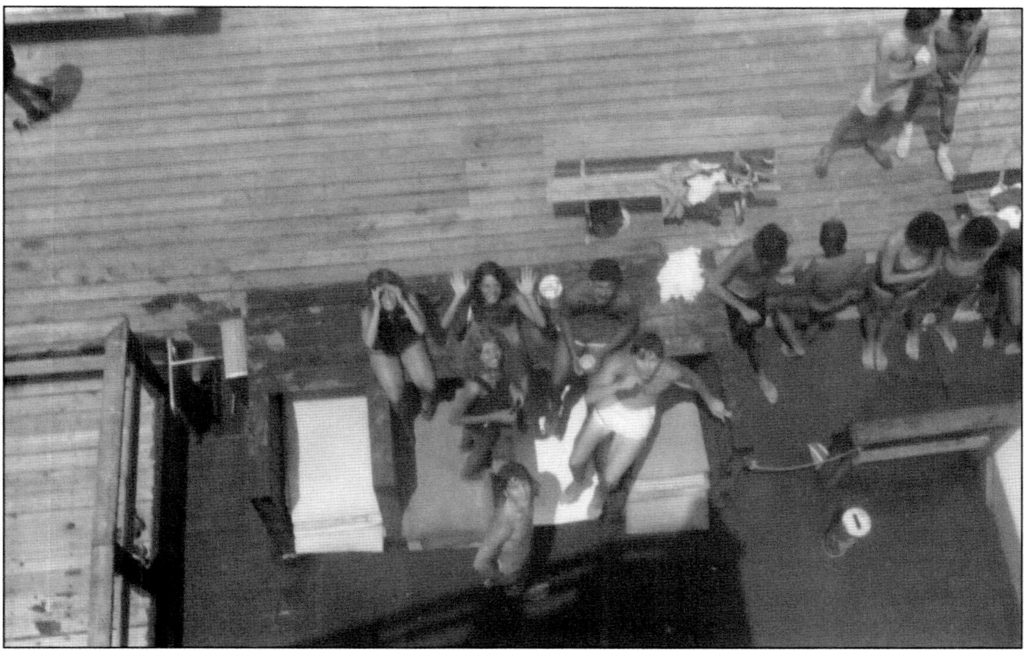

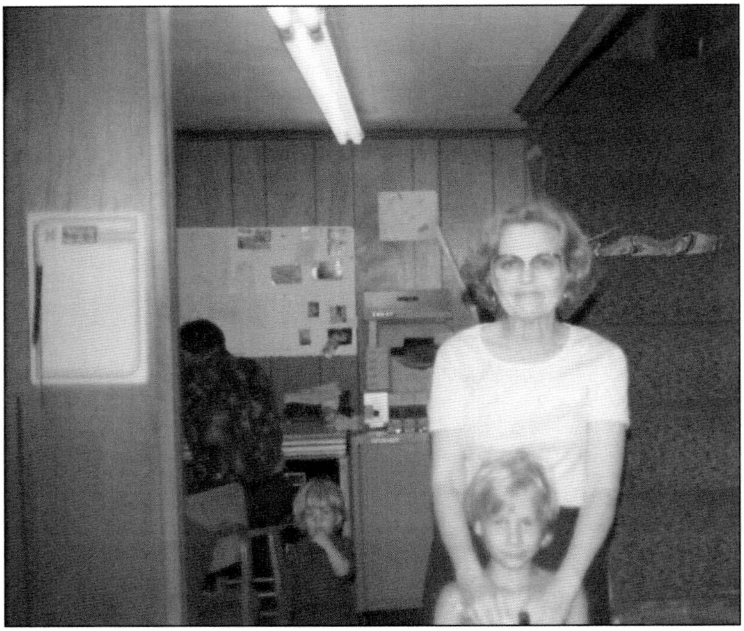

Bill and Helen Howard's office was located below their Fun Pier apartment. Helen is shown here with her grandson Alex in the office. Fun Pier was a family affair, not only for the Fialas, but also for the Howards, as numerous members of both families worked for the pier. (Courtesy Debbie Fiala-Davis.)

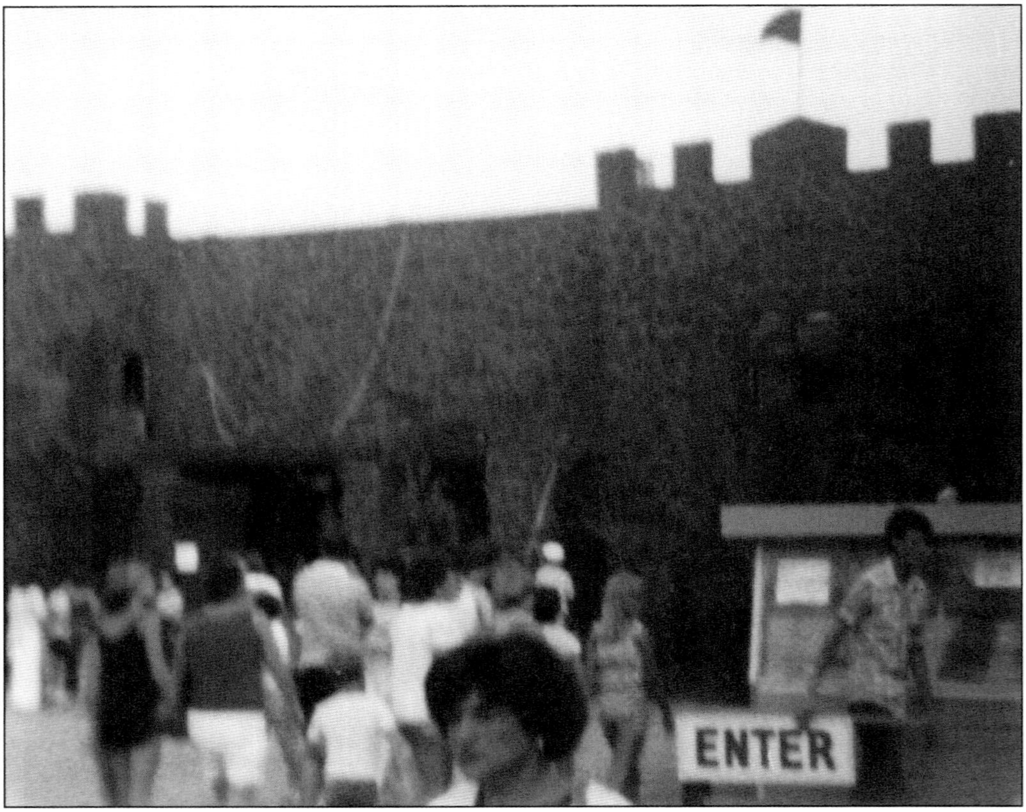

The new and improved Castle Frankenstein is still under construction in this photograph. Only the brick facade has been completed. As Sheila Rubin recalled, the artists' work began inside the castle. This ride needed to become a walk-through attraction, as the track had been badly damaged. (Courtesy Mike Bailey.)

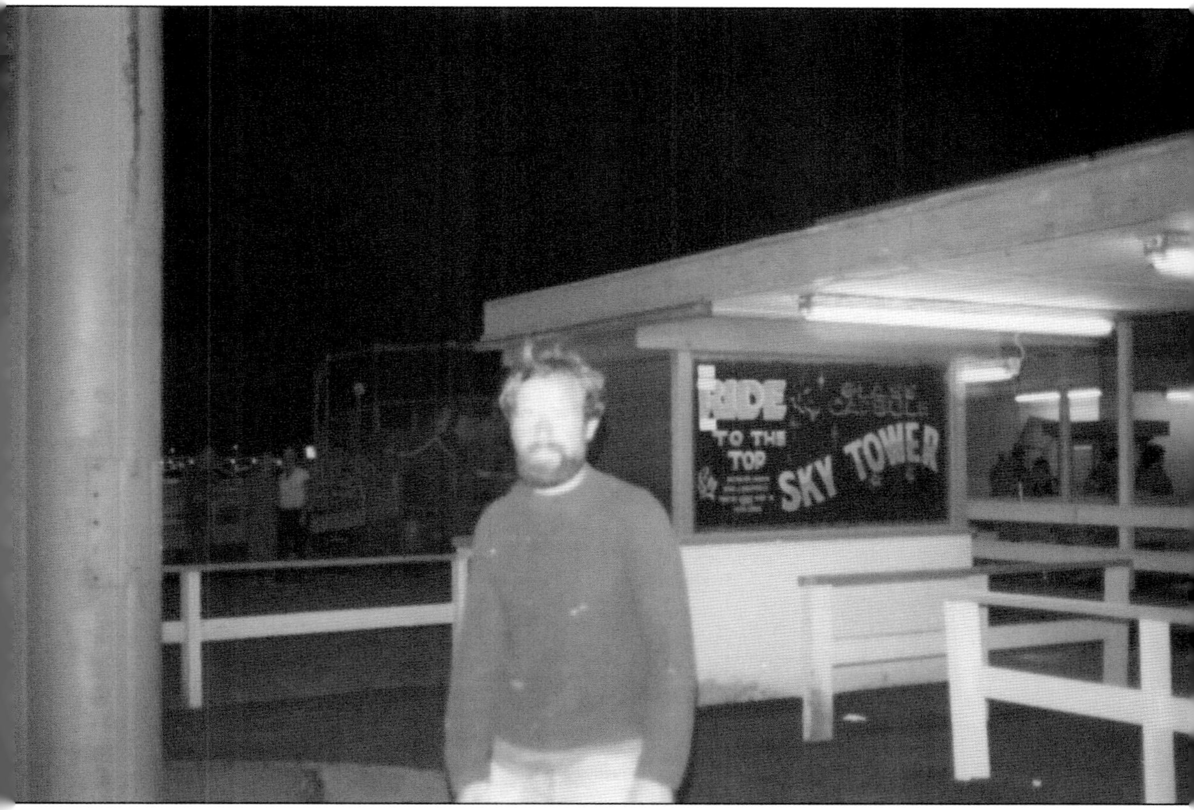

In this photograph, Peter Savard is pictured working on the Sky Tower, which in its later years had become prone to mechanical breakdowns. Since the motors of the Sky Tower were located at the top of the ride, few were both skilled enough and brave enough to climb out onto the top of the capsule to perform the repairs needed. By the early 1980s, customers were no longer able to ride the revolving capsule to the top of Sky Tower. Sky Tower would remain on the pier but nonoperational until all its parts except for the center pole were removed in the spring of 1985. The pole was finally dismantled and removed in May 2009. (Courtesy Debbie Fiala-Davis.)

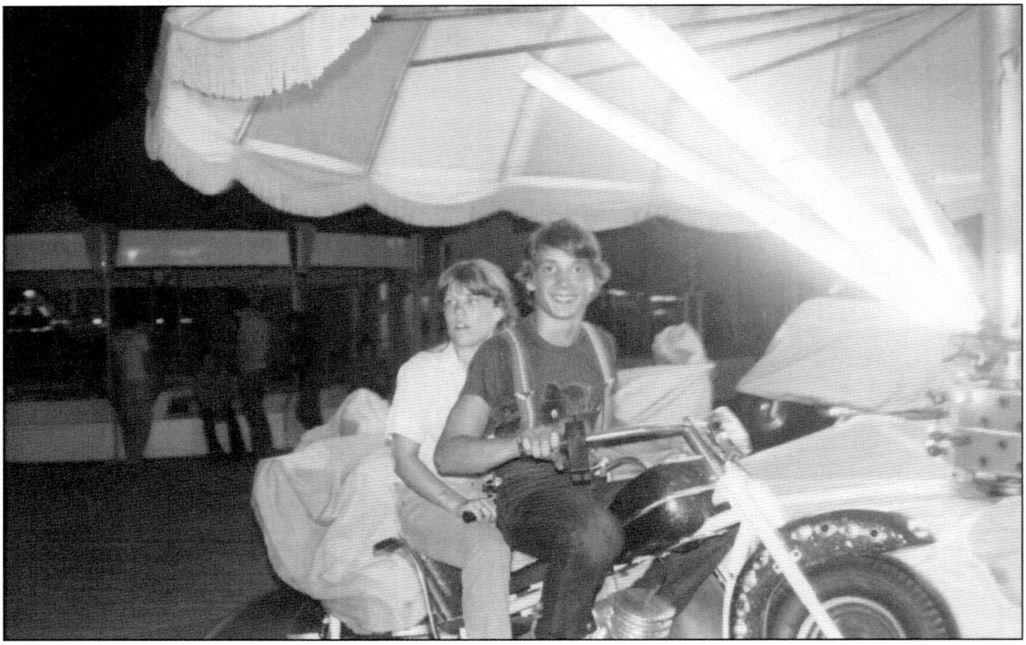

Debbie Fiala-Davis and friend Mick take a final ride on an umbrella ride before the pier closed at the end of the summer season in 1979. In those days, Labor Day weekend signaled the end of the season. (Courtesy Debbie Fiala-Davis.)

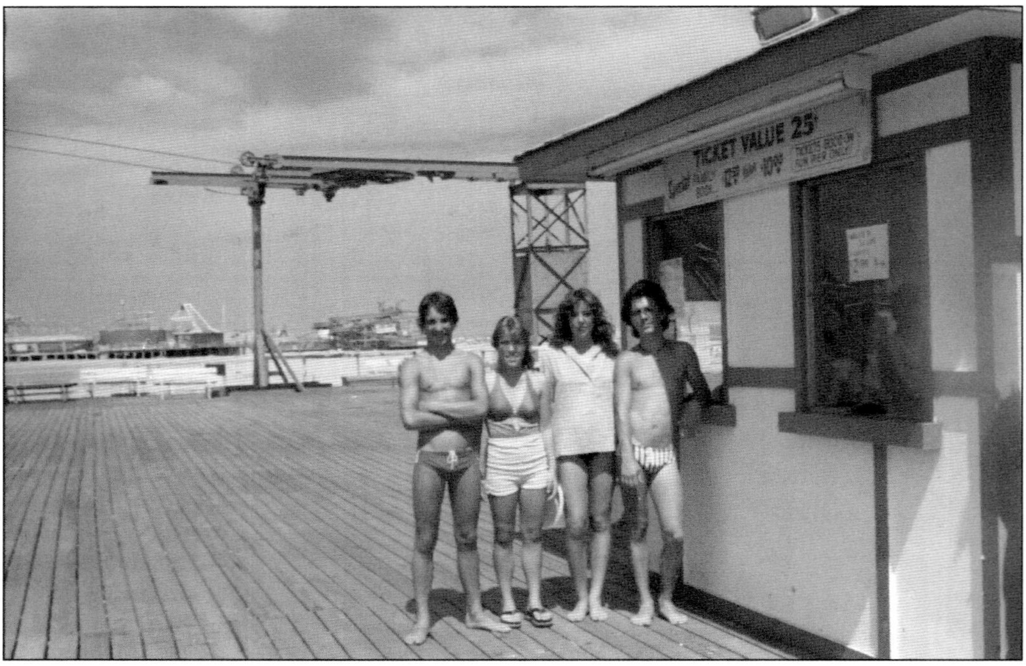

This photograph shows the ticket booth to the north, which was located next to the waterslide. Pictured here are, from left to right, Mick ?, Debbie Fiala-Davis, Sue ?, and John ?. Note the cables and mechanism for the Ski Ride. (Courtesy Debbie Fiala-Davis.)

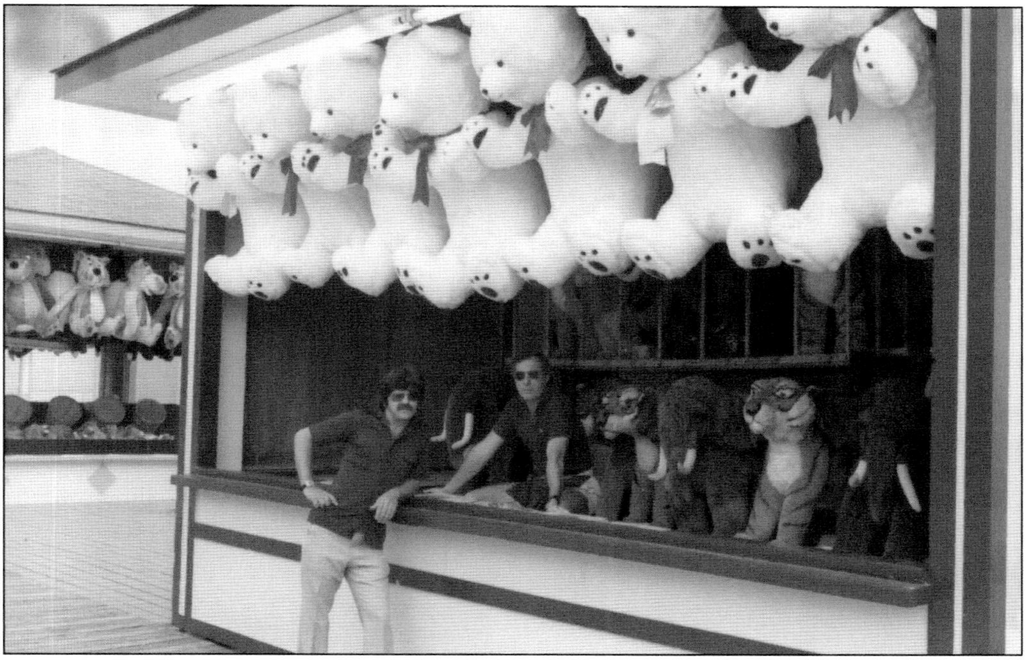

When all the piers on Wildwood were separately owned, Fun Pier was the one most known for games. After Bill Howard purchased the pier from Joe Barnes, not only were the then-current games enhanced, but many more were built on the pier. Wayne Mueller (left) was known to work many of the games; one such game was Fool the Guesser. (Courtesy Debbie Fiala-Davis.)

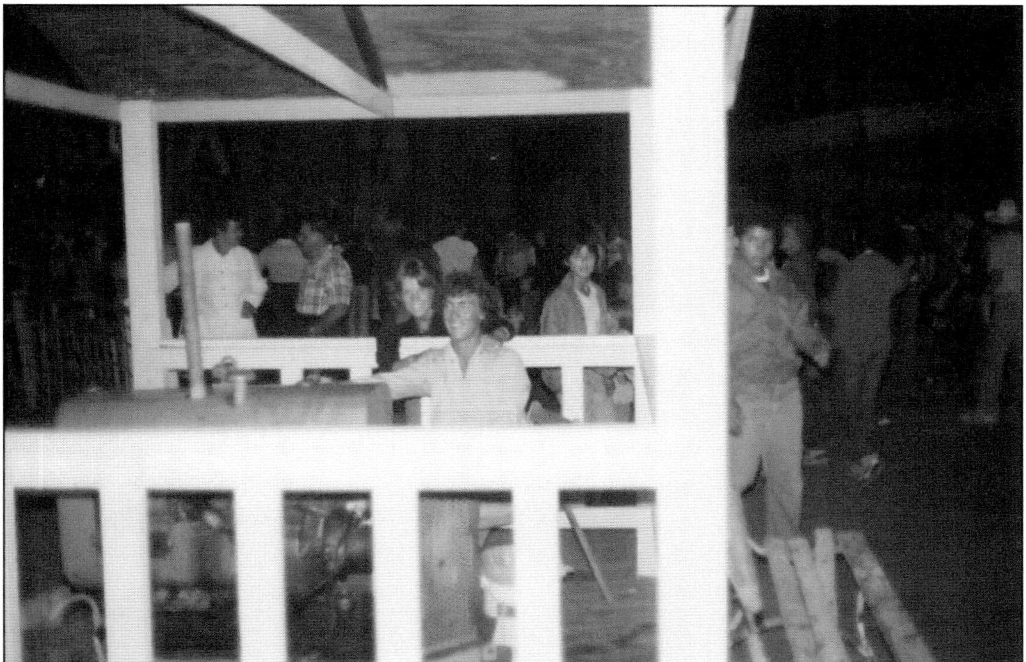

This tractor engine powered Fun Pier's Scrambler. This allowed the Scrambler to move a bit faster than most. Many of Fun Pier's employees had nicknames, such as ride operator "Smarty Pants," pictured here with Debbie Fiala-Davis. (Courtesy Debbie Fiala-Davis.)

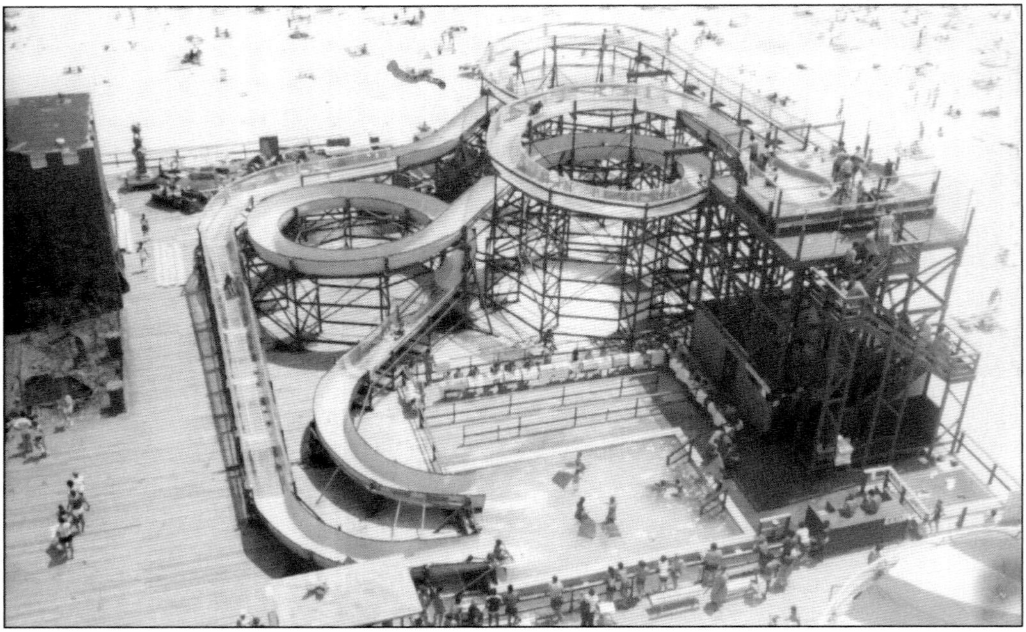

This aerial photograph shows the full size of the waterslide. Note Castle Frankenstein on the left. Also behind the waterslide are the cars from the Ski Ride. Though always popular, the waterslide suffered after a 1980 accident in which a panel became loose and fell out. A few riders got the shock of their life as they shot directly out at the beach instead of going down into a cool pool. (Courtesy Debbie Fiala-Davis.)

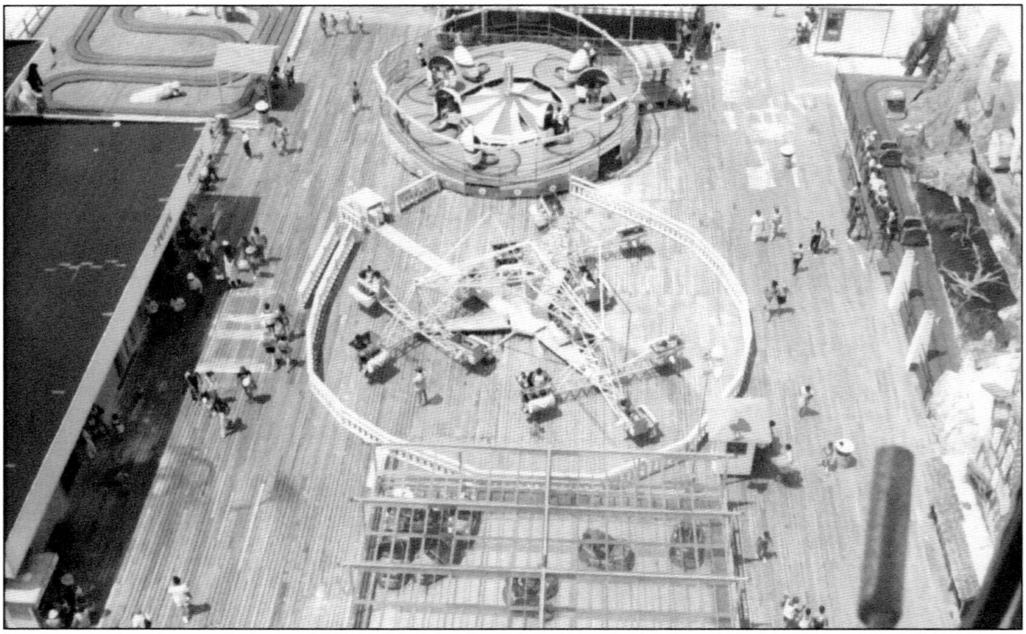

This aerial photograph from the Sky Tower capsule shows the arcade on the left, followed by a kiddie car ride with some former props from Devil's Inn, such as the hippo, rhino, and elephant. The bumper cars are directly below the Sky Tower, the Scrambler is in the center, and the Tilt-a-Whirl is at the top of the photograph. Lost World and Crazy House are on the right. (Courtesy Debbie Fiala-Davis.)

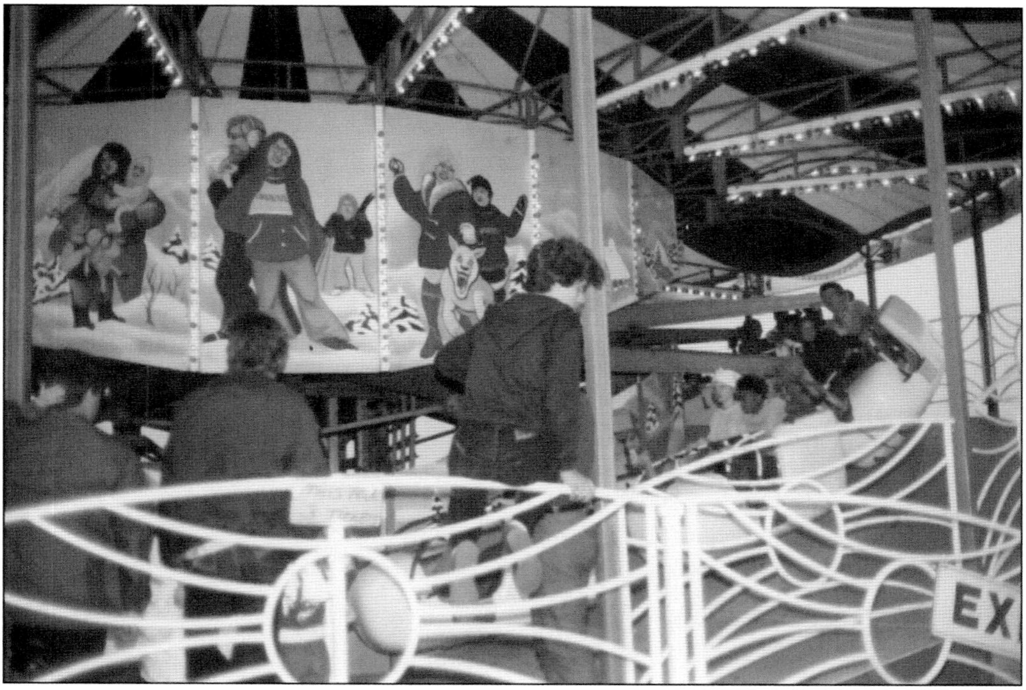

The Flying Bobs was an Allan Herschell Company ride. Flying Bobs are still in existence in other amusement parks. A version of this ride named Rock and Roll still exists in Wildwood on Morey's Surfside Pier. While the theme of the ride may be different, the thrill of the ride is all the same. (Courtesy Debbie Fiala-Davis.)

Go Karts were popular on the pier. However, Fun Pier began to feel the heat of the competition as Hunt's Pier and Morey's Piers were beginning to get the bulk of tourist traffic in the summer. These crucial years would determine the fate of amusement industry on the Wildwood Boardwalk. (Courtesy Debbie Fiala-Davis.)

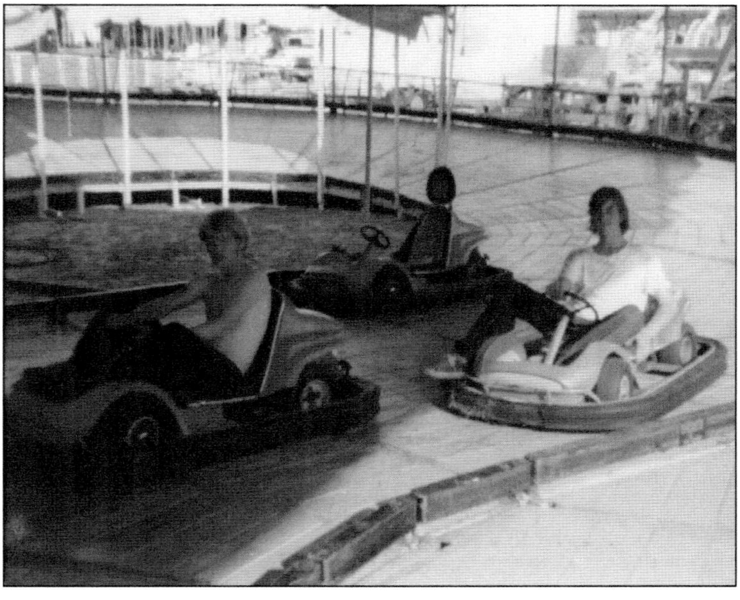

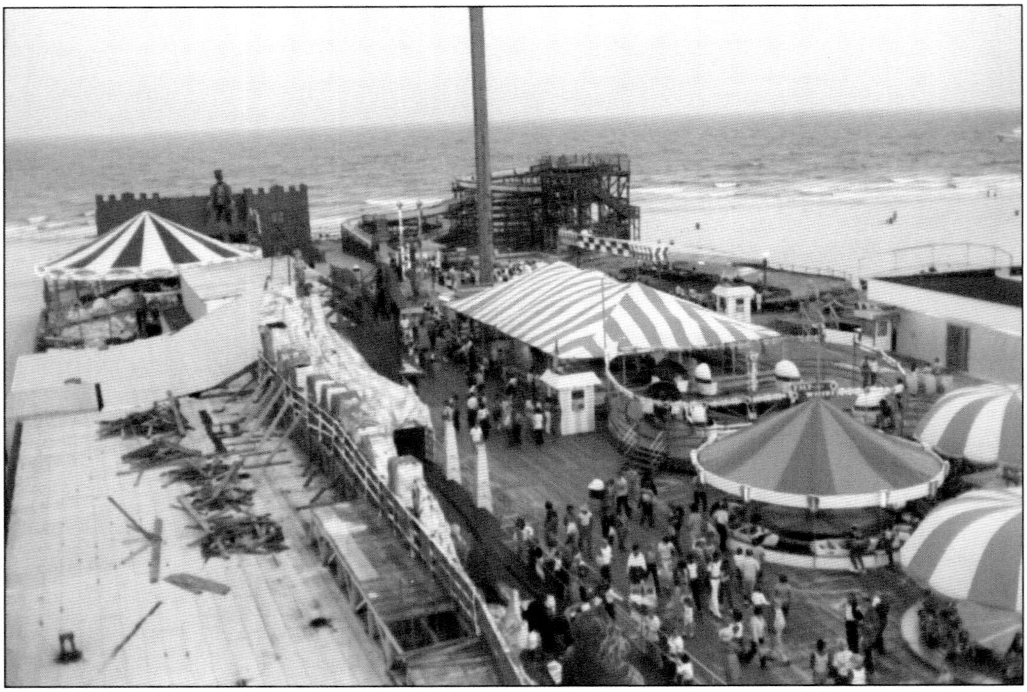

Pictured here in the summer of 1979, the pier had quite a lot of attractions to offer patrons. Castle Frankenstein always stood out, as it was located directly at the back end of the pier. Frankenstein's monster stood 22 feet tall and was elevated 10 feet above the entrance doors. (Courtesy Debbie Fiala-Davis.)

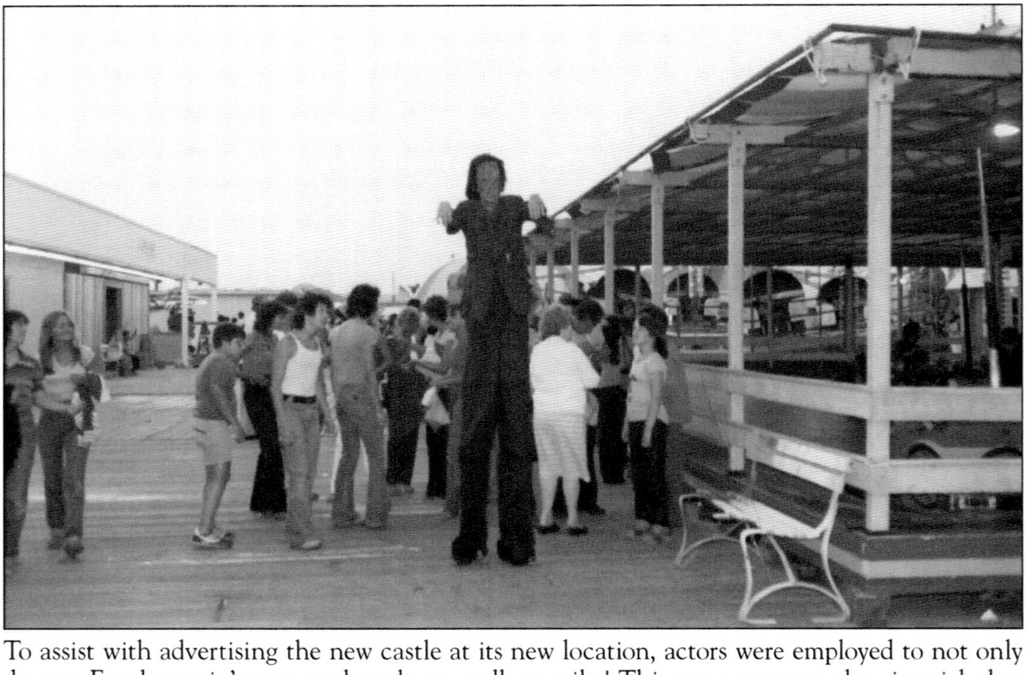

To assist with advertising the new castle at its new location, actors were employed to not only dress as Frankenstein's monster but also to walk on stilts! This was a very popular gimmick that Dennis Easy thought up, and at times, Easy himself had to wear the stilts. The actor pictured here is unidentified. (Courtesy Debbie Fiala-Davis.)

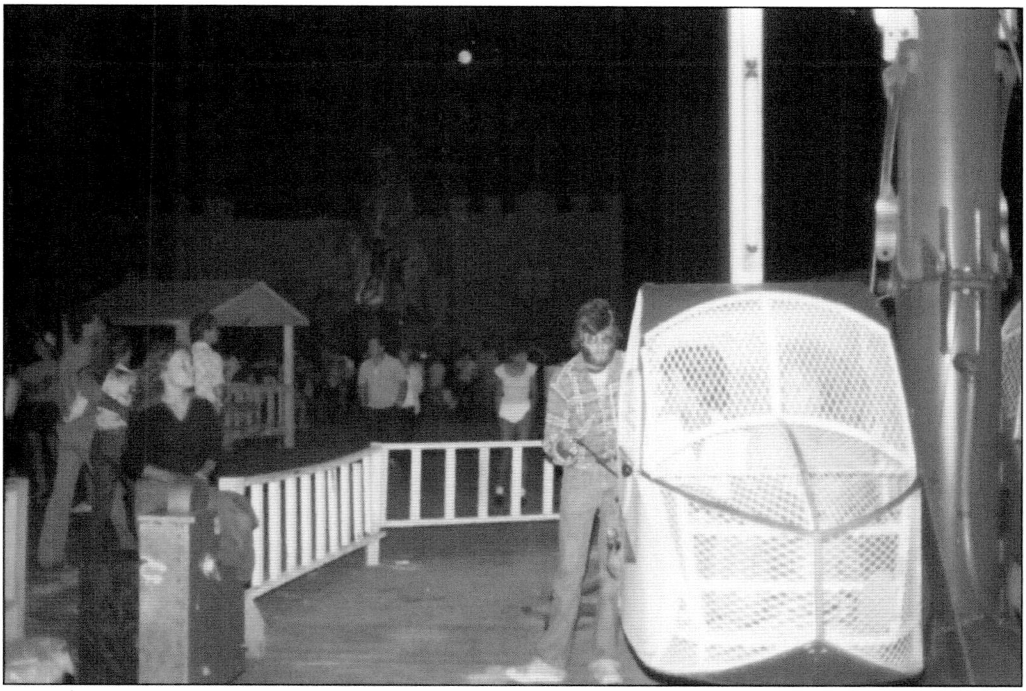

Salt and Pepper Shakers started on Marine Pier, but by the late 1970s, Marine Pier had been purchased by the Morey organization. Fun Pier continued to offer the ride. In this photograph, Debbie Fiala-Davis (left) oversees safety regulations. She took a highly active role on the pier. She sold tickets in the booth by the waterslide and operated kiddie rides. Her father also assigned her a concession stand, where she sold homemade lemonade, hot dogs, cotton candy, and pretzels. At the end of the night, she kept the books. (Courtesy Debbie Fiala-Davis.)

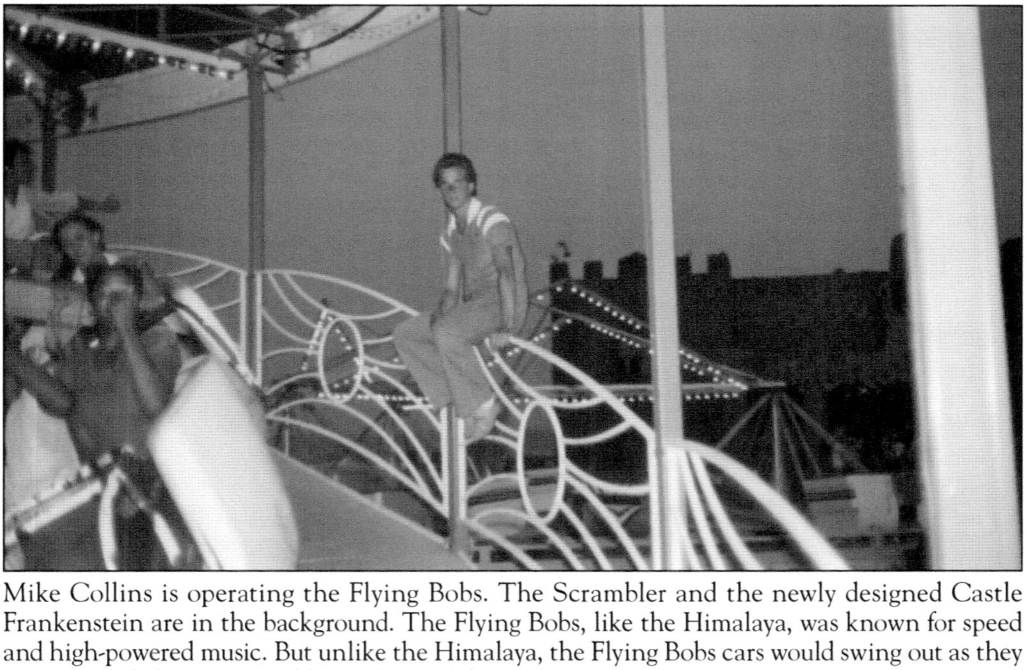

Mike Collins is operating the Flying Bobs. The Scrambler and the newly designed Castle Frankenstein are in the background. The Flying Bobs, like the Himalaya, was known for speed and high-powered music. But unlike the Himalaya, the Flying Bobs cars would swing out as they went around. (Courtesy Debbie Fiala-Davis.)

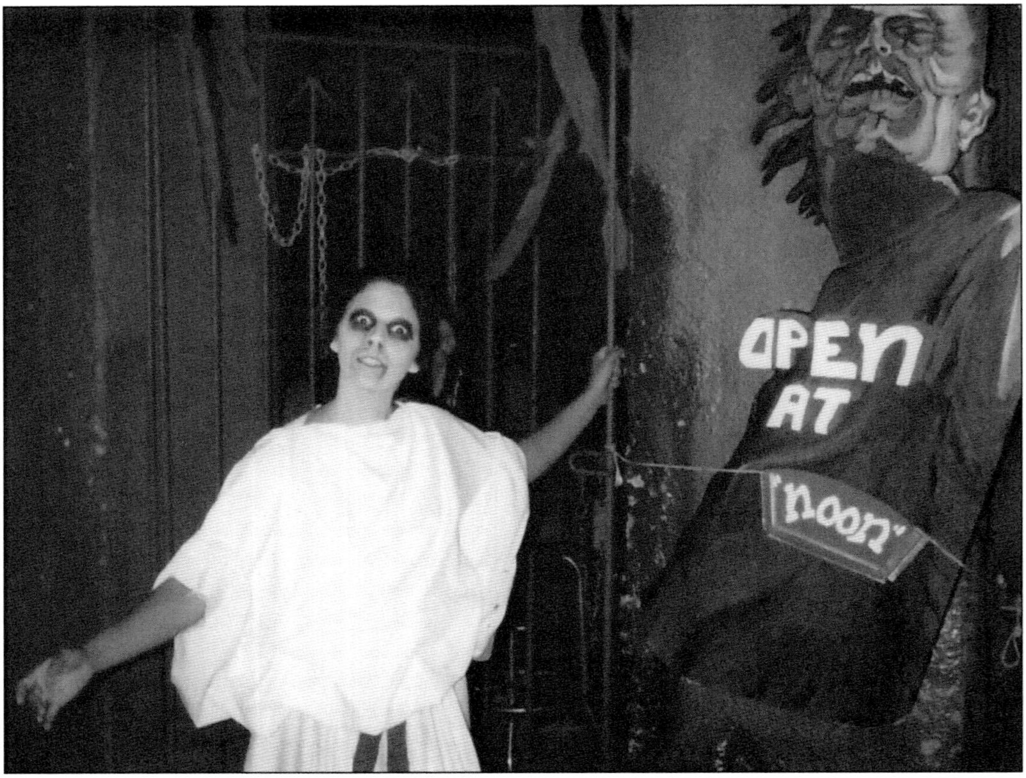

In the photograph below, Sheila Rubin poses against her own tombstone in the graveyard scene of the all-new Castle Frankenstein. To the this day, Sheila is a very talented artist in Canada; Fun Pier's Castle Frankenstein would be her only time as an amusement display artist and actress. The brickwork on the new castle was done by Garden State Brickface, which also did work on Brigantine Castle. Rubin painted the large sign on the gatepost of the castle, which is next to her in the image above; she remembers the sign was so large that when she finished it one night, she scared herself. (Above, courtesy Lee Durland; below, courtesy Debbie Fiala-Davis.)

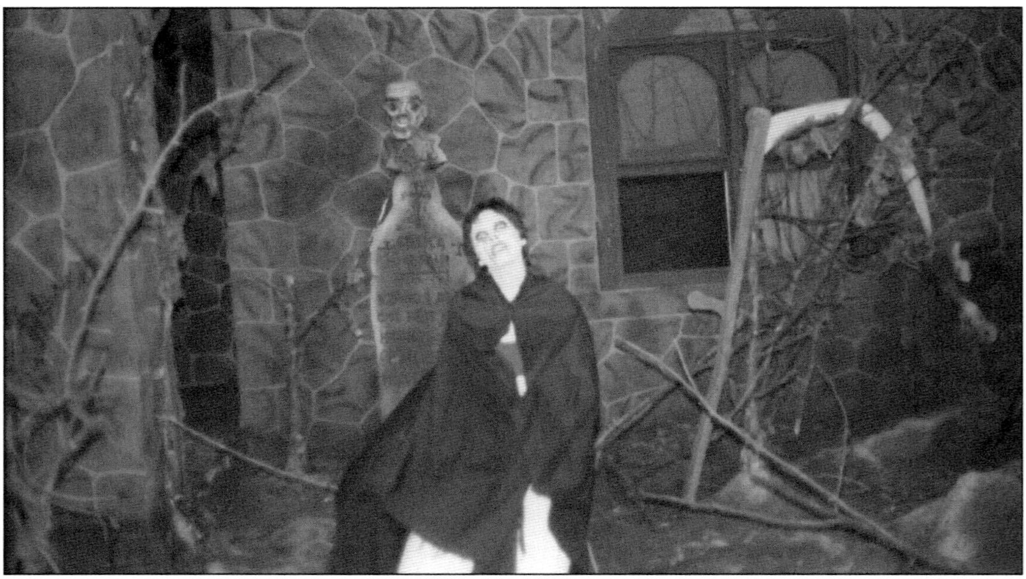

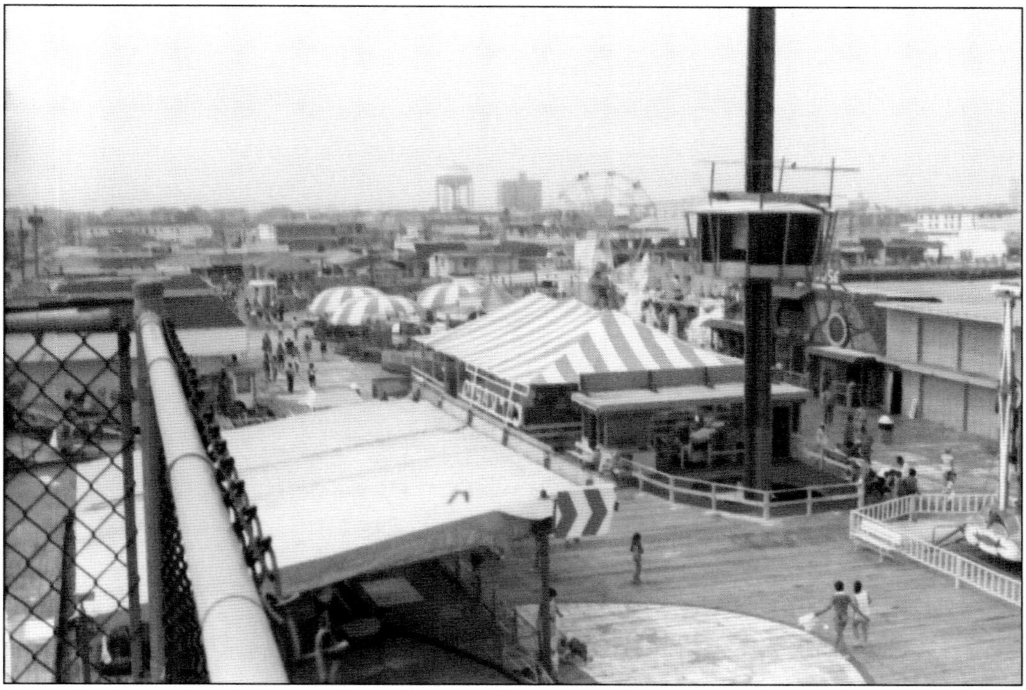

Viewed from atop the waterslide, here the Sky Tower is no longer secure for riders. Also, the Mirror Maze building has been changed to a storage facility. An interesting note is that a portion of the Mirror Maze was taken out and put into the first floor of Crazy House. This addition to Crazy House enhanced the walk-through experience as well as tipping its hat. (Courtesy Debbie Fiala-Davis.)

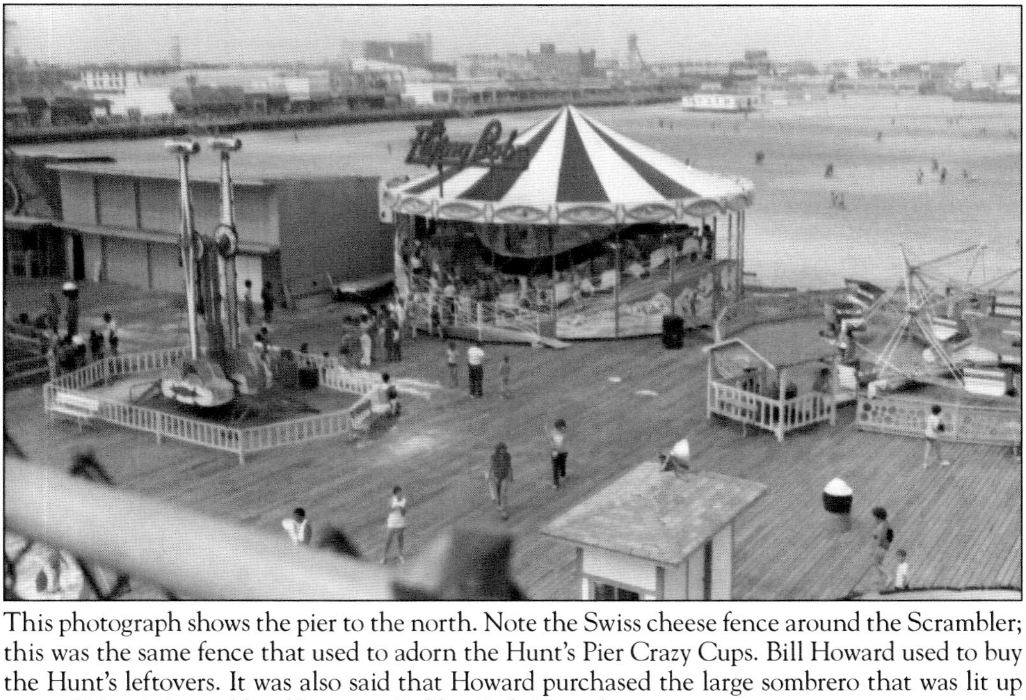

This photograph shows the pier to the north. Note the Swiss cheese fence around the Scrambler; this was the same fence that used to adorn the Hunt's Pier Crazy Cups. Bill Howard used to buy the Hunt's leftovers. It was also said that Howard purchased the large sombrero that was lit up atop of Hunt's Scrambler. (Courtesy Debbie Fiala-Davis.)

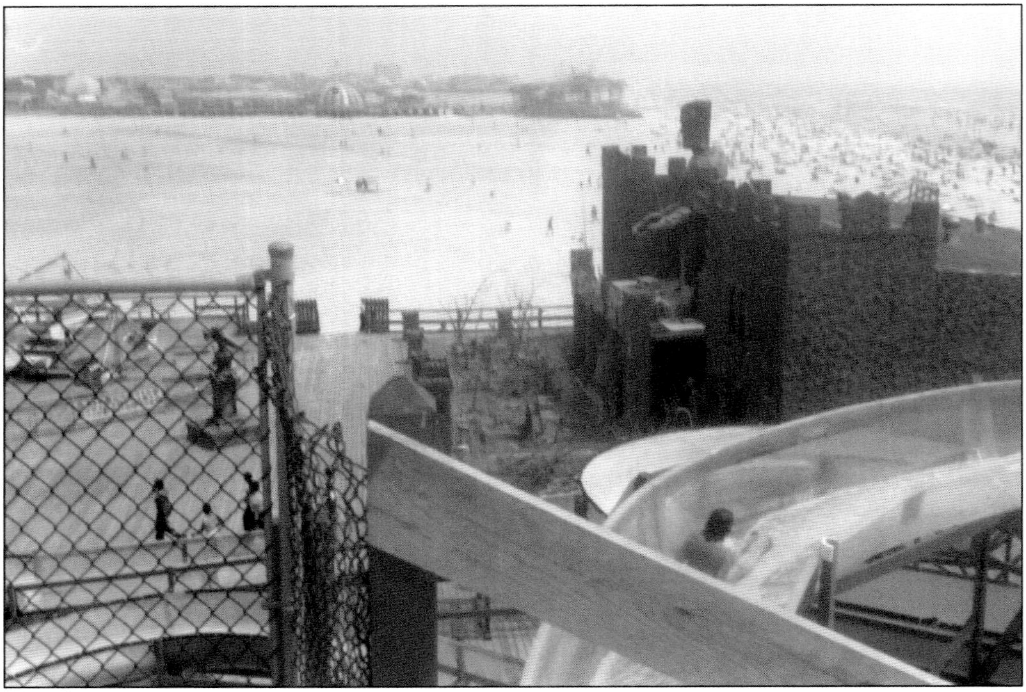

Here is another photograph looking at the Castle Frankenstein. The original plan was to keep the castle open during the evening hours only, from 6:00 p.m. until close. However, some patrons seem to enjoy these types of walk-through attractions during the afternoon hours. As the need to keep revenue going was a must, the castle quickly began to keep operational hours from noon until close. (Courtesy Debbie Fiala-Davis.)

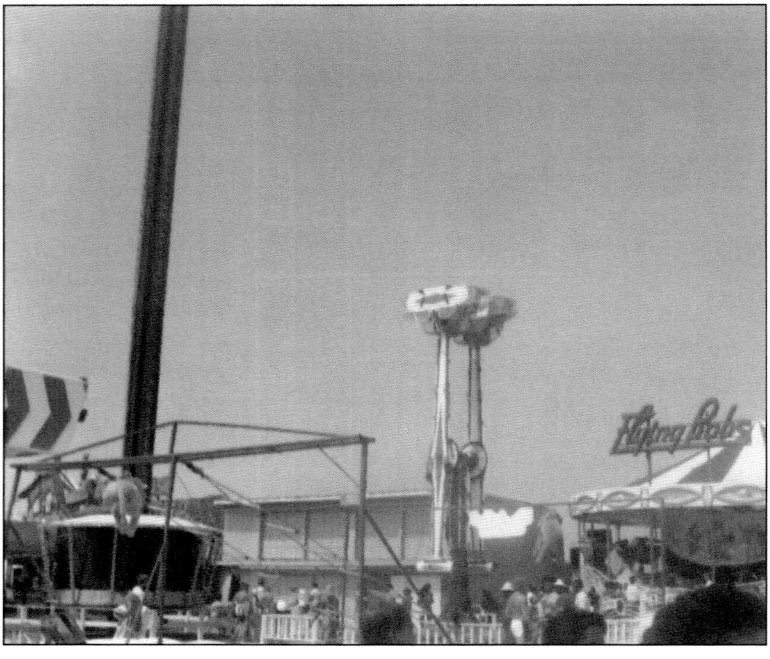

The former Mirror Maze building became a shooting gun game station for a short time before finally being reduced to a storage facility. Ideas for another walk-through attraction were under consideration but eventually were scrapped. The building was destroyed by fire in November 1984. (Courtesy Debbie Fiala-Davis.)

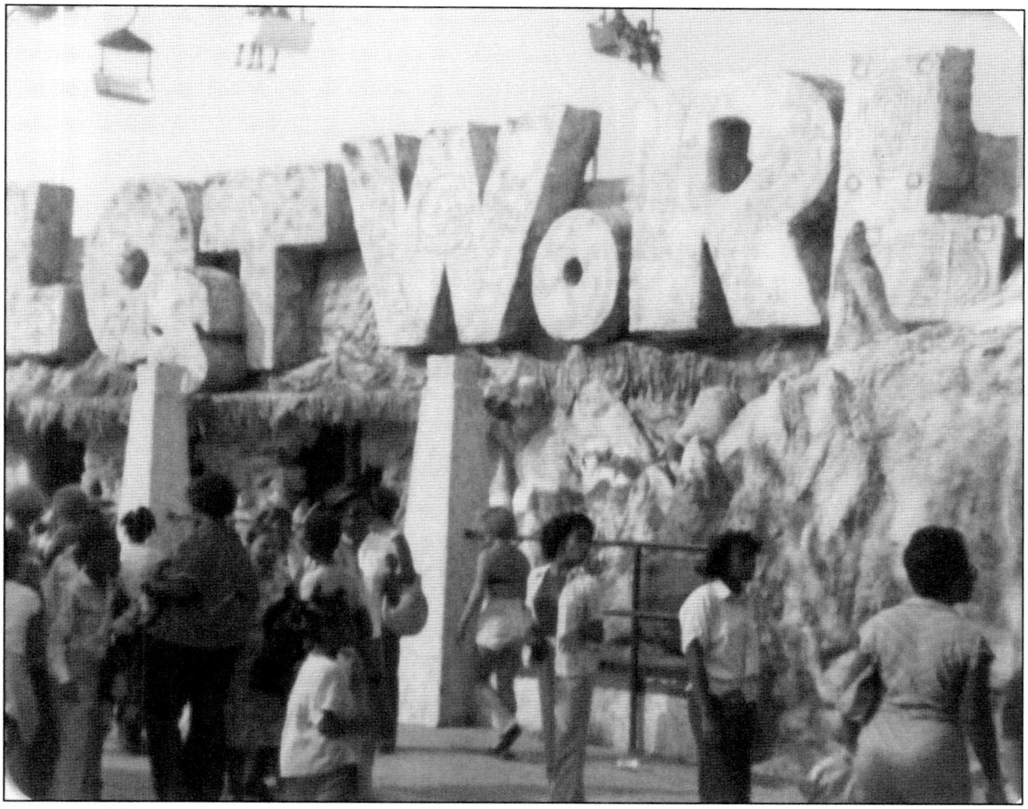

Lost World was a long holdover on Fun Pier. This ride had taken on many different titles and themes. By late 1974, Devil's Inn was not doing well, and the pier management under J.D. Floyd considered tearing it down. After Joe Barnes denied them this request, pier manager Glenn Bergathon sought out Freddy Mahana. Mahana's lead artist, Jim DeMusz, was brought in to retheme the ride based on the Lost World, the new title that Mahana came up with. (Courtesy Mike Bailey.)

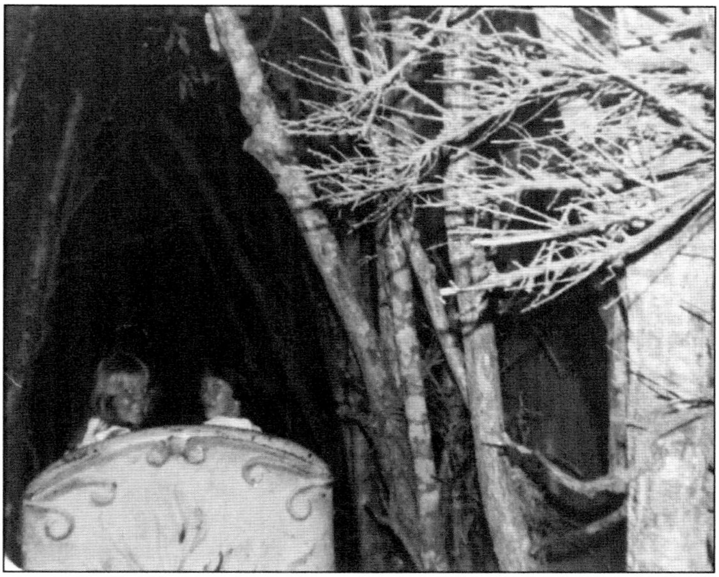

This is a rare photograph of the interior of the Lost World. This ride was half ride-through and half walk-through. Jim DeMusz made numerous displays and murals for this ride. Actors dressed as Aztec cannibals and Inca warriors. Before the ride ended, an actor would turn off the car and demand the riders "get out" and "walk left." Sometimes, they even banged a large stick that resembled a club against the ride car. (Courtesy Mike Bailey.)

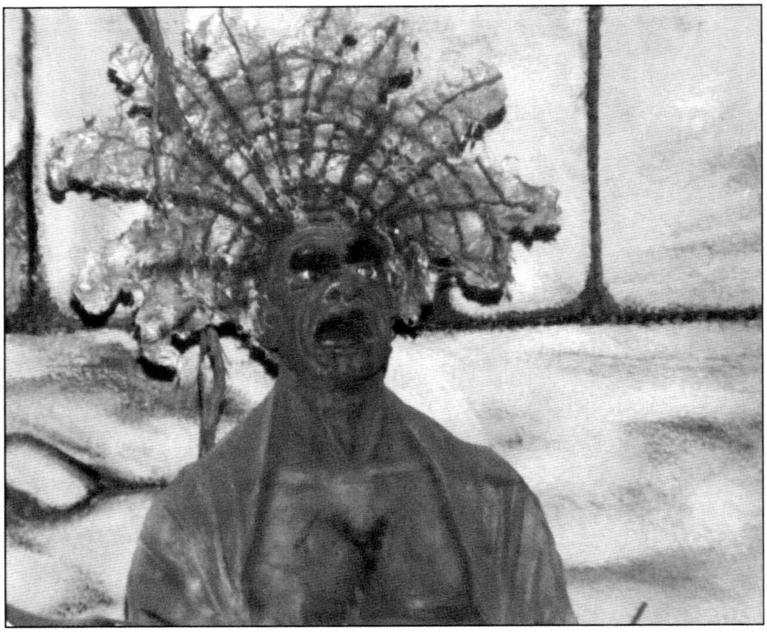

The Chief was an indoor prop accompanied by audio. After exiting the car and walking through a tree maze, the customer would encounter the Chief, who explained that to escape the Lost World, one would have to walk down a narrow flight of stairs into the dark caverns. (Courtesy Mike Bailey.)

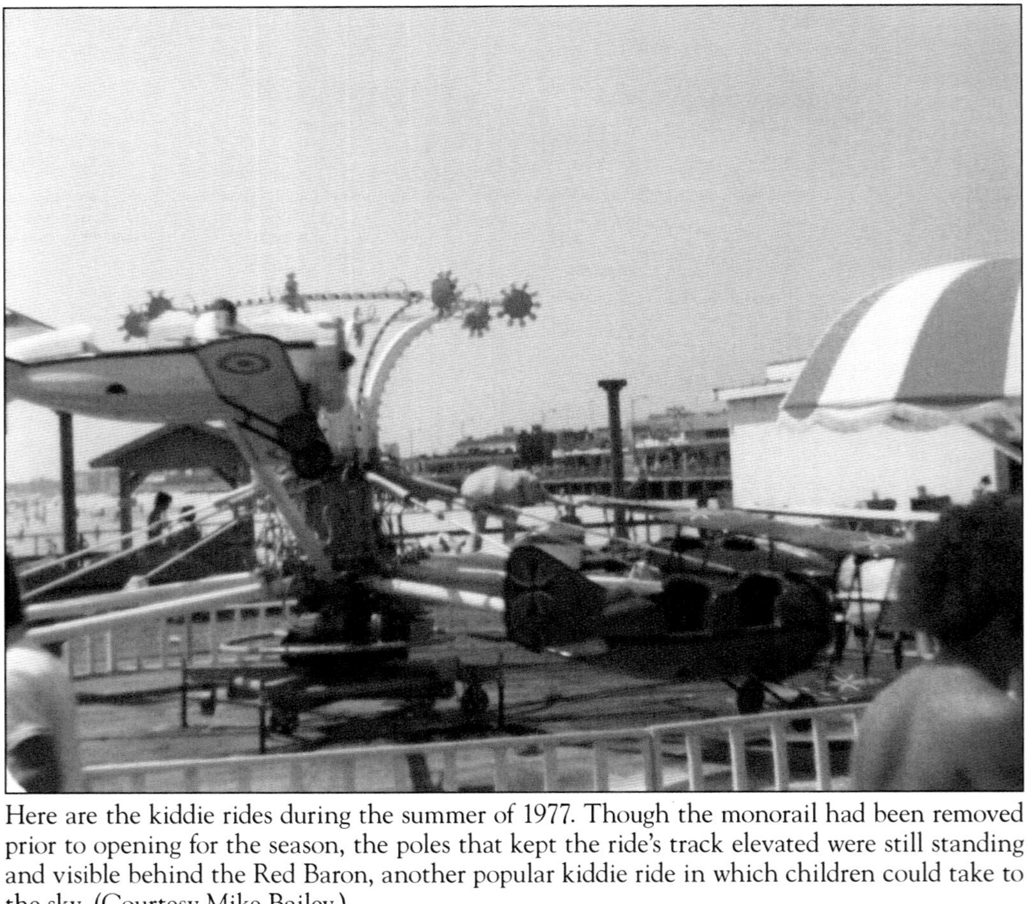

Here are the kiddie rides during the summer of 1977. Though the monorail had been removed prior to opening for the season, the poles that kept the ride's track elevated were still standing and visible behind the Red Baron, another popular kiddie ride in which children could take to the sky. (Courtesy Mike Bailey.)

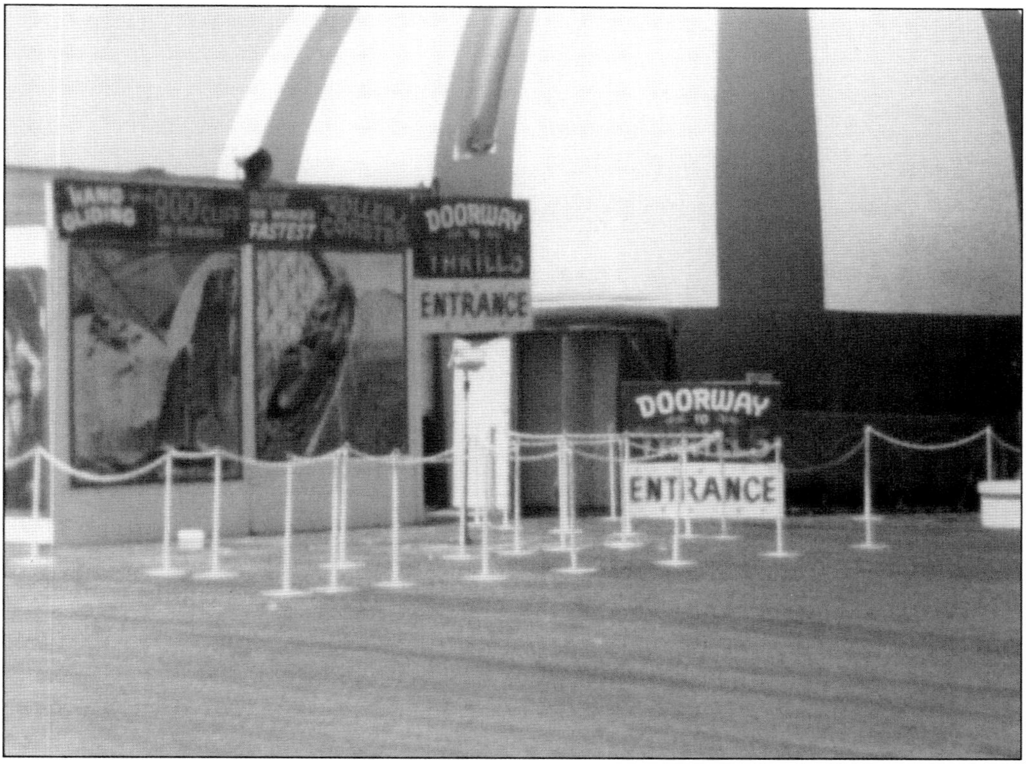

During the 1970s, Cinema 180s were popular boardwalk attractions. This one on Fun Pier was titled Doorway to Thrills. No 3D glasses were needed, and no seating was necessary either. The wrap-around screen simulated the thrill of hang gliding and other popular thrills. (Courtesy Mike Bailey.)

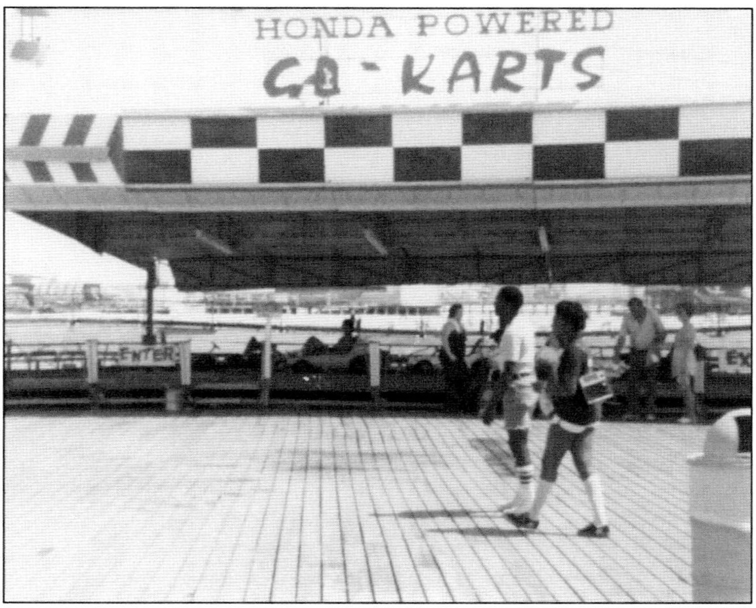

This photograph shows Morey's Mariner's Landing to the north during the summer of 1977 on Fun Pier. Go-karts have always been a popular attraction. Note the Ski Ride car in the upper left corner. Only a decade after this photograph was taken, the Morey family would purchase Fun Pier from Bill Howard. (Courtesy Mike Bailey.)

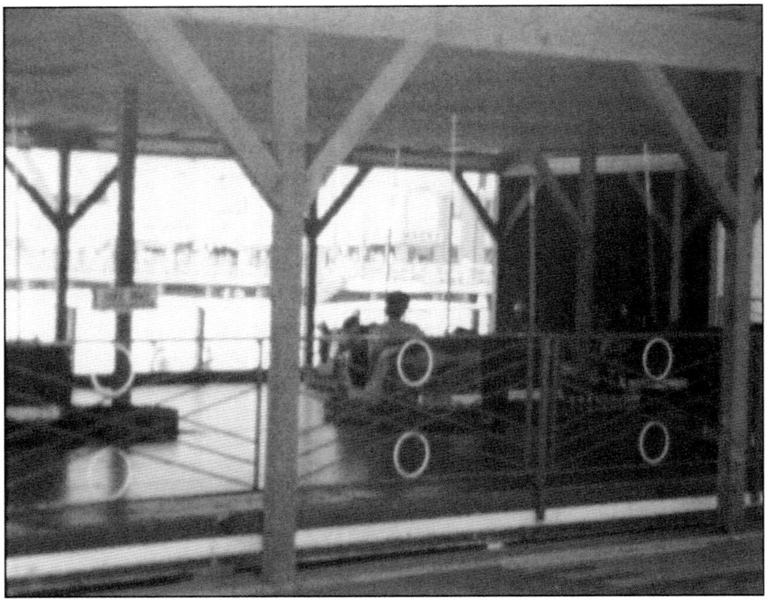

This is another photograph of the gas-powered Honda go-karts. As the Howards were involved in other amusement parks and state fairs, the cars would be taken with them. Bill Howard's other amusement endeavors included Martin's Fantasy Island in Niagara Falls and Marshall Hall Amusement Park on the Potomac River. (Courtesy Mike Bailey.)

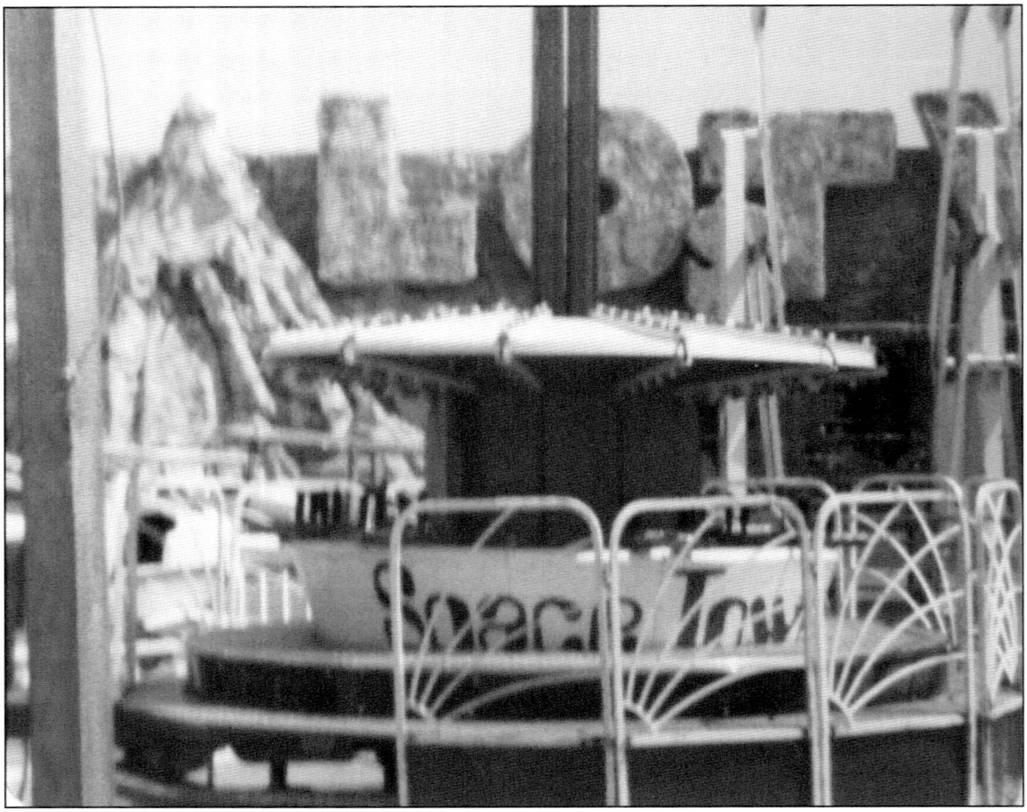

Since Sky Tower could no longer safely climb to its original height, it was reopened as a scaled-down or mini version called the Space Tower. Where Sky Tower would take riders to heights close to 50 feet, Space Tower would take children up around 12 feet. This ride was short-lived on the pier. Most riders wanted the spectacular view of Wildwood from Sky Tower. (Courtesy Mike Bailey.)

A rider comes down from the Sky Tower, looking down on the Spider ride with Tilt-A-Whirl in the background. Lost World's loading station is to the left. (Courtesy Mike Bailey.)

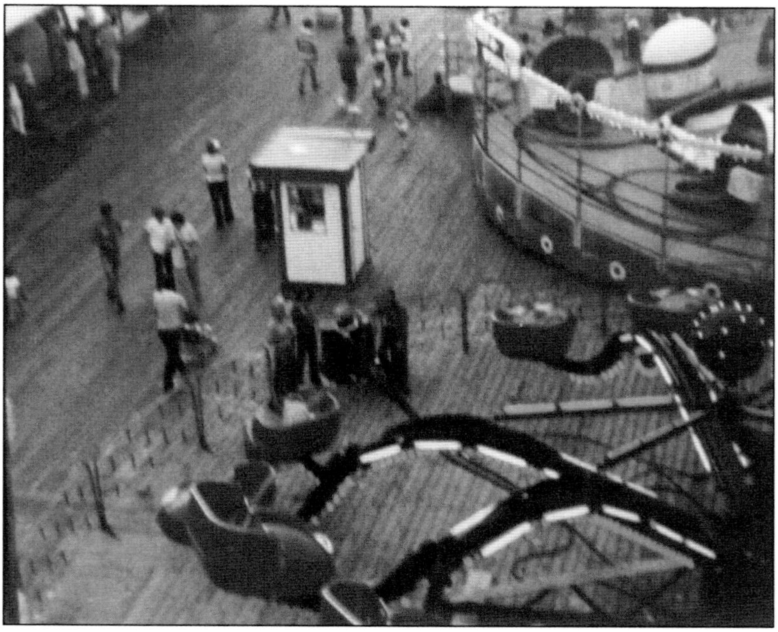

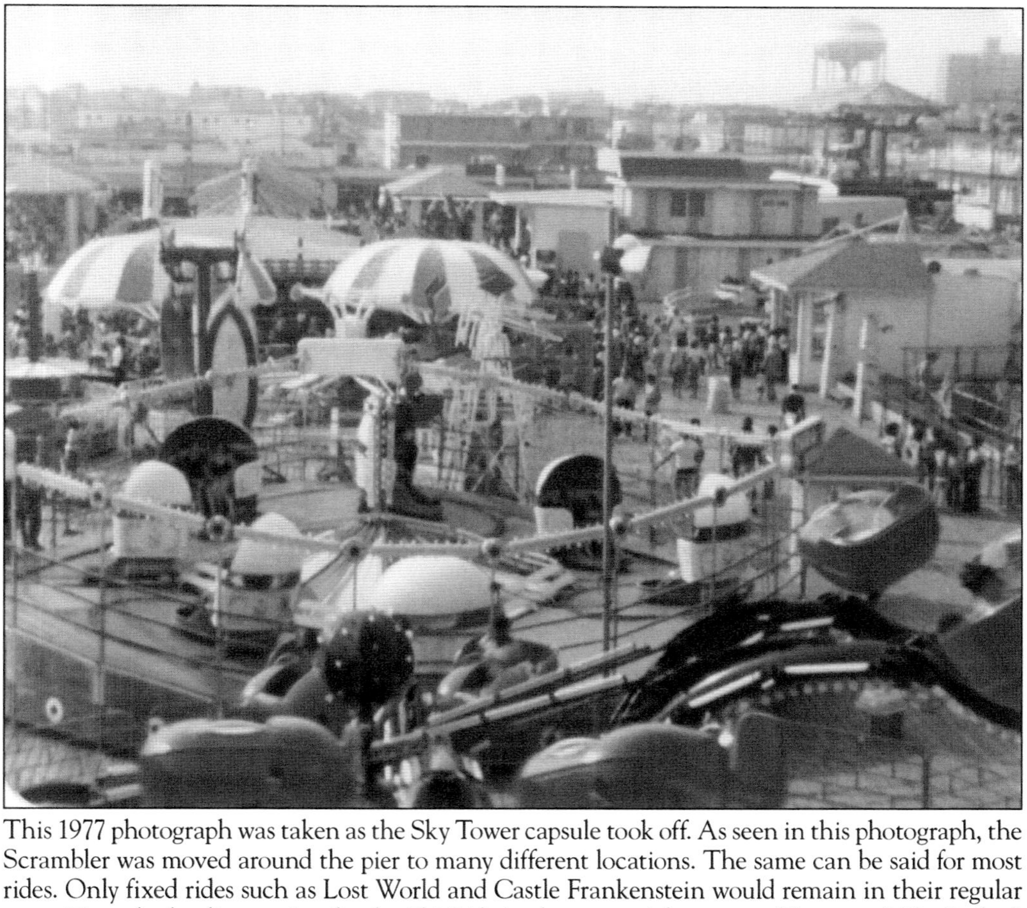

This 1977 photograph was taken as the Sky Tower capsule took off. As seen in this photograph, the Scrambler was moved around the pier to many different locations. The same can be said for most rides. Only fixed rides such as Lost World and Castle Frankenstein would remain in their regular spots. Note the loading station for the Ski Ride in the upper right corner. (Courtesy Mike Bailey.)

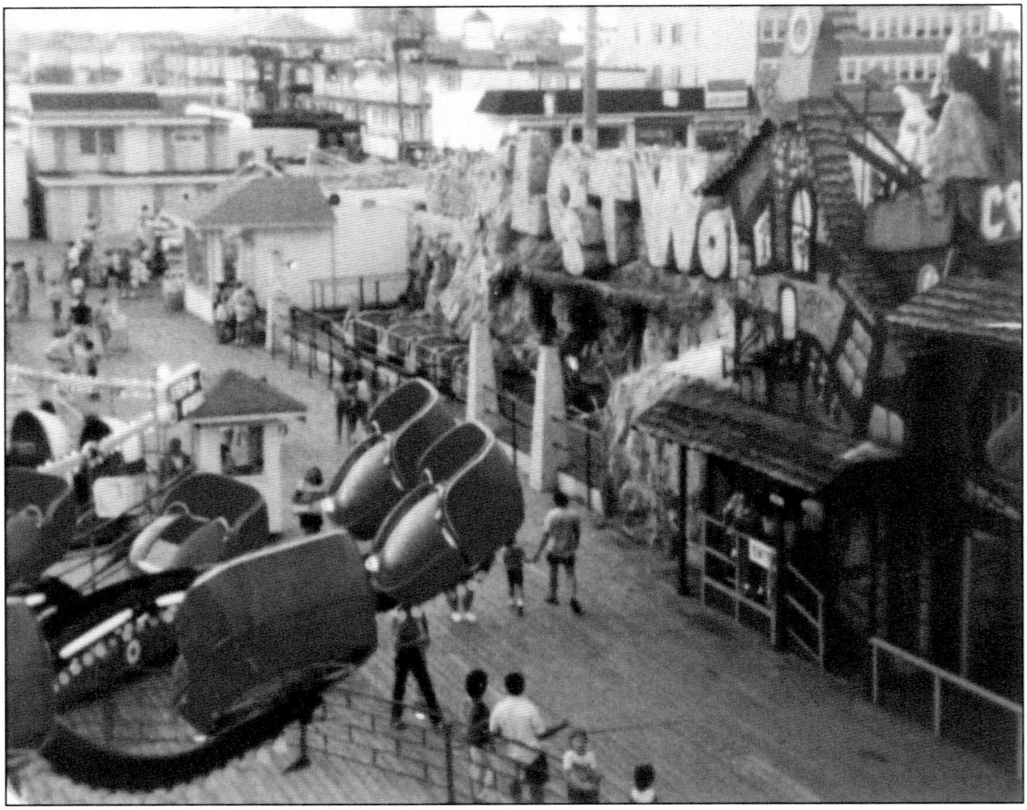

The iconic gorilla that stood by Lost World for most of its run is missing in this photograph. During the hurricane of 1976, King Kong fell and broke. The following summer, Sheila Rubin would visit Fun Pier and take it upon herself to repair him. The foot and face of the gorilla were badly damaged. The foot was the most difficult part to repair, as it provided stability for the giant statue. Sheila did the repair so successfully that pier owner Bill Howard asked Rubin if she would stay on, loaning her talents for their newest attraction in 1978, Castle Frankenstein. (Courtesy Mike Bailey.)

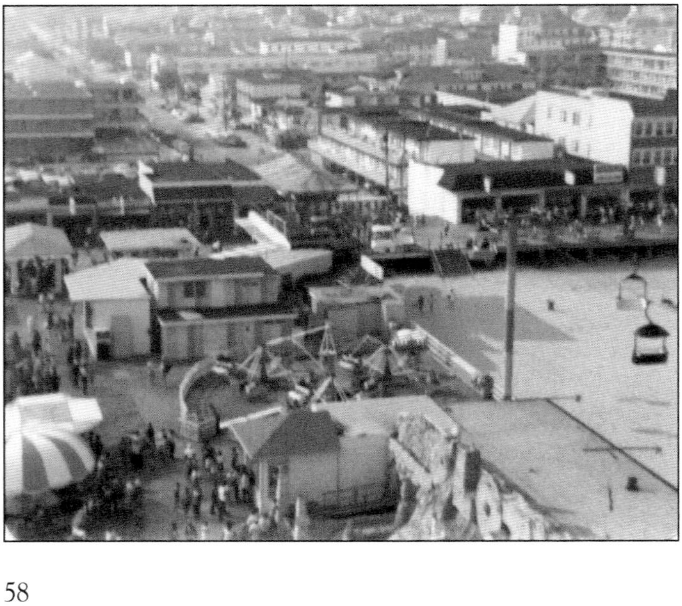

Note the two-level office building in front of the Scrambler. The first floor was the main business office for Fun Pier management, while the second floor contained the rooming apartments. The building to the right was also used for living quarters, and additional living accommodations were located right behind the Crazy House. (Courtesy Mike Bailey.)

At the top of the Sky Tower during its revolution, one was treated to a magnificent panorama of the northern part of the Wildwood Boardwalk, including Morey's Mariner's Landing, Hunt's Pier, and Sportland Pier. Note Mariner's Landing Cinema 180 and waterslide. The Ramagosa family played a hand in all these waterslide creations, but a waterslide never did appear on Ramagosa's Sportland Pier, as the Aqua Slides sat directly across the boardwalk from the pier. (Courtesy Mike Bailey.)

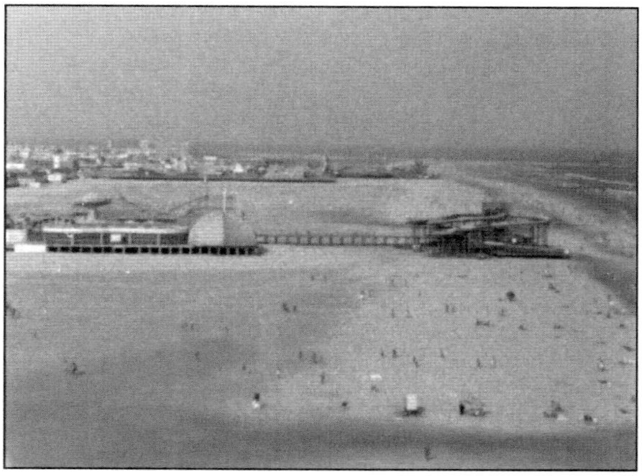

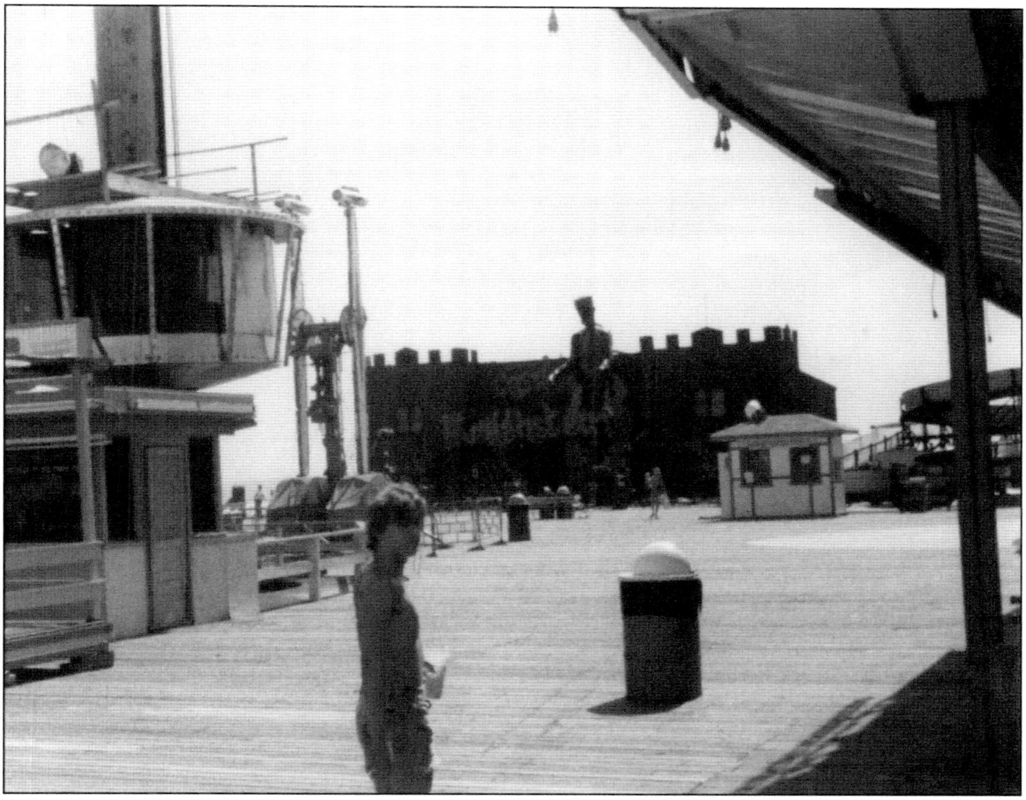

The start of another fun day on the pier shows little action. The Sky Tower is looking like it has seen better days, and by this time, another ride had been placed directly in front of the loading area that was used for the tower. It was only a matter of time before the once-magnificent Sky Tower would be removed from the pier and become another part of Wildwood Boardwalk history. Castle Frankenstein still stood larger-than-life, and no matter where people found themselves, it always appeared as though the monster was looking down upon them. (Courtesy Angelo Quisito.)

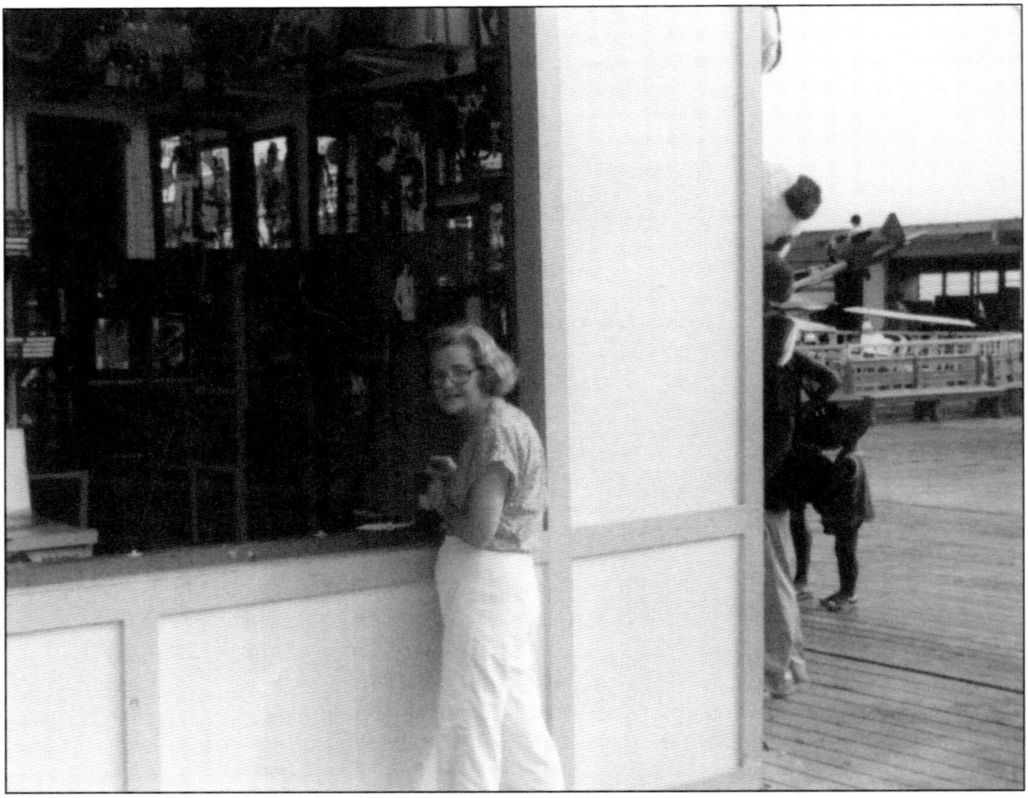

Helen Howard checks up on the game concessions. She had been involved in the carnival industry for most of her life. She and her husband, Bill, became regular fixtures before purchasing the pier from Joe Barnes in November 1976. (Courtesy Angelo Quisito.)

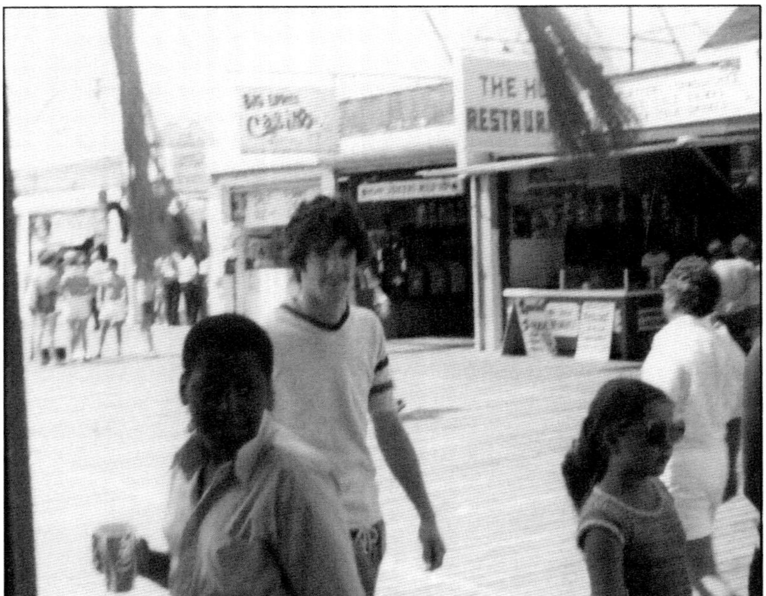

Jim Pietrowski (in a white shirt with stripes on the sleeve) worked at Fun Pier from 1975 to 1982, starting with the stand-up bottle game, five-pin bushel baskets, and mini-basketball concessions on Fun Pier. The Hub restaurant, located directly across from the pier, became a regular hang out for employees. (Courtesy Angelo Quisito.)

Judy Sableski works the Milk Can game. Sableski and her late husband, Eddie, had been involved with the gaming concessions from the early years of Fun Pier. The Sableskis were long-standing family members of Fun Pier. During the many summers, patrons got to know many of the Fun Pier employees. (Courtesy Angelo Quisito.)

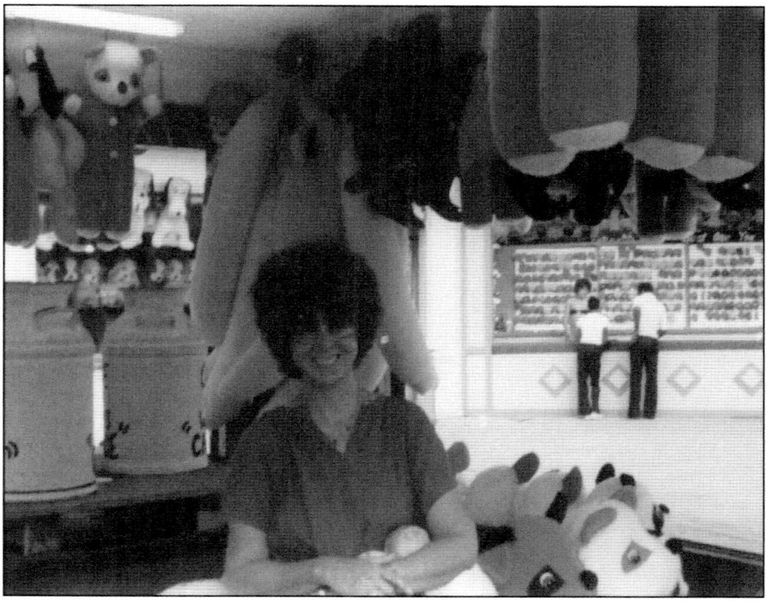

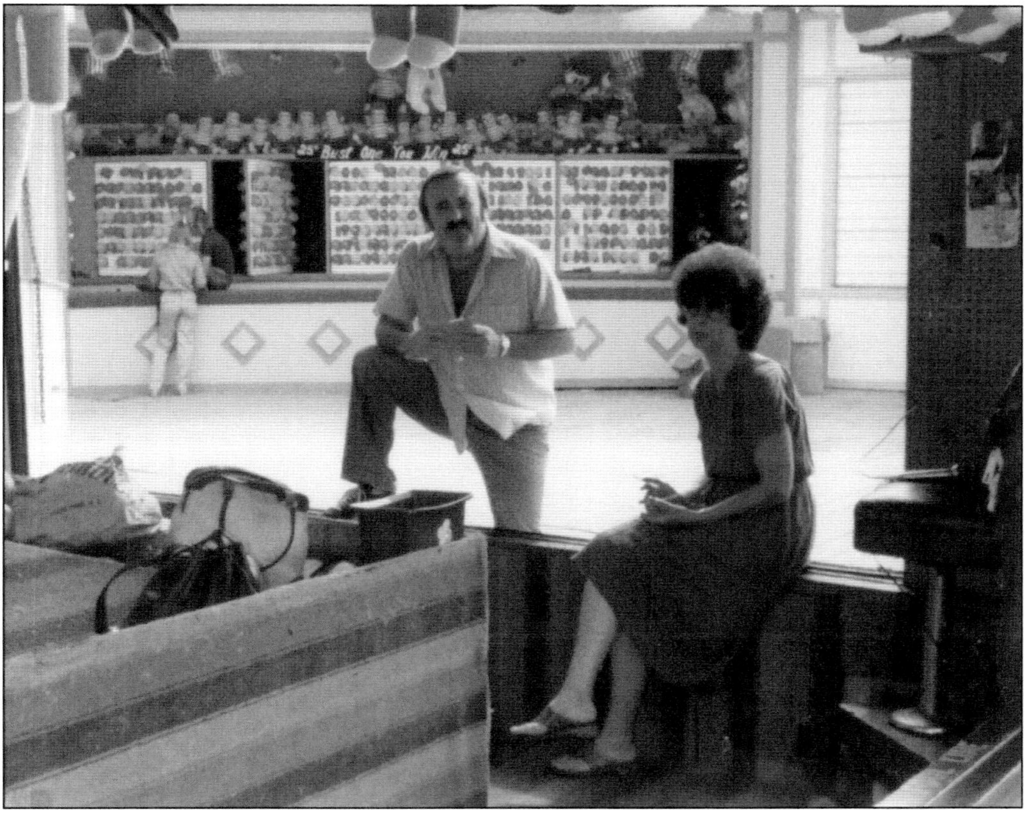

Peter Barnes and Judy Sableski are pictured here at her Milk Can game. Barnes was always on the pier, even after his father sold it. He also ran a few games and was involved with Universal Design, Ltd. After Fun Pier was sold to Morey Development, Barnes became one of the owners of Season's restaurant. (Courtesy Angelo Quisito.)

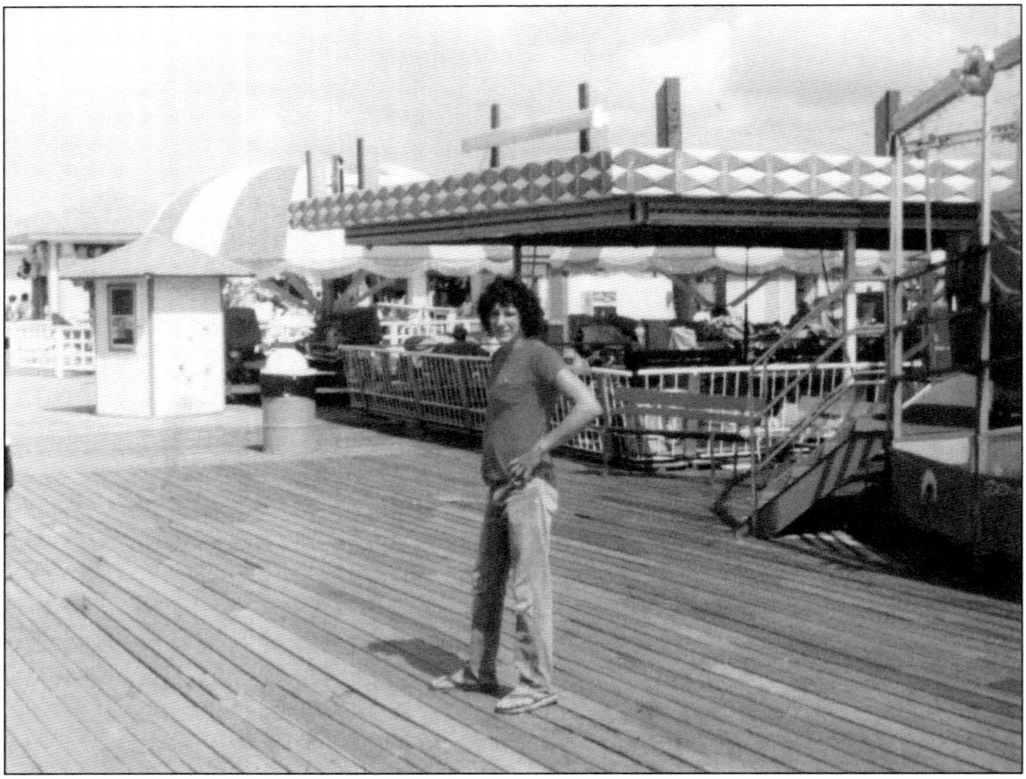

Angelo Quisito worked for Eddie and Judy Sableski at the Milk Can game on Fun Pier from 1979 to 1981. For the Milk Can game, the patron tossed a softball into the top of a milk can. In 1981, Quisito drove the trucks to New York City to pick up the stuffed-animal prizes. (Courtesy Angelo Quisito.)

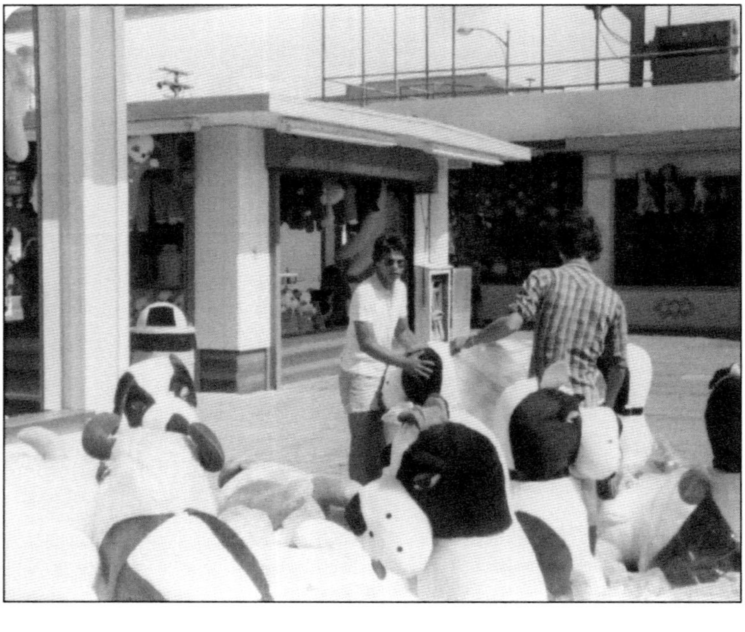

Erroll Rubin used to drive the trucks once or twice a week to pick up the prizes for the games and bring tractor-trailer loads back to Fun Pier. He also continued to manage the Dime Pitch game. Note the Ski Ride loading station on top of the game concessions. (Courtesy Angelo Quisito.)

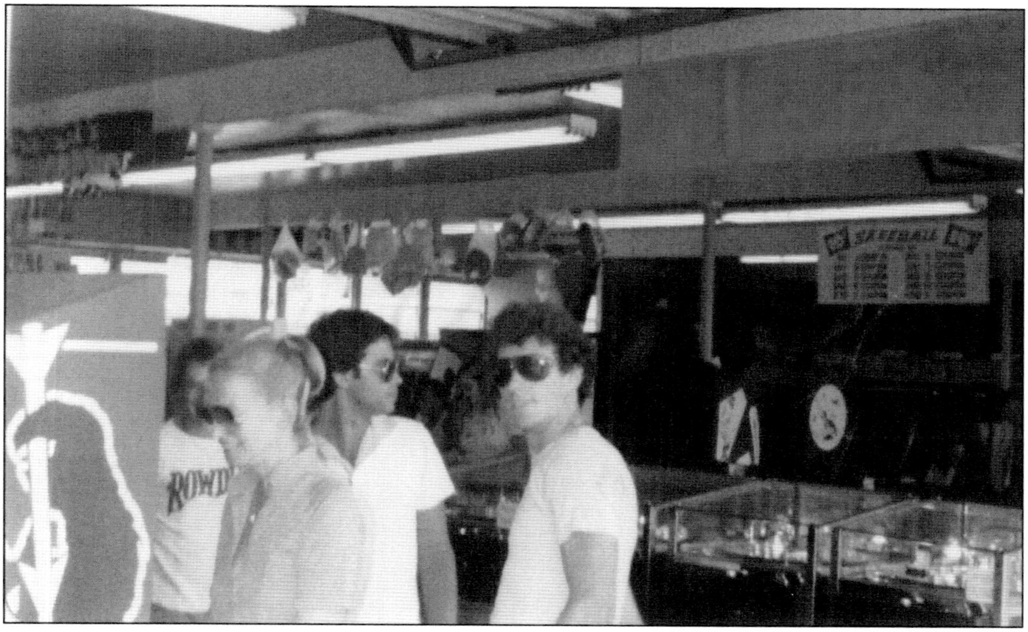

Many boardwalk visitors couldn't resist spending some of their entertainment dollars playing the popular arcade games of the era or games that would net a prize for the winner, like the balloon game shown below. An always-popular game with both customers and employees, the object was to throw a dart and pop the balloon, revealing a number that was associated with a prize. Of the many games that were on Fun Pier over the years, the balloon game was most popular with kids. At the end of each summer season, there would be hundreds of stuffed-animal prizes left over that Bill Howard and his son-in-law Peter Fendeller would sell in the off-season at Christmastime in Atlanta, Georgia. (Both, courtesy Angelo Quisito.)

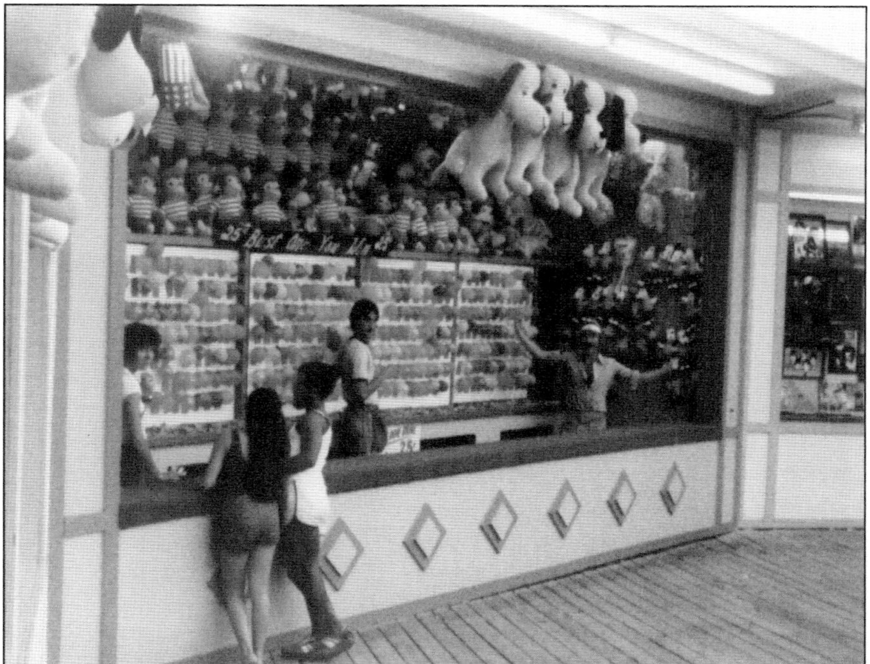

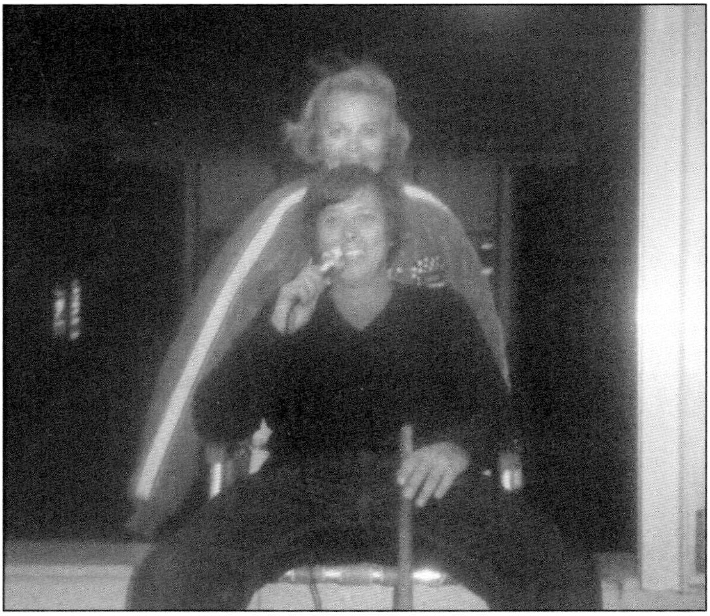

Helen Howard is pictured with "Crazy Albert" Butler in 1984. Butler ran the Dime Pitch game, the highest-grossing game on the pier. He was such an entertainer while running the game that he was given the nickname "Crazy Albert," and he became an icon to other game operators on Fun Pier. (Courtesy Albert Butler.)

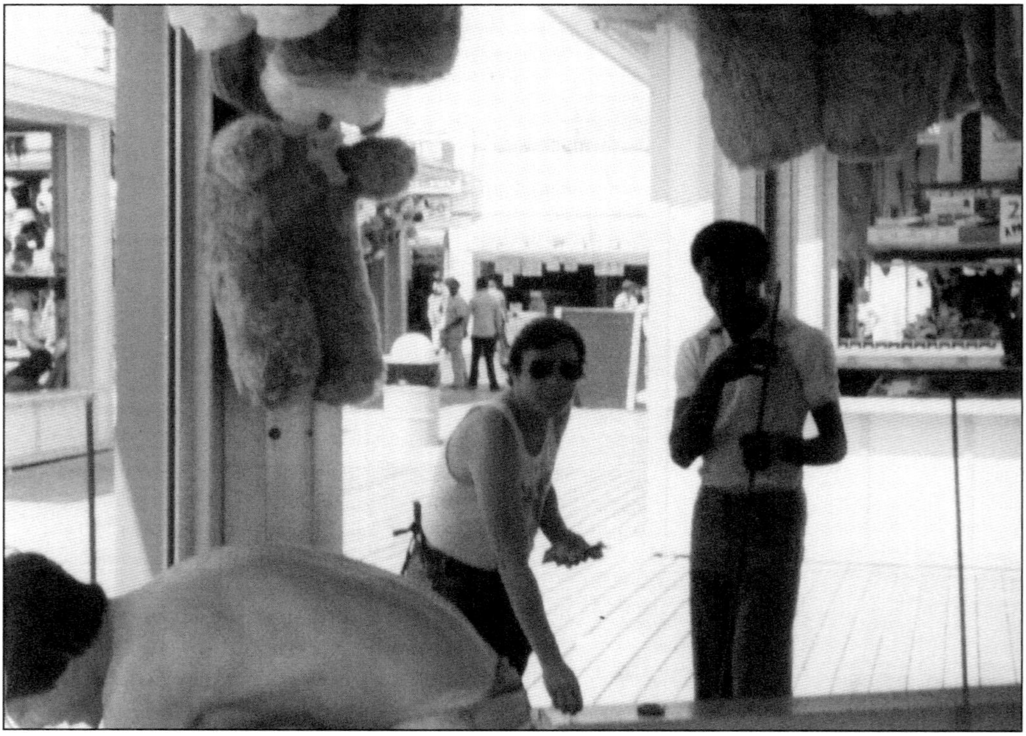

Pictured here are game concessions with employees. The game concessions generated the most revenue for the pier, especially in the 1970s and 1980s. The games would open before the rides would. The gaming industry on the Wildwood Boardwalk is still a big business that continues to have many different concessions, not only on the amusement piers but also along the boardwalk. The games, along with the many pizza and T-shirt shops, made up the Wildwood Boardwalk. Many lifelong friendships have been made as a result of working the games during the summer seasons. (Courtesy Angelo Quisito.)

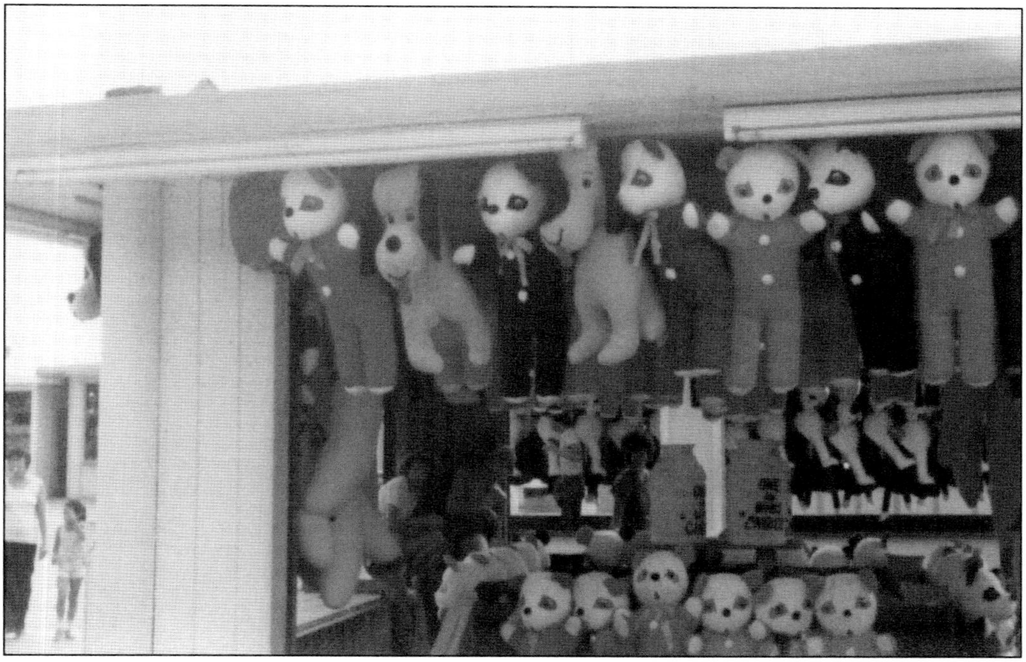

Judy Sableski continued to operate the Milk Can game long after her husband, Eddie, passed away. They started their business on the pier during Joseph Barnes's ownership and continued to operate games during Bill Howard's ownership. (Courtesy Angelo Quisito.)

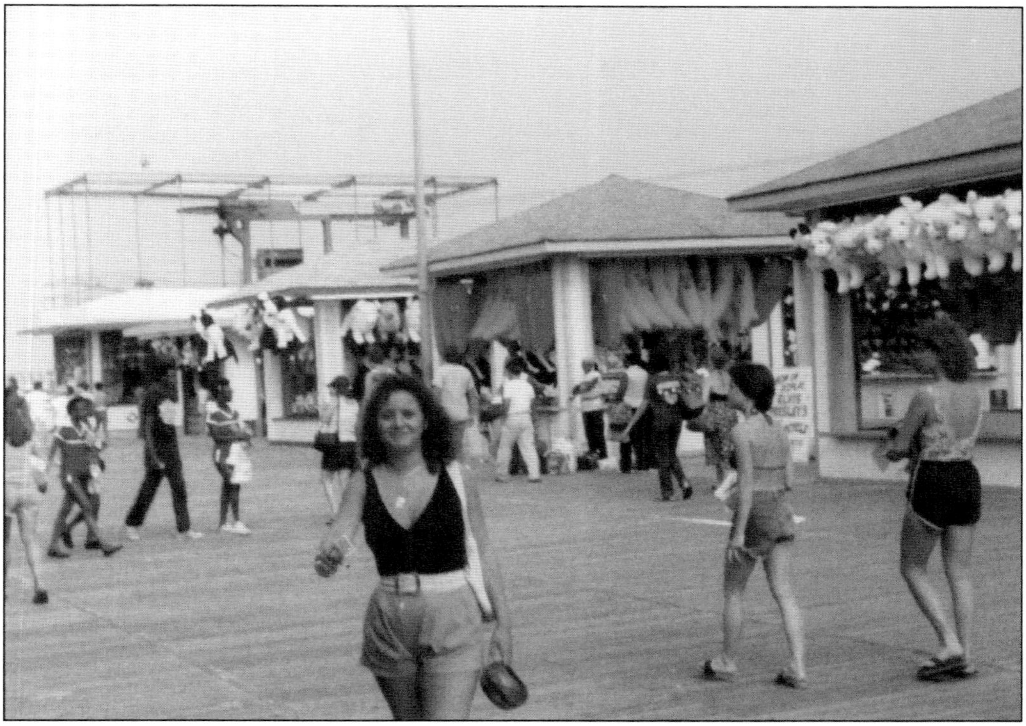

In this 1979 photograph, games dominate the front of Fun Pier, though the classic Ski Ride loading station is still visible, reminding patrons of where the fun still is. The Fun Pier gang liked to mingle with the customers and make the most of each day. (Courtesy Angelo Quisito.)

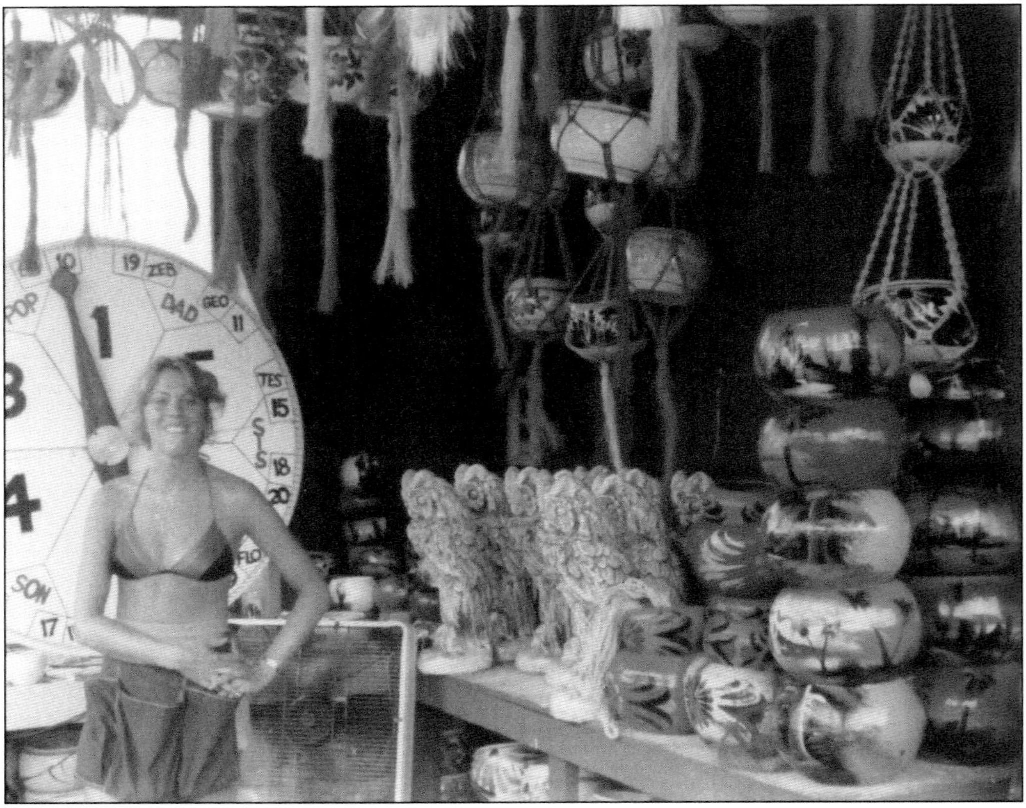

In the wheel game, 25¢ is placed on a name or number, and the attendant (Lori in this photograph) spins the wheel to get a winner. Eddie and Judy Sableski imported the hanging pots from Mexico. This was a very popular game; however, by the time a tractor-load of these pots got to Wildwood, half of them were already damaged. (Courtesy Angelo Quisito.)

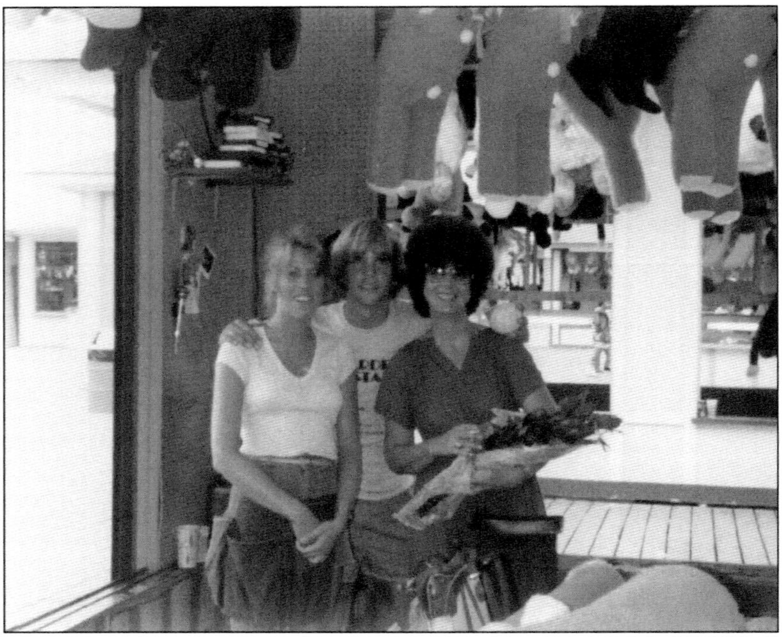

Lori ? (left) and Judy Sableski work the Milk Can game with another attendant. Lori and some of the other girls working the games were from Kutztown State College. During this time, there were many people from Ireland coming to the Wildwoods to work during the summer months. (Courtesy Angelo Quisito.)

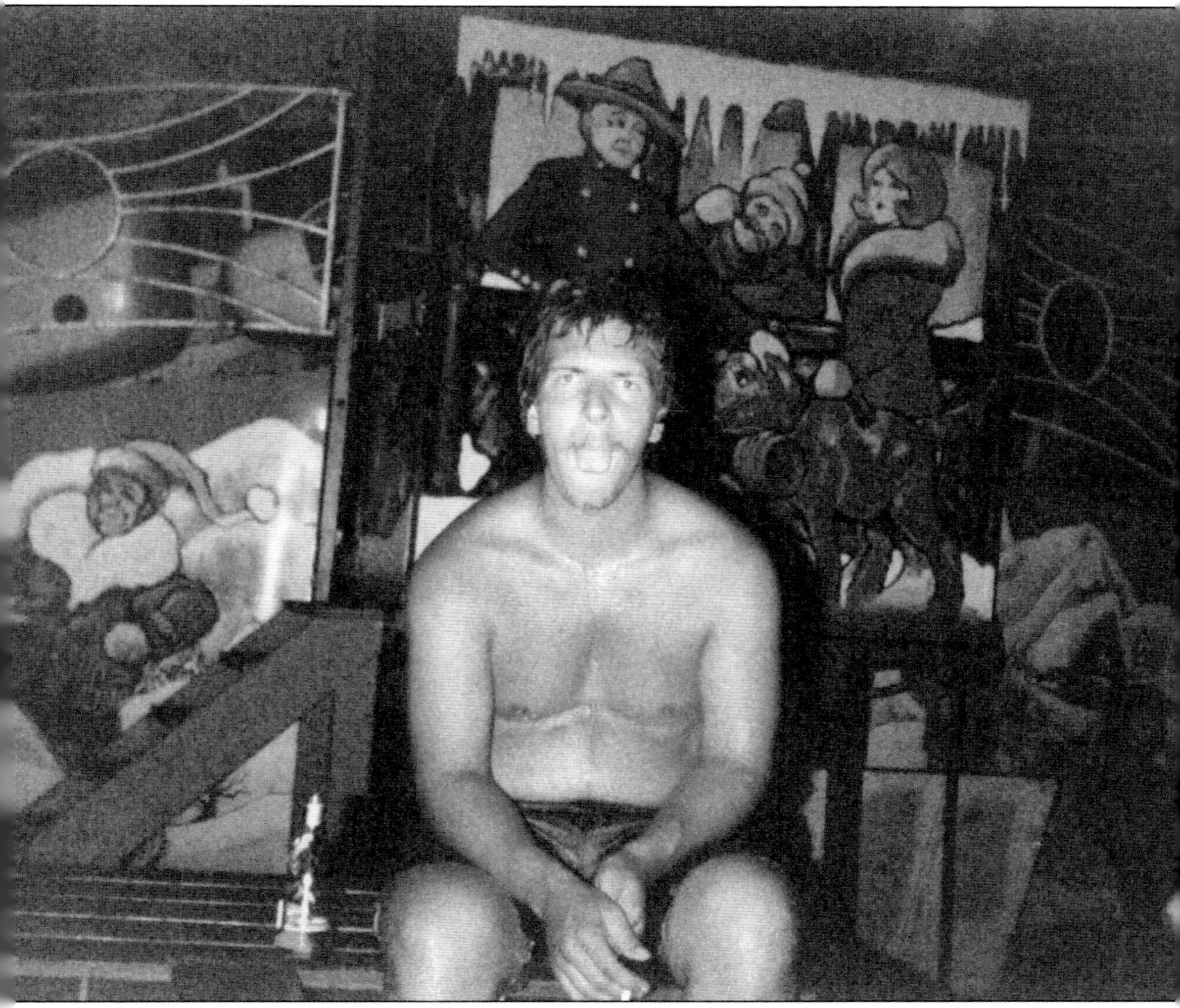

Mike Bailey is out of makeup in this photograph. He started on Fun Pier in 1976, working the kiddie rides. In 1977, he was moved over to be an actor inside Lost World. Bailey took his role seriously and would go down to the Fun Shop to buy his makeup. Inspired by both the rock group KISS and the Aztec theme, Mike Bailey and David Ulysses painted their faces to look like they really were from a Lost World. Bailey also bought a large dog collar that he wore around his neck. The duo took every chance possible to terrorize the patrons. In order to prepare for this, they would shut all the lights out and run through the entire ride in the dark. This way, they would know where every trap door and every opening was. There was no air-conditioning inside the ride, and shirts and shorts were optional, given they were supposed to look like savages. Bailey and Ulysses would put on such a performance that some patrons would run out of the fire doors, which would take them directly out onto the Wildwood Beach. Unbelievably, Ulysses would continue to chase to them down the beach! (Courtesy Lee Durland.)

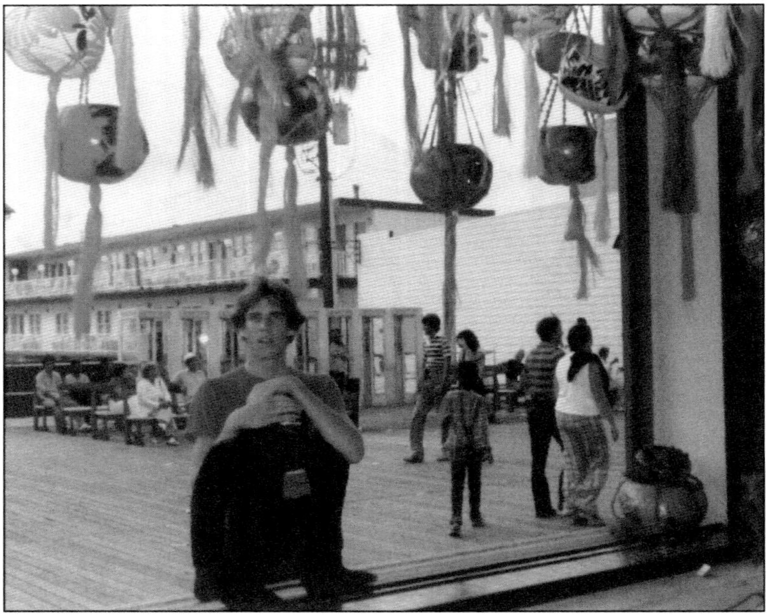

Pictured here are many of the pottery prizes for the wheel game, facing the front of the pier. As time went on, it became necessary to add different prizes in order to keep the patrons' interest. The pottery game was one of Judy Sableski's games. The pottery came from Mexico, and the pier employees would make the trip down to Mexico and back. (Courtesy Angelo Quisito.)

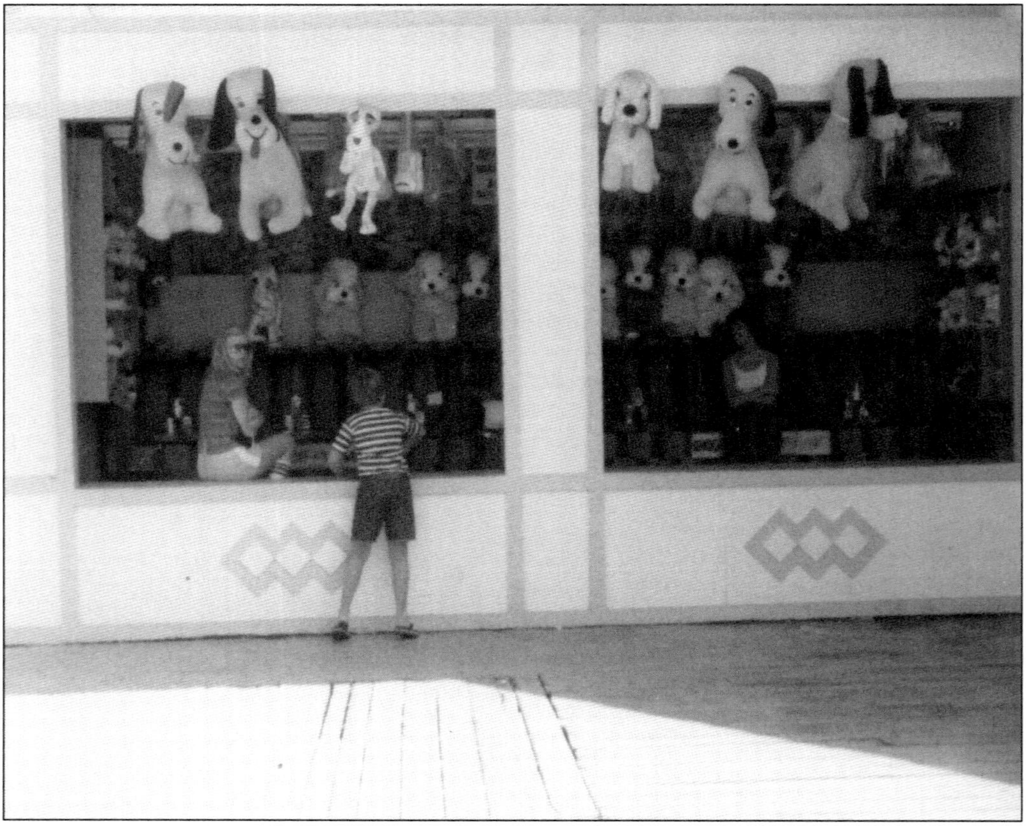

This is the bean toss game. The skill for this game was to knock the cans down with beanbags. While not always busy during the day hours, the games would usually be bustling at night, except on Saturdays and Sundays when the buses came in—at that point, the games were busy day and night. (Courtesy Angelo Quisito.)

Through the years, many different employees would come and go so frequently that it was difficult to keep track of all of them. One thing most of the former pier employees say is that they made the greatest profit working the games. (Courtesy Angelo Quisito.)

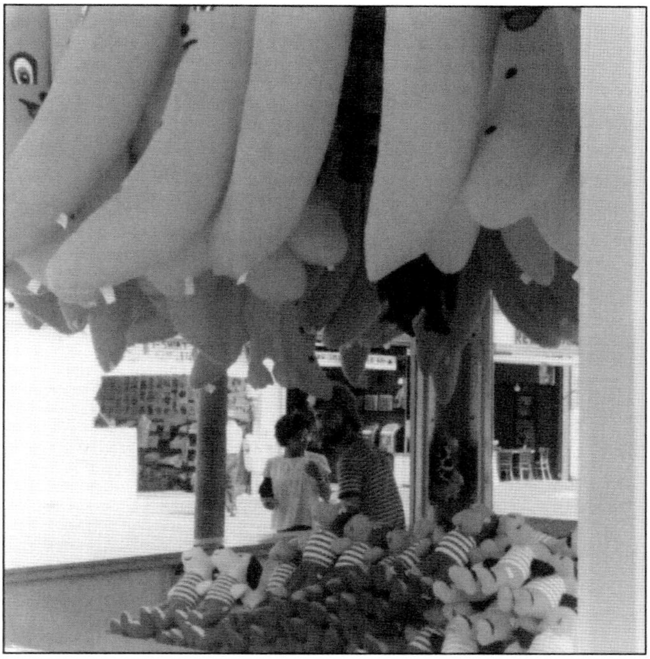

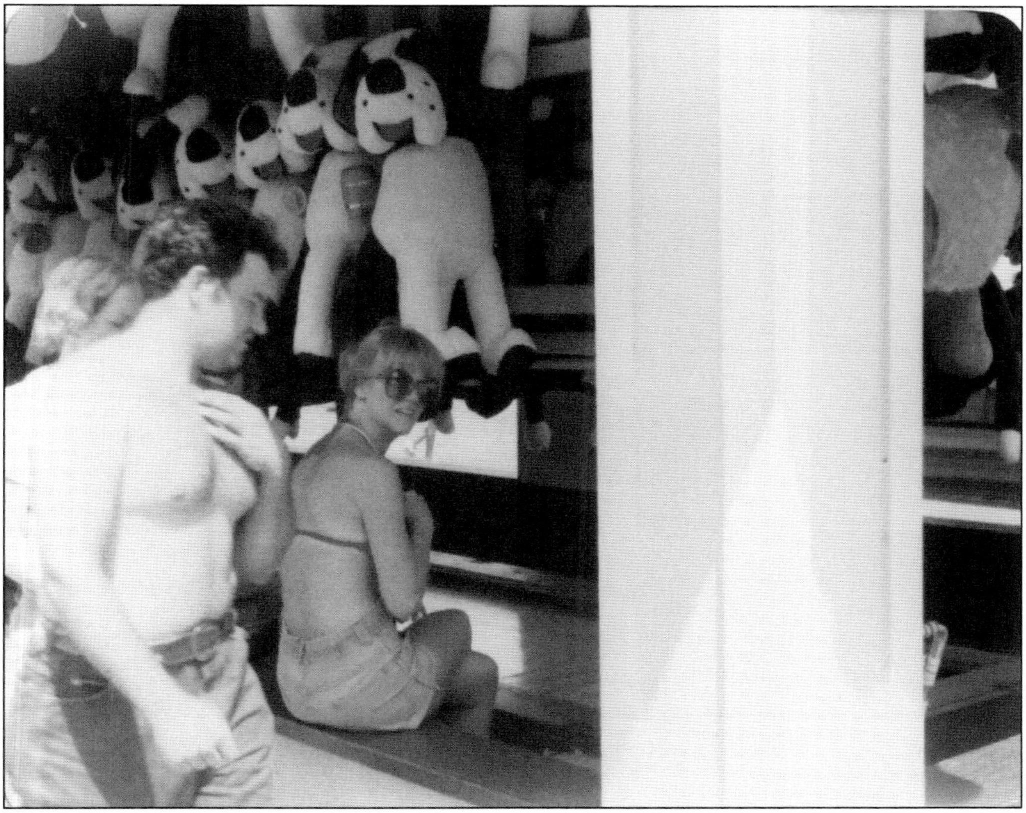

Jan (seated) operates the Dime Pitch. For this game, dimes were tossed in the center of a Lucky Strike cigarette pack. The brand had a red circle in the middle. The whole board had a few hundred of these, and they were flattened and hardened with urethane. (Courtesy Angelo Quisito.)

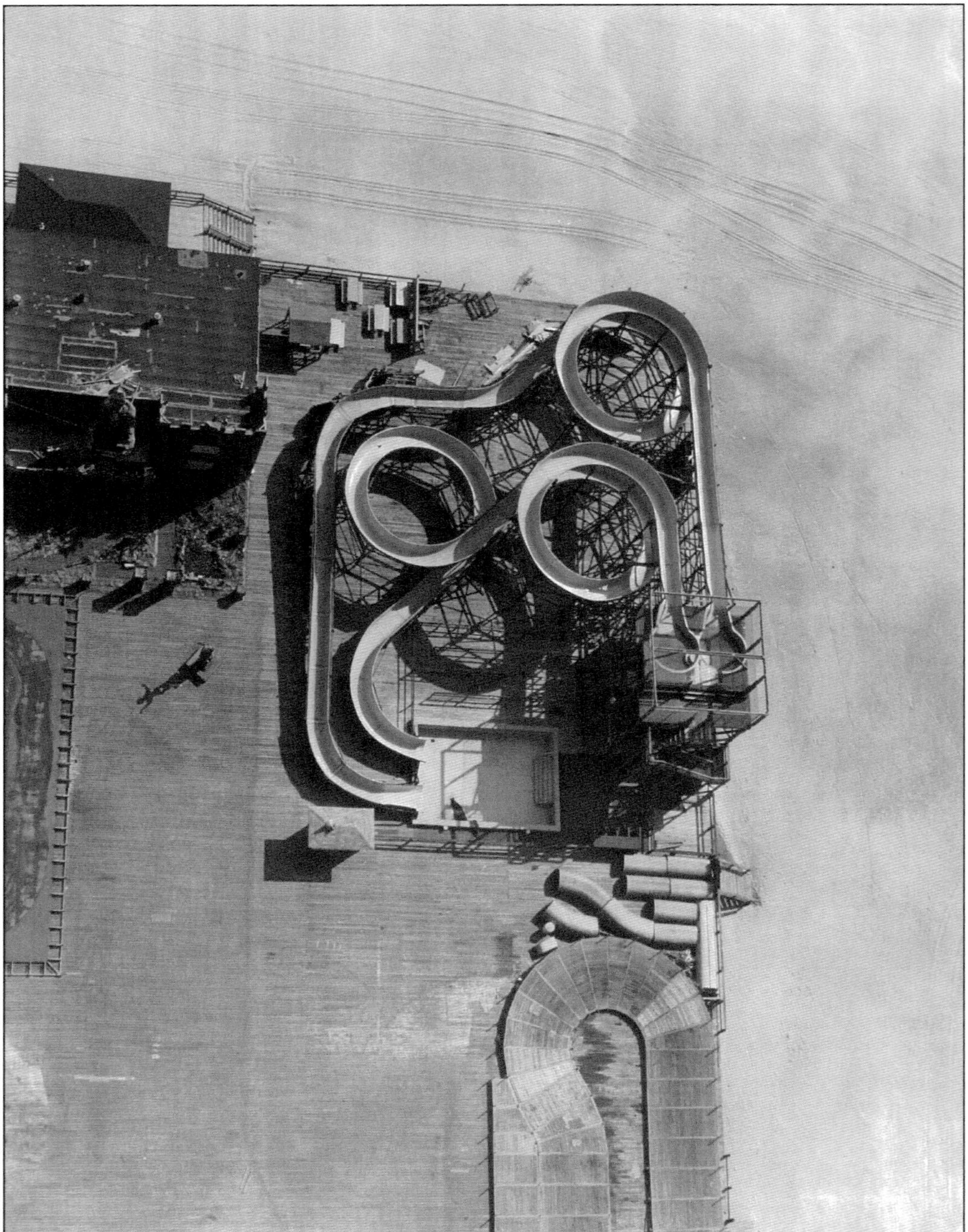

Fun Pier appears here during the off-season. The Castle Frankenstein building started out as Seascape during the 1960s. It was rethemed into Castle Frankenstein in 1973 before being moved to the back end of the pier. The move caused severe damage to the car tracks, which could no longer be used. The track was torn out and everything cleared to turn the building into a walk-through. Note the snack bar behind the castle and the steps that lead down to the beach. Peter Savard built this snack bar as well as the benches for patrons to enjoy their snacks. (Courtesy Richard Ramagosa.)

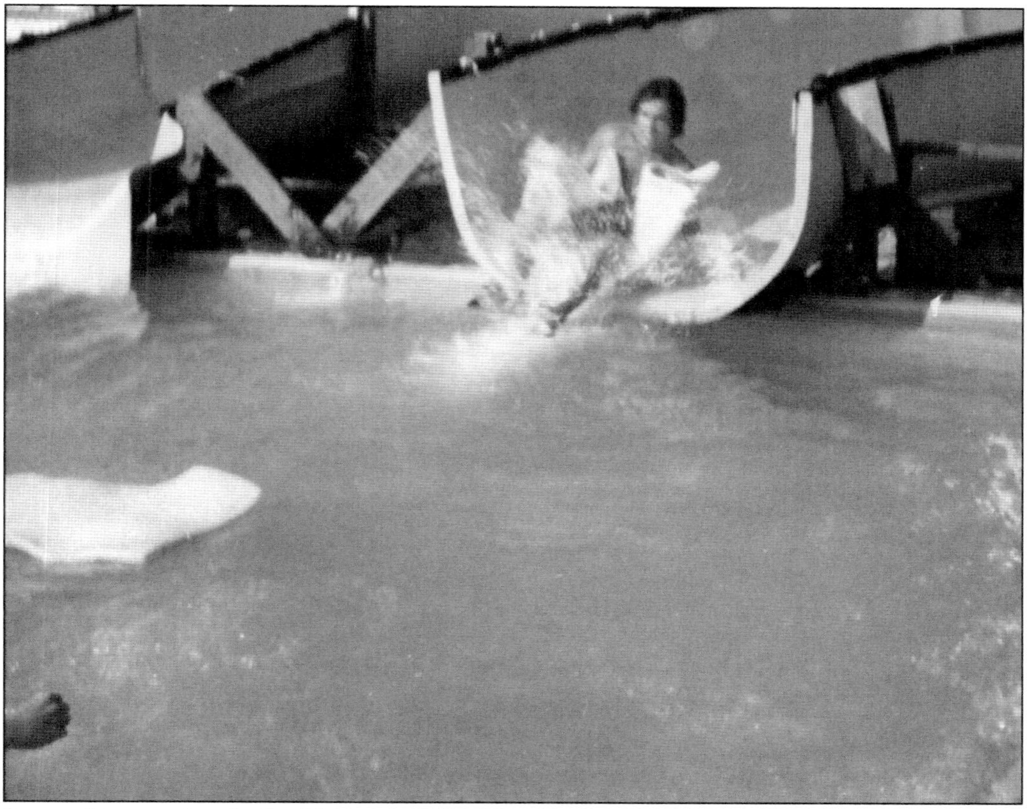

Pictured here is the thrill of the waterslide. After landing into the pool, many would then take advantage of clowning around with others. Even the Fun Pier Gang would take part in this as a way of interacting with the patrons. Under the management of Southerner Art Fiala and his family, Southern hospitality was extended on the pier. The Fiala family is still remembered to this day in Wildwood for their generosity and compassion. The family still resides in Alabama and has fond memories of their days and nights on Fun Pier. (Both, courtesy Lee Durland.)

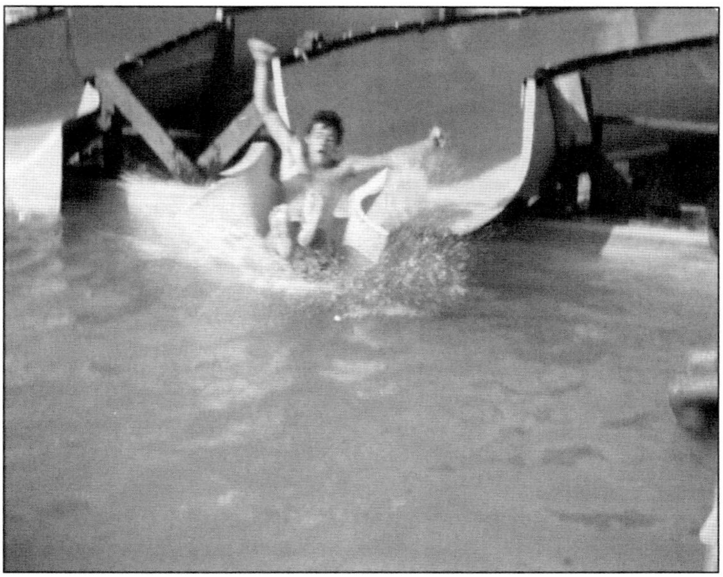

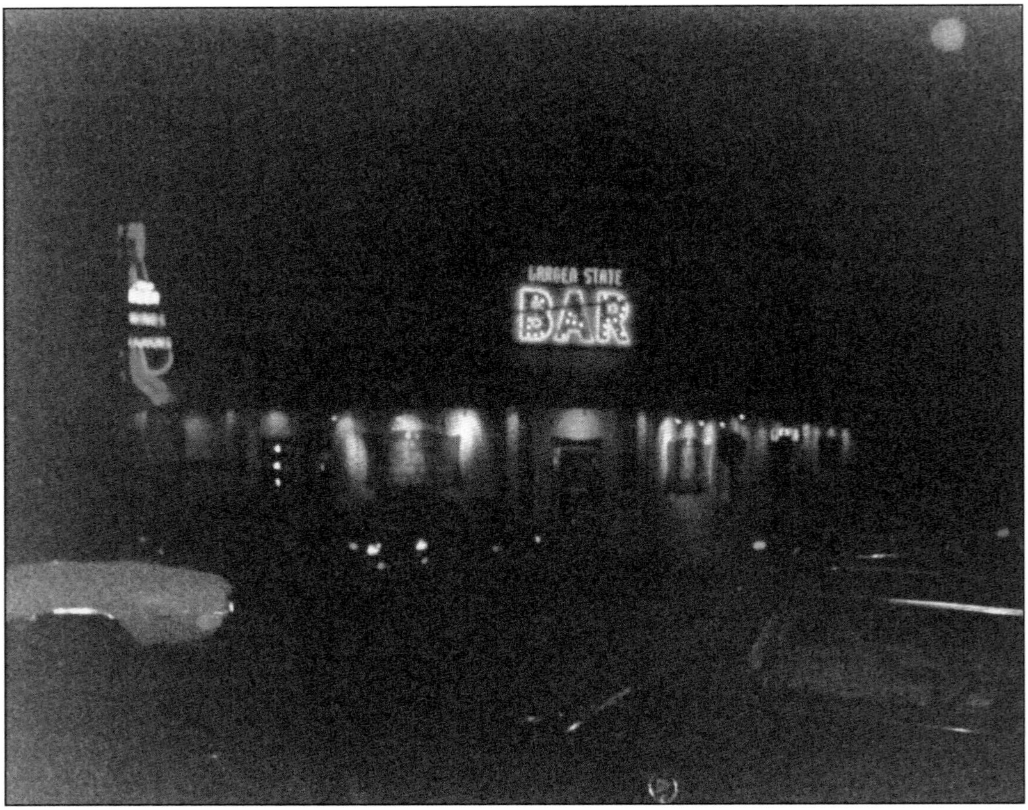

This is the Garden State Bar and liquor store as it appeared in 1979. After working long nights on Fun Pier, many employees would walk here for some drinks. This was one of the few hangouts for the Fun Pier Gang. The Garden State Bar was always open till 5:00 a.m., and the Fun Pier Gang would always arrive between 12:00 and 1:00 a.m. (Courtesy Lee Durland.)

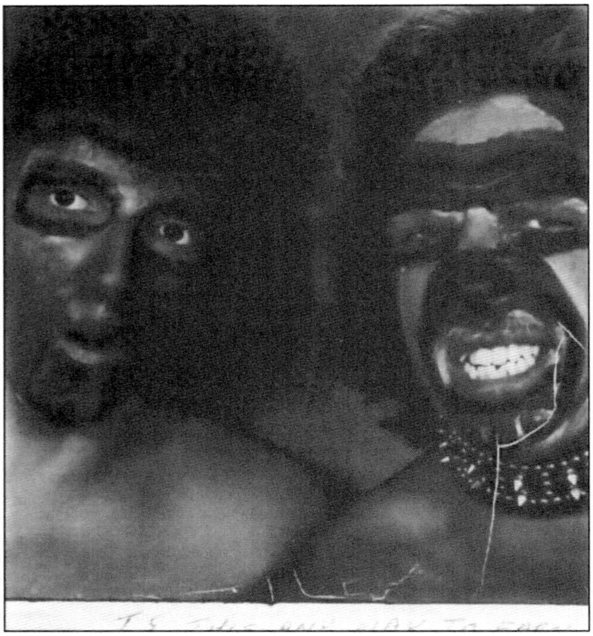

This photograph, taken at a photo booth on the Wildwood Boardwalk in the summer of 1978, shows David Ulysses (left) and Mike Bailey in Lost World makeup. Ulysses and Bailey put on quite a show for the customers who dared to venture through the Lost World. Note the dog collar around Bailey's neck—this was Mike's trademark during his time working the dark ride. The night this photograph was taken, Ulysses and Bailey stayed in character after working Lost World, walking all around the Wildwood Boardwalk. (Courtesy Mike Bailey.)

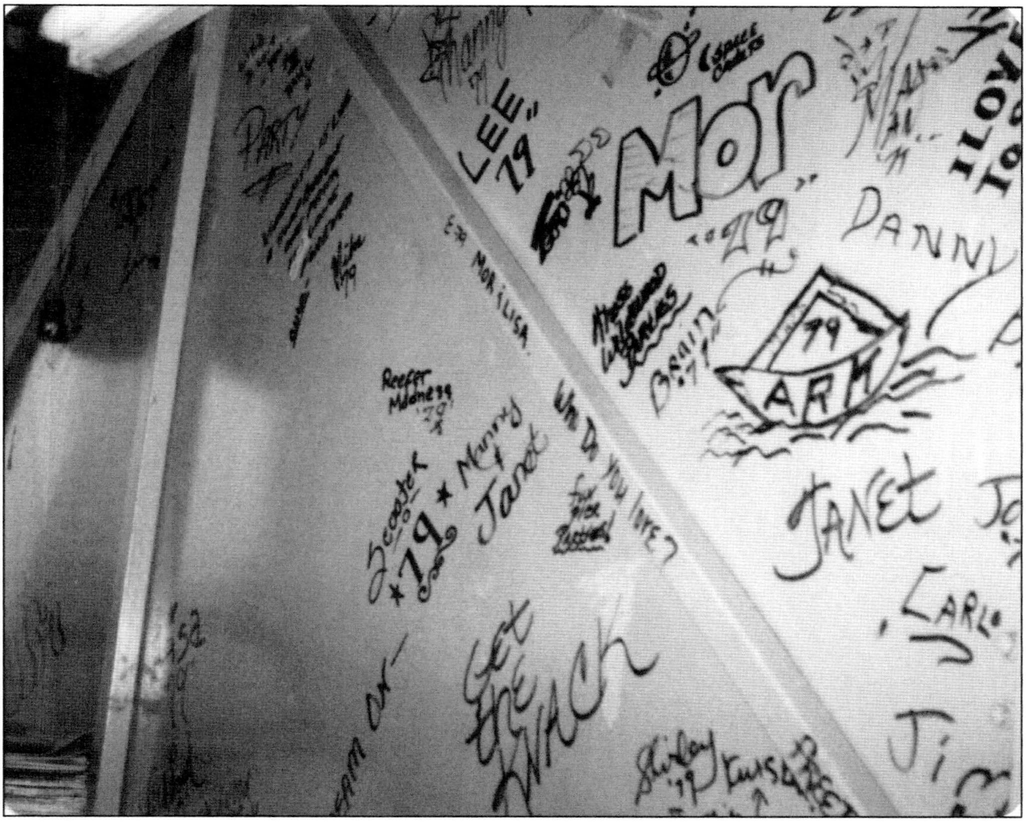

Inside the Flying Bobs ride, the panels became a sort of yearbook for the employees. As seen in this photograph, many people came through and signed their names in remembrance of all the fun they had on the pier. (Courtesy Lee Durland.)

This photograph shows one of the operators of the Flying Bobs. The ride required a strong handle on the current hit songs. The combination of the music along with the speed of the ride continues to thrill people to this day. The current music was always a strong sell for this ride. Note the glass milk bottle. (Courtesy Lee Durland.)

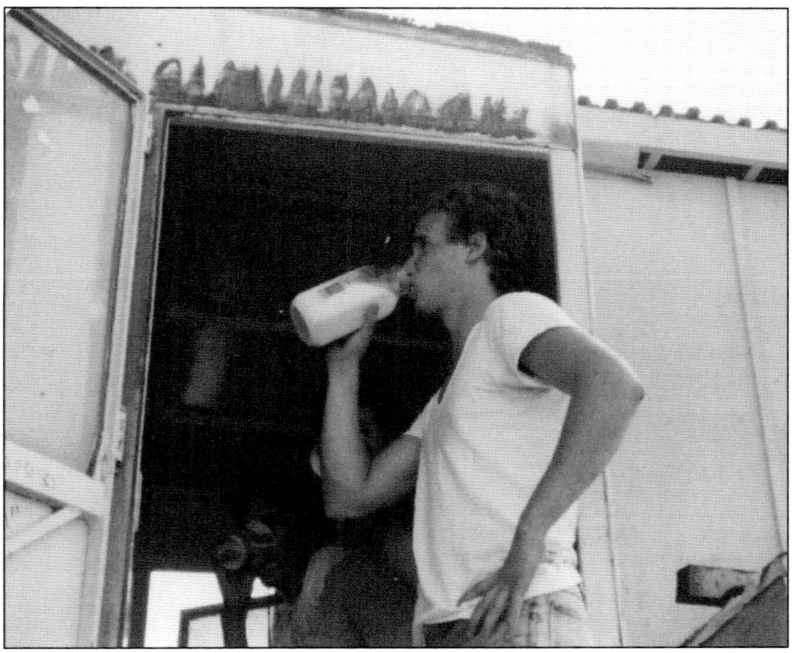

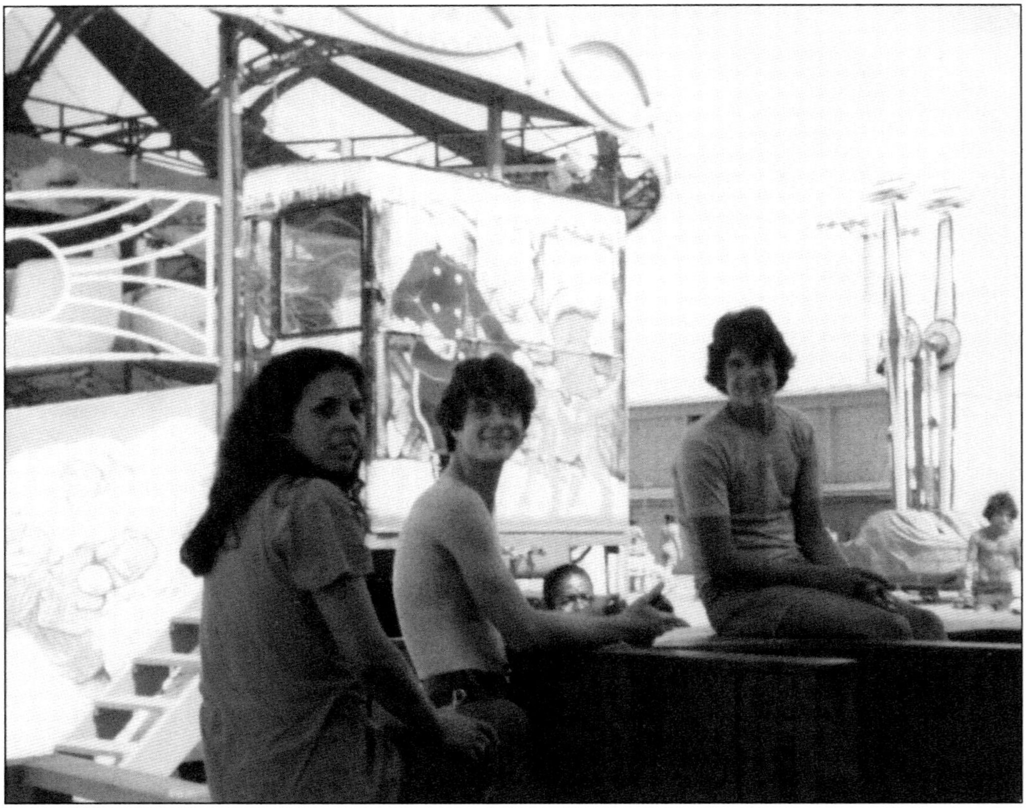

Pictured here are Sheila Rubin (left), Dennis Easy (center), and Lee Durland. Durland worked the waterslide for most of his days on Fun Pier. Here, the three take a break and share some laughs. (Courtesy Lee Durland.)

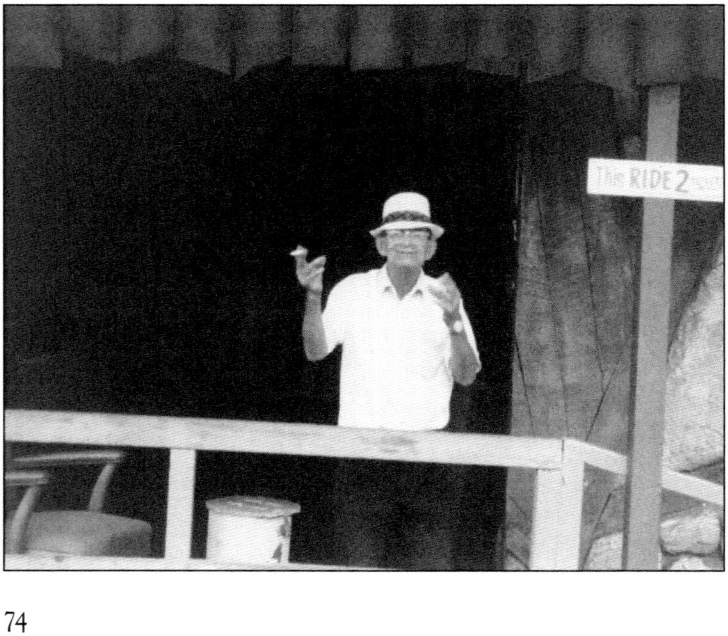

"Shorty" Franchville is pictured here at his normal perch at the entrance to Crazy House. Shorty, as he was called by all that knew him, was quite a character. He could make even the most serious person laugh. He was a regular fixture on the pier, especially at the Crazy House. In the years when the monorail would ride over any time, he would hear Peter Frampton and would start to dance. (Courtesy Lee Durland.)

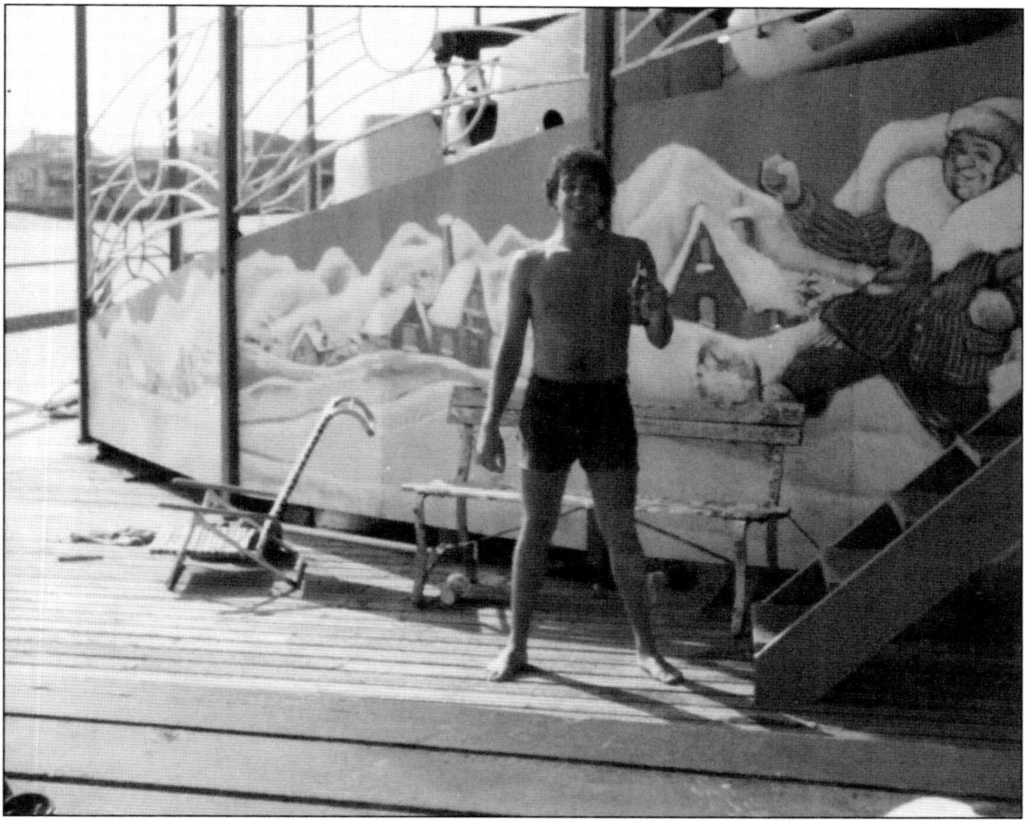

Mark "from Ark" takes a break while working the Flying Bobs. Many different DJs would come and go as a means of keeping up with popular music. However, fellow employee DJ Martin Morley was able to change with the times and the music. (Courtesy Lee Durland.)

Art "Scooter" Fiala Jr. is pictured here at his 17th birthday party in the second-floor apartment on Fun Pier. According to those who attended, this was an all-night event. It was not called Fun Pier for nothing, and the gang did everything they could to help Scooter celebrate his big 17th birthday. (Courtesy Lee Durland.)

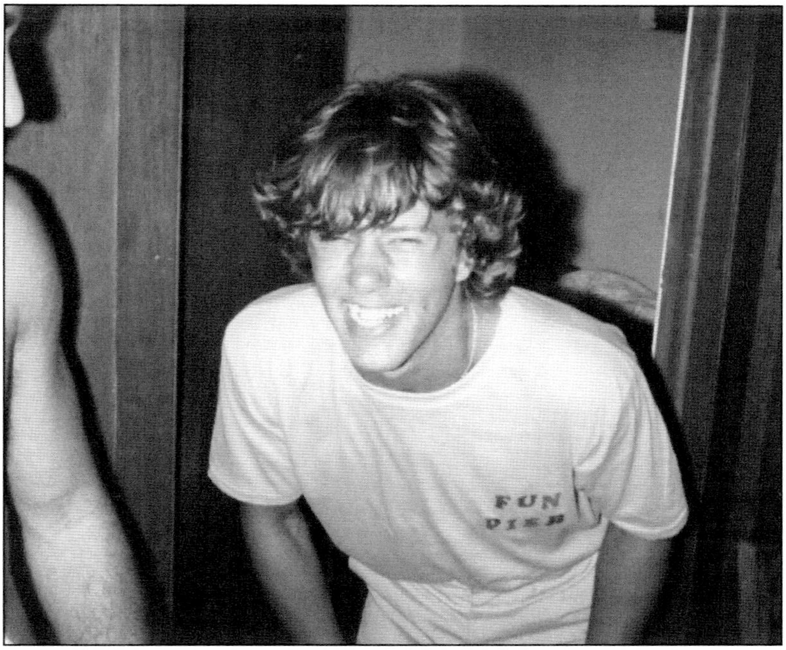

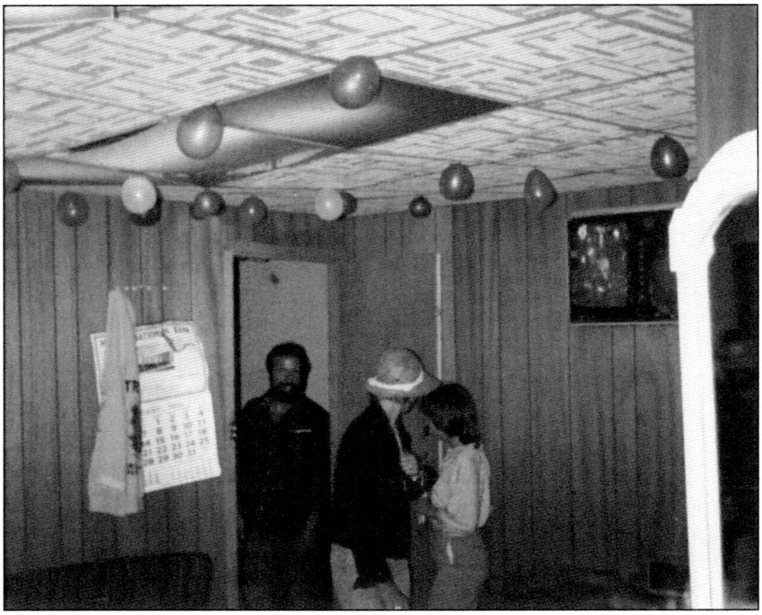

Peter and Kathy Savard join Scooter's 17th birthday party. This was not a typical party, as it was taking place during regular business hours on Fun Pier. As described by those in attendance, there was a lot of "back and forth," meaning they alternated between working on the pier and partying in the apartment. (Courtesy Lee Durland.)

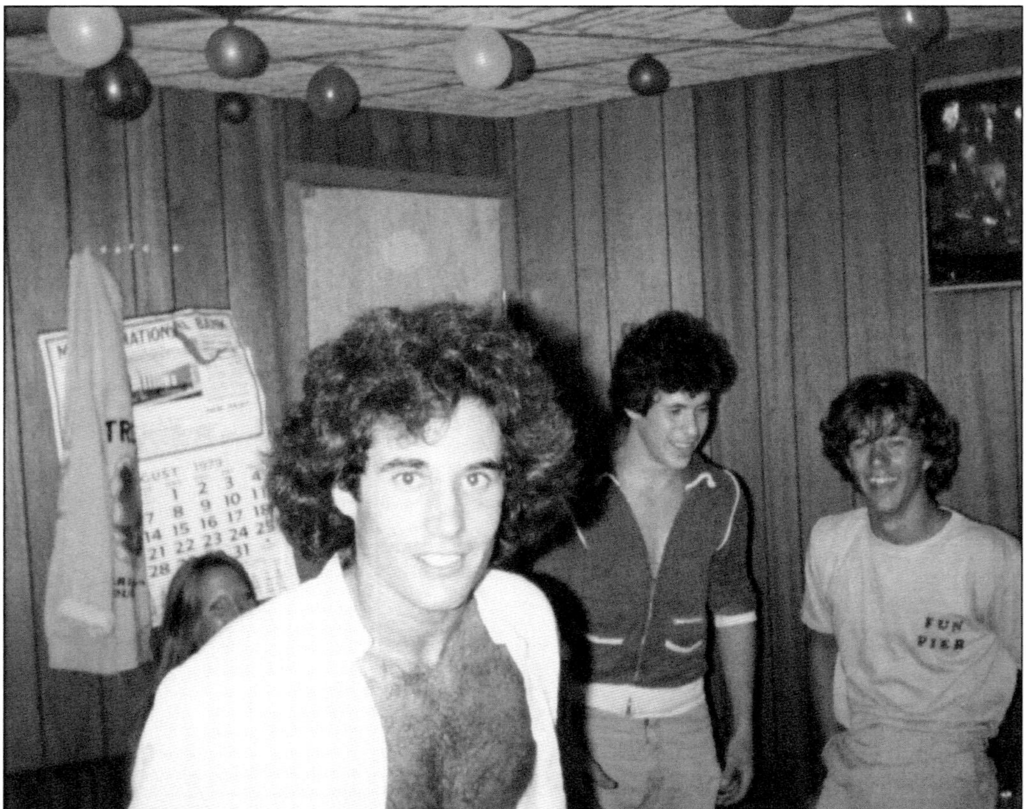

Martin Morley (left), Manny Ferrer (center), and Scooter Fiala get the party started at the apartment. Morley was known as a DJ and always had the latest music. At that time, Morley was very into disco. He could get even the hardest rock 'n' roll buff to listen to disco. (Courtesy Lee Durland.)

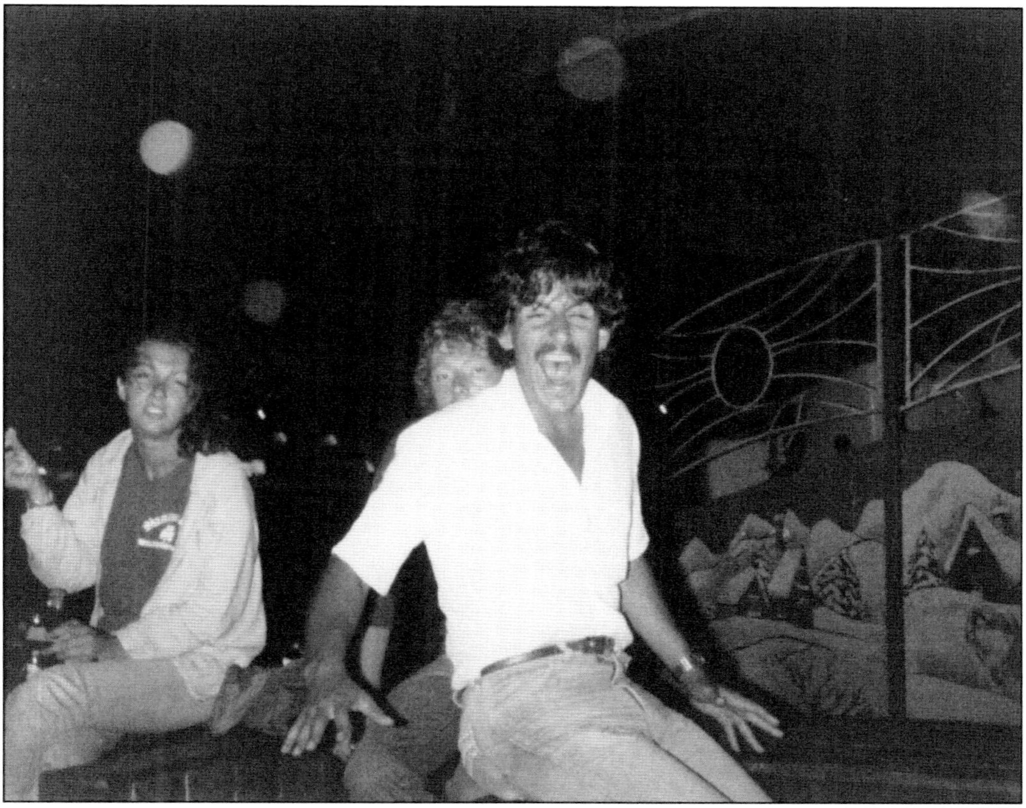

More people meant more fun on the Flying Bobs. Nights were wild and crazy on Fun Pier. Marty Morley was known as the leader of the party. Morley always played the latest music and even brought his own form of entertainment both to the pier and parties. (Courtesy Lee Durland.)

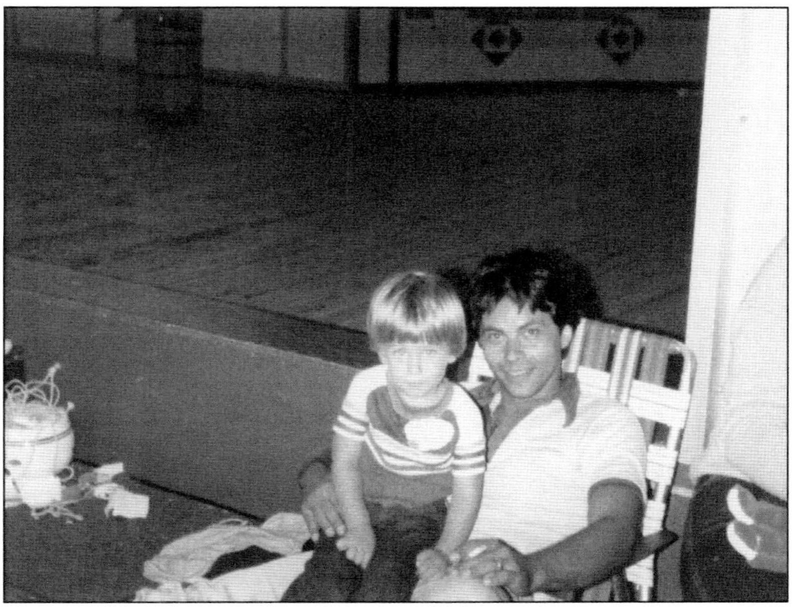

Erroll Rubin appears here with his son Jacob at his game concession. Rubin was managing quite a lot of the games and had many employees. He was known as a great boss by many and is highly regarded by those who worked for and with him. (Courtesy Lee Durland.)

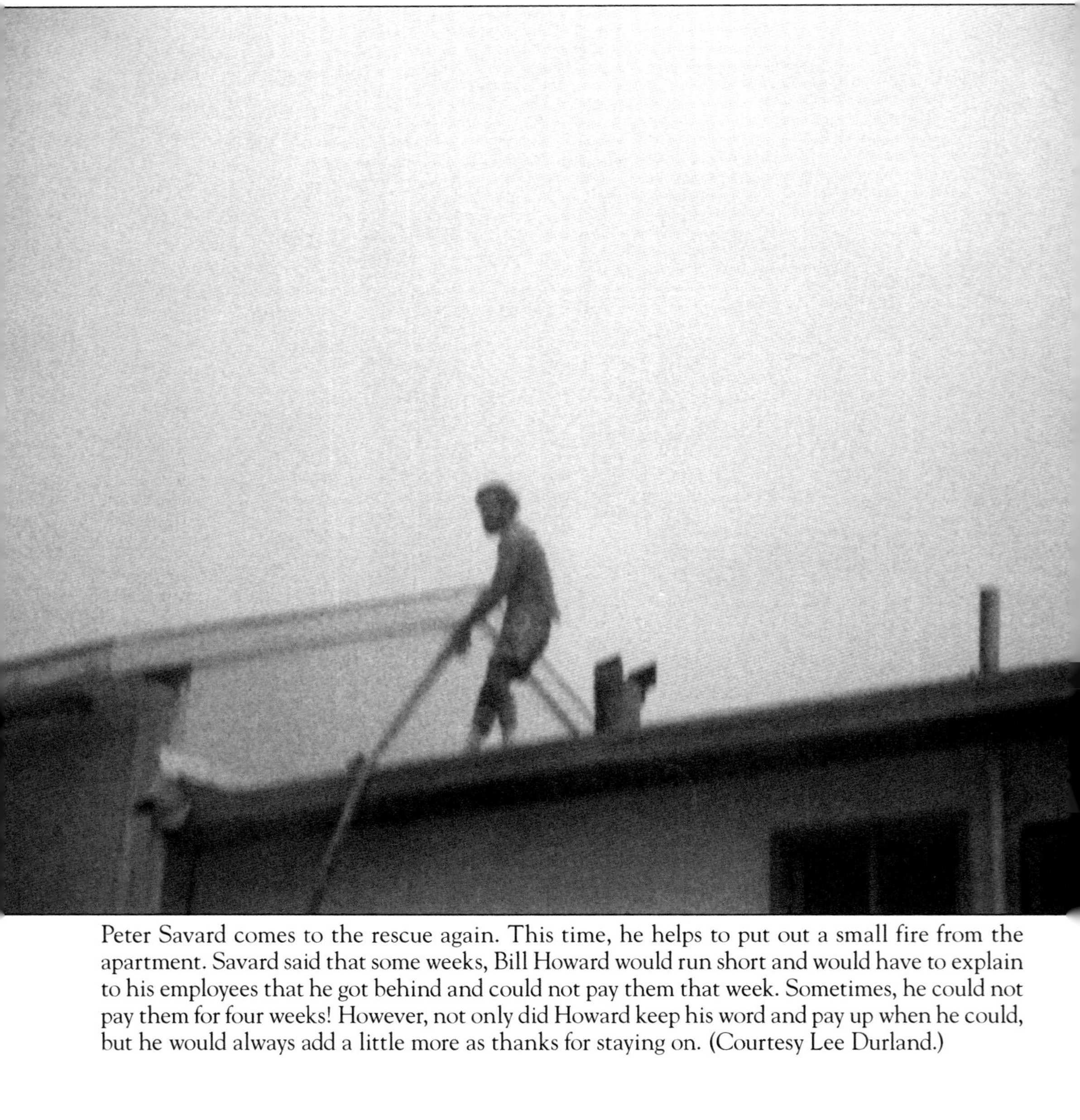

Peter Savard comes to the rescue again. This time, he helps to put out a small fire from the apartment. Savard said that some weeks, Bill Howard would run short and would have to explain to his employees that he got behind and could not pay them that week. Sometimes, he could not pay them for four weeks! However, not only did Howard keep his word and pay up when he could, but he would always add a little more as thanks for staying on. (Courtesy Lee Durland.)

Both the Howards and the Fialas were Southern families. The Howards were from Georgia and the Fialas from Alabama. As the sign says, "Hey ya'll don't do that do this. Come on down to the stomping and strolling, Rockin & Rollin days of the 50's. So stop on by and bop on down to the great music! 10:00 o'clock pm Friday at the Flying Bobs Fun Pier." (Courtesy Lee Durland.)

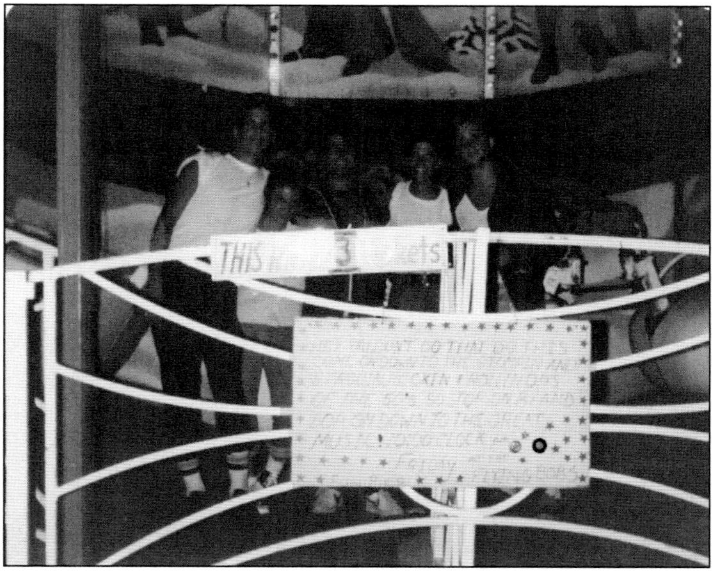

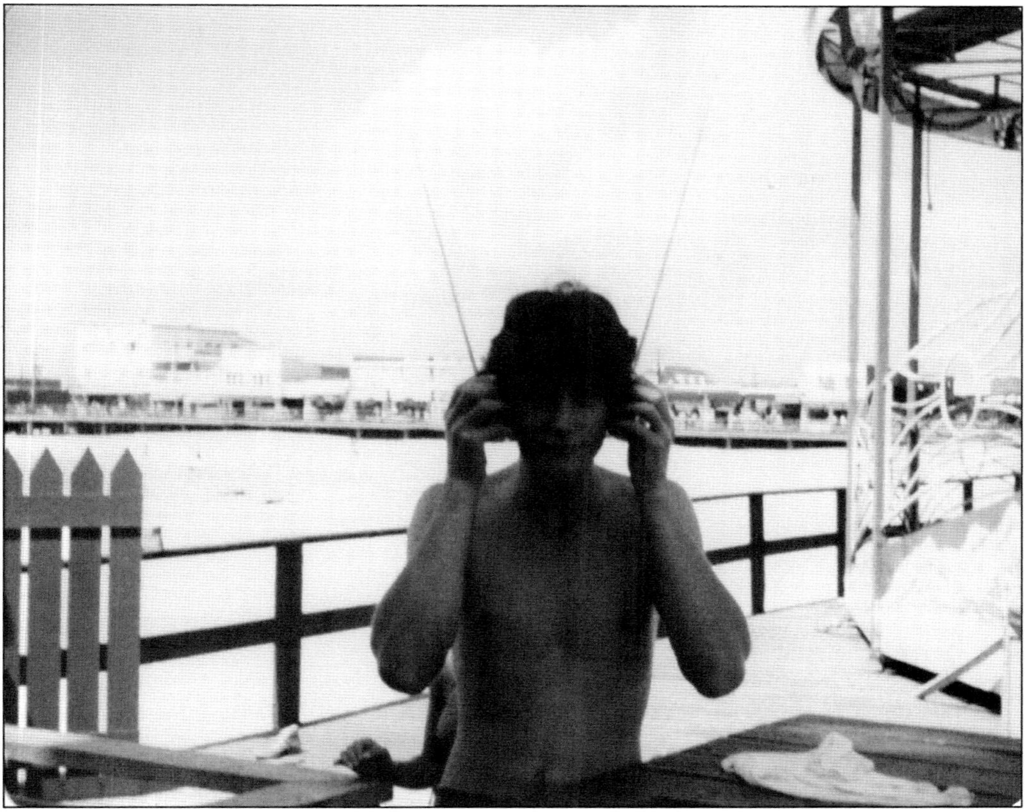

Dennis Gibson, who called himself "Captain Easy," was the cocreator of the second Castle Frankenstein, which was the one located at the back of the pier. Dennis and his then-wife Sheila used chicken wire, paper towels, masking tape, and primer paint to begin production on the many creations they made for the castle. Some of their creations, such as the gargoyles that stood at each corner of the castle, were one of a kind. Each gargoyle looked significantly different from the others. Dennis and Sheila were indeed very talented artists. (Courtesy Lee Durland.)

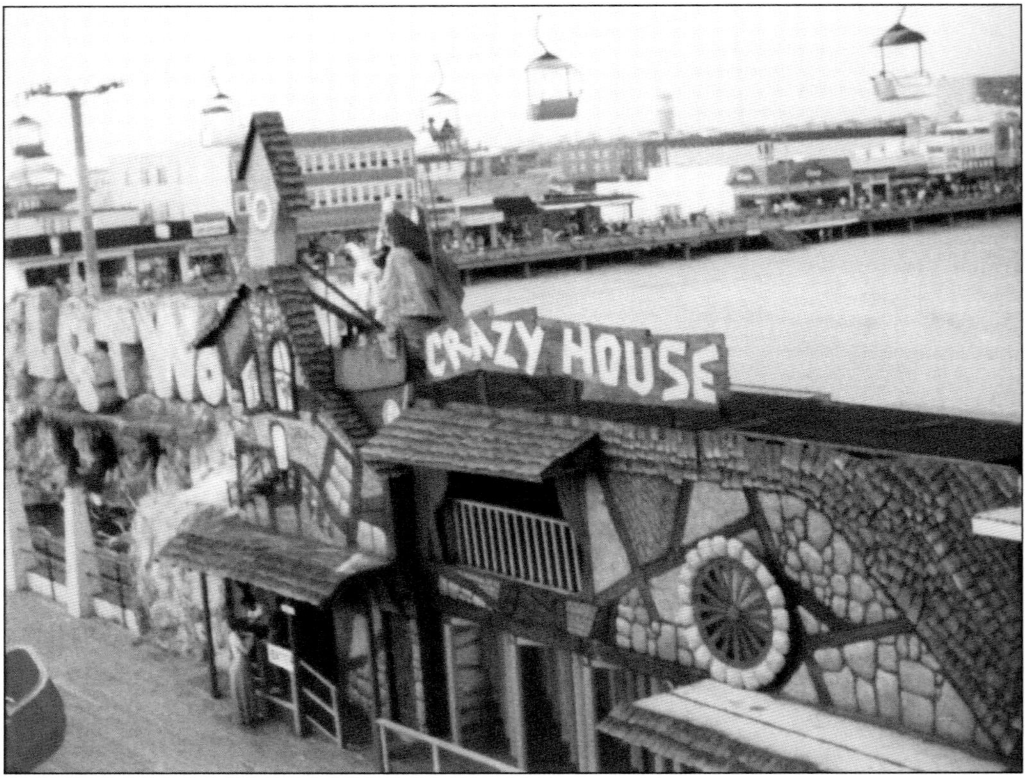

The eye-catching facades of Lost World and Crazy House were highlighted by the Ski Ride cars. The Ski Ride took patrons not only over the northern beach side of Fun Pier but also over the rooftops of the rides. Note Gino's Kentucky Fried Chicken on the boardwalk. The restaurant later became Wildwood's only Roy Rogers. (Courtesy Lee Durland.)

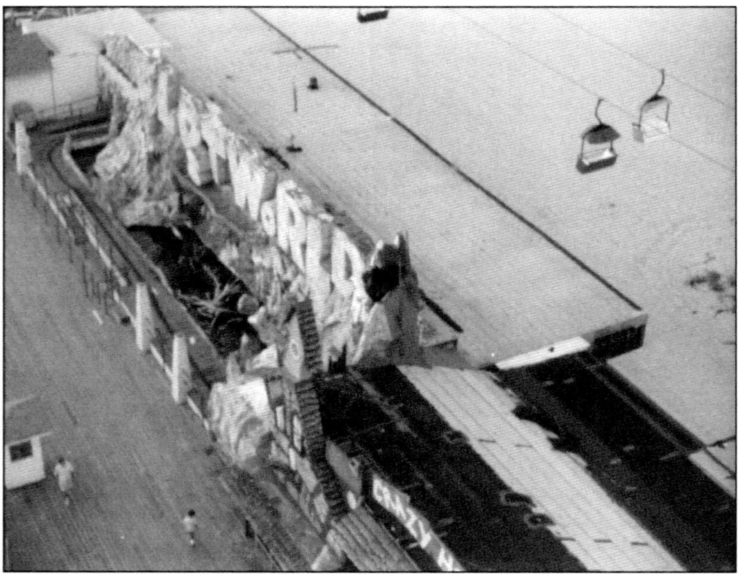

This aerial photograph shows the loading station of Lost World. Note the small bridge to the left of the ride next to the office. This bridge was where the patrons would walk out. The bridge was removed, and King Kong was moved into its place. Patrons would then exit through the gorilla's legs until the walk-through section of the ride was closed down. (Courtesy Lee Durland.)

Peter Savard (left) is conversing with pier owner Bill Howard over new planks that have to be installed. Most of Savard's work took place behind the Castle Frankenstein dark ride. Art Fiala, in the hat in the background, lends a hand. (Courtesy Kathy Savard.)

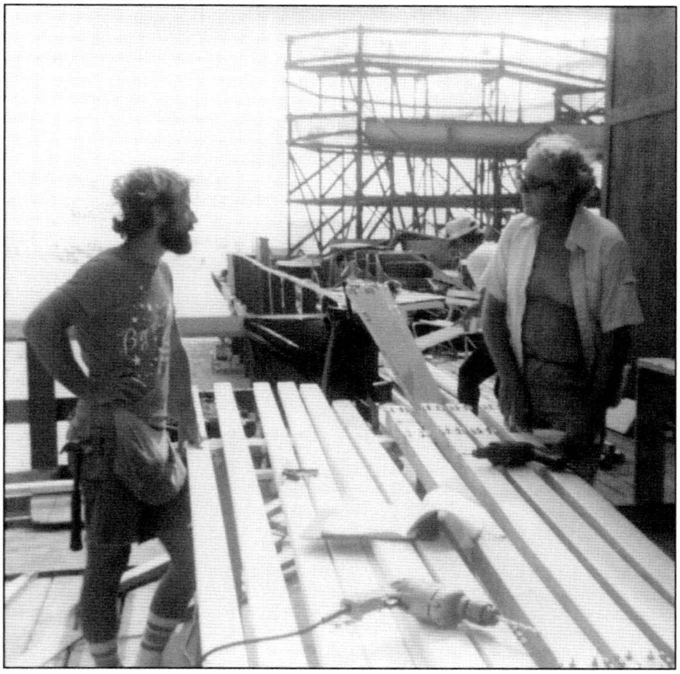

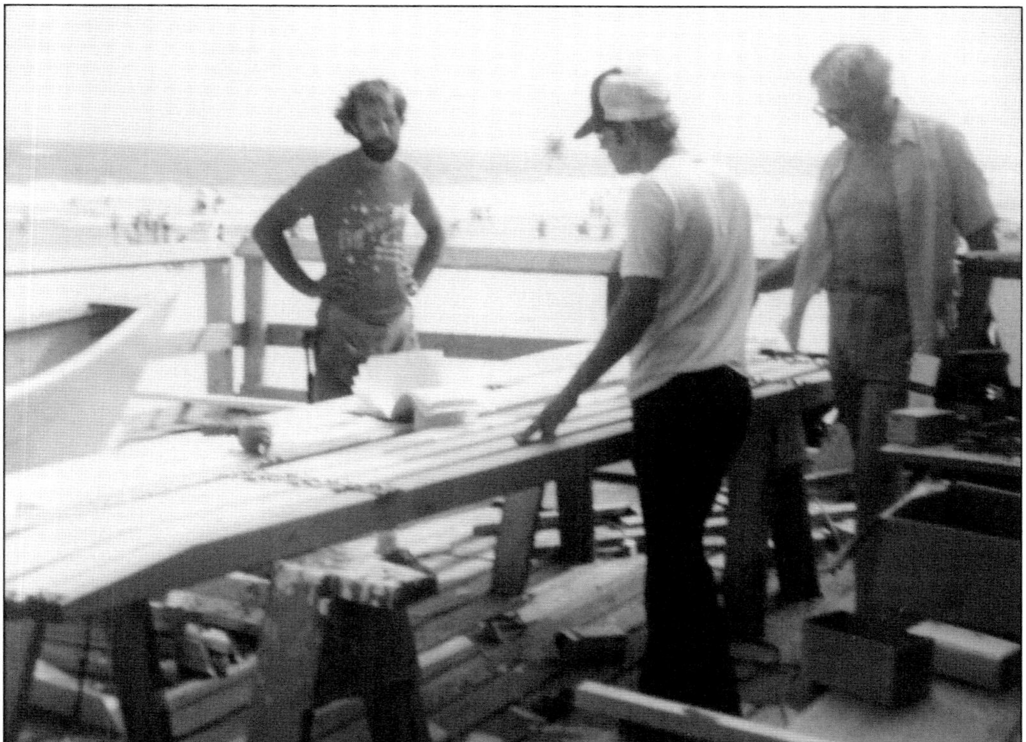

Peter Savard (left) and Art Fiala (center) inspect the replacement planks for Fun Pier. The planks had to be just right, and they were the right men for the job. They still maintain a close friendship to this day. This was a typical workday on Fun Pier. Bill Howard is on the right. (Courtesy Kathy Savard.)

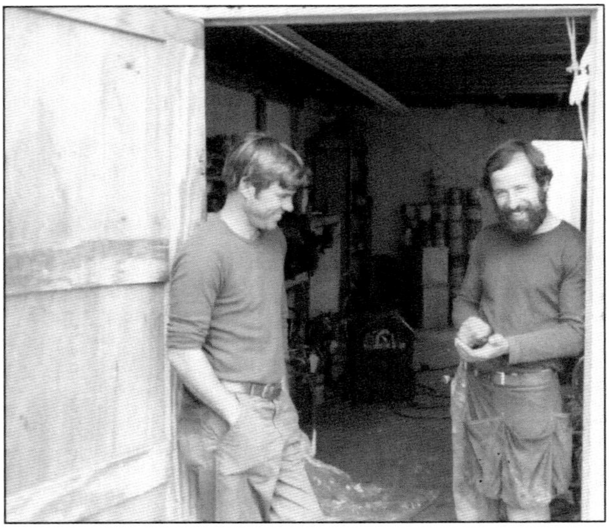

Art Fiala (left) and Peter Savard are pictured inside the maintenance shop on the pier. No matter how much they got finished in one day, the workload always seemed to be doubled on the following day. Savard continues to be a leading carpenter in the Wildwoods to this day. Fiala is also still a carpenter and mechanic in Alabama. (Courtesy Kathy Savard.)

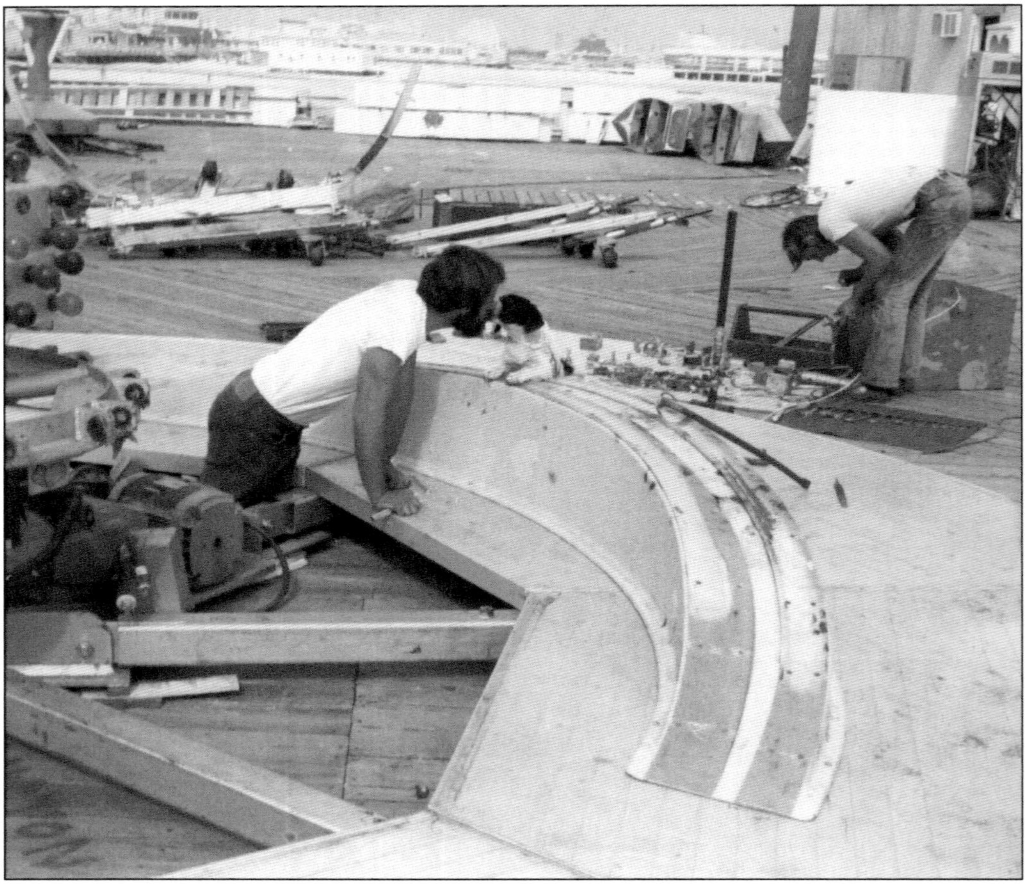

In the spring, all of the rides are put back into place. Here, Peter Savard is given a good-luck kiss by his dog, Sadie. Many of the rides on Fun Pier were carnival attractions. While others piers such as Hunt's Pier had mostly custom-made rides that could not be moved, Fun Pier's carnival rides were not only dismantled, but most were then taken on the road to different carnival attractions that Bill Howard was involved with. (Courtesy Kathy Savard.)

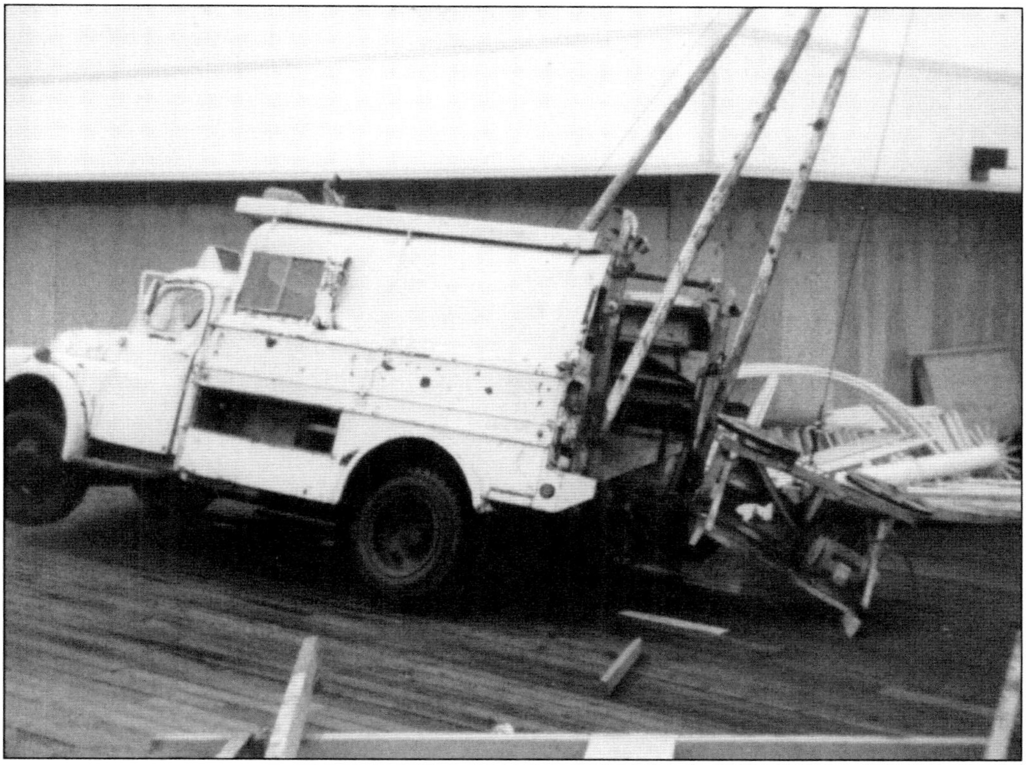

The Zoom Boom truck was always on Fun Pier. This was a former telephone company truck that was mainly used by Peter Savard. At the beginning of the season, before the pier would open for business, he would drive the Zoom Boom all over the pier as a way of testing the integrity of the board planks. Many times the Zoom Boom would crash through the boards and onto the beach. Although very primitive, it was an effective method of finding out which boards needed to be replaced, according to Savard. (Both, courtesy Kathy Savard.)

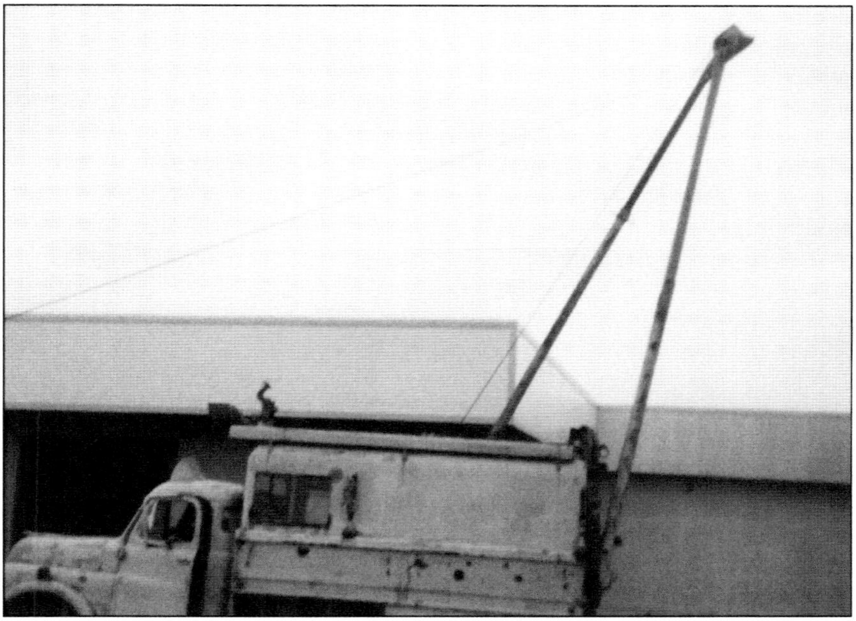

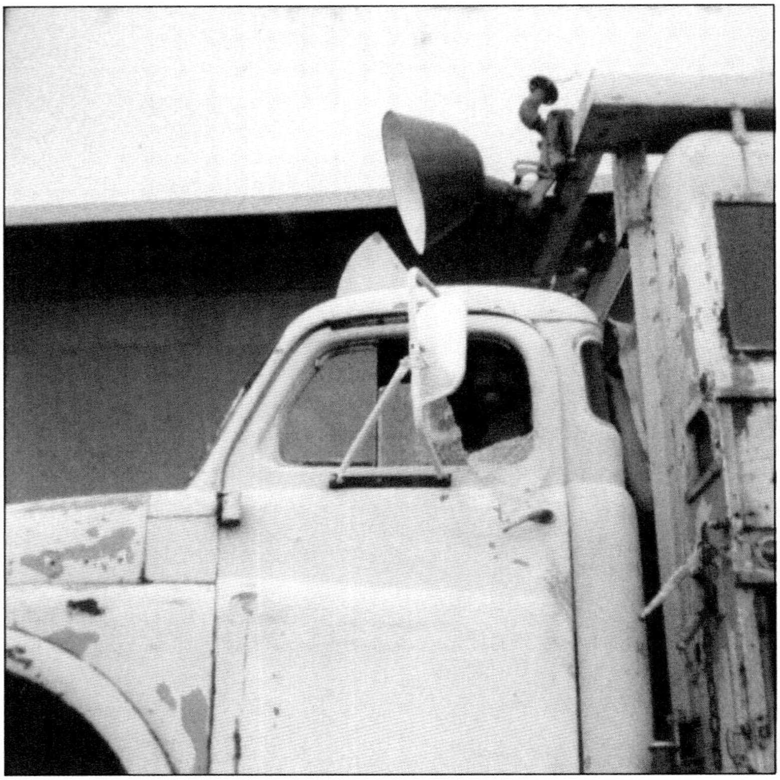

Peter Savard is ready for action as he operates the Zoom Boom. Savard says sometimes he would get away with some shakes when riding this truck along the pier. He would make note of what planks needed to be replaced and where. However, other times, he and the Zoom Boom would crash straight down to the beach. When this happened, they usually had to get a tow truck to pull it back up and onto the pier using cables. (Courtesy Kathy Savard.)

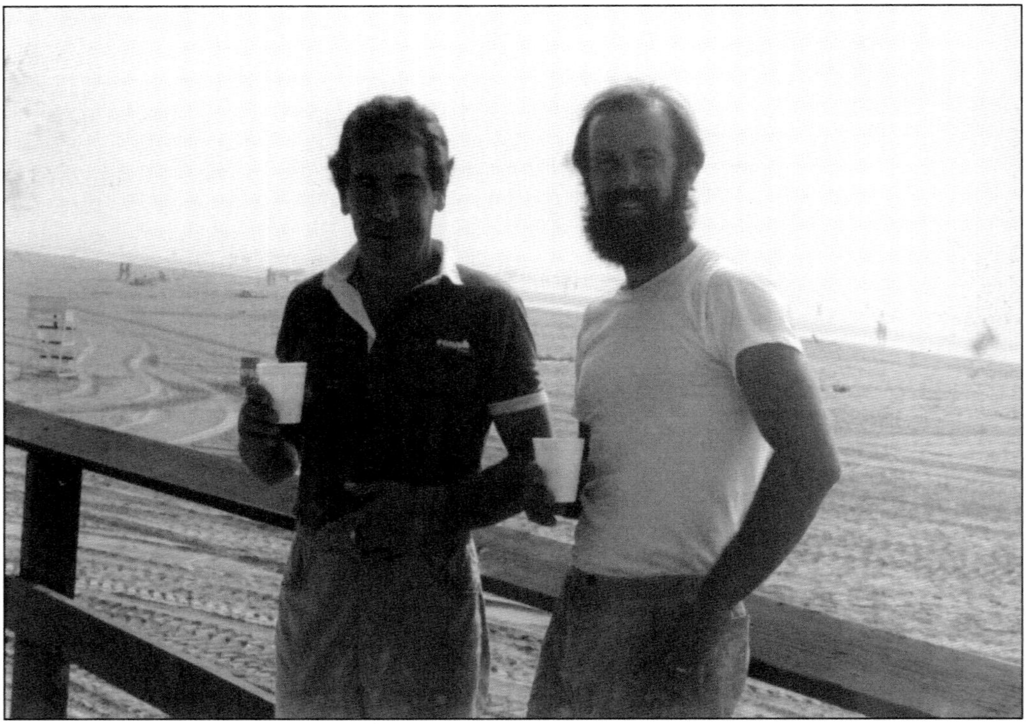

Here, Joey Faranolla (left) and Peter Savard take a much-needed break on Fun Pier. Faranolla was Savard's carpentry mentor. (Courtesy Kathy Savard.)

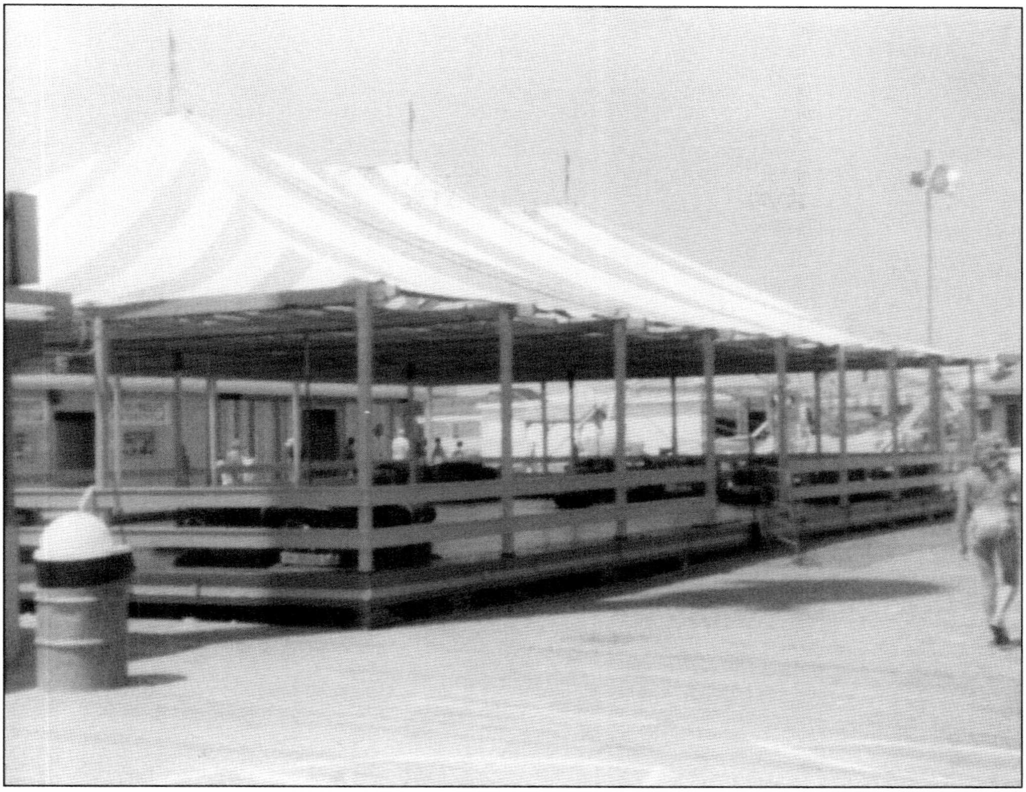

Through the years, many rides came and went on Fun Pier. Mulberry Street Fair was another of Bill Howard's many endeavors. Portable rides always came in handy, as Howard could just pack them up and take them from fair to fair. According to most of the former Fun Pier Gang, Howard got his start at state fairs. (Courtesy Kathy Savard.)

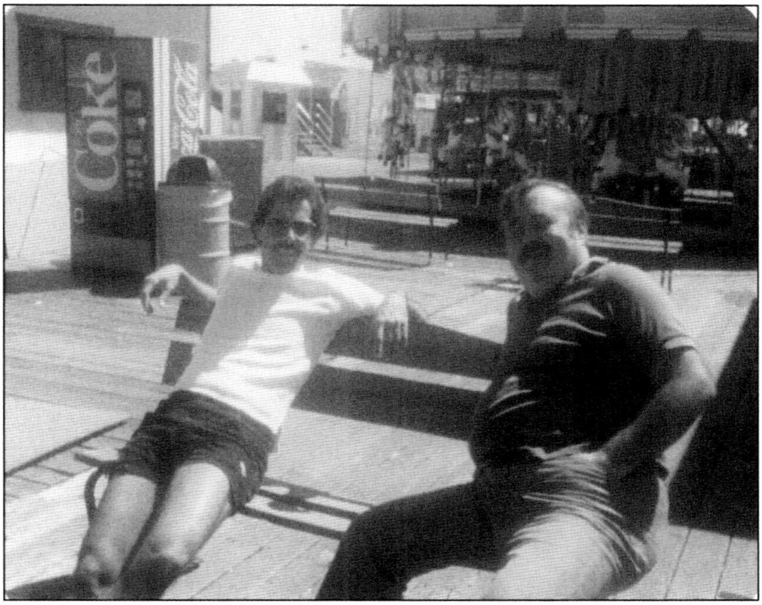

Garry Ross (left) is pictured here with Peter Barnes. Ross started out owning one of the games and eventually came to own and manage several, not only on Fun Pier but also at other Wildwood Boardwalk locations. In addition to the games on Fun Pier, he also had games on Sportland Pier and Casino Arcade. (Courtesy Albert Butler.)

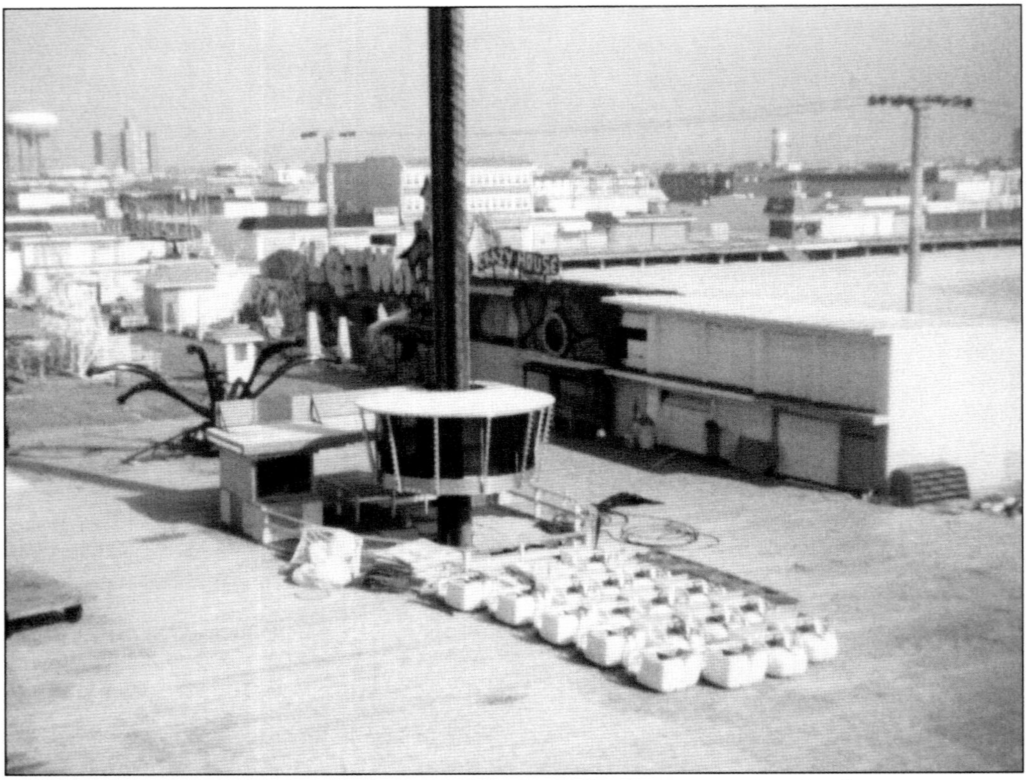

Here are some end-of-the-season photographs. The dark rides came in handy when storing away the rides cars for the Spider and Flying Bobs. Note that the Spider is nothing but arms, while the Flying Bob cars await their winter storage. It is common practice for most seasonal businesses to carefully pack everything up for the following season. Peter Savard had spent over 15 years working on Fun Pier. Savard started with Joe Barnes and continued to work for the Howards. Once the dark rides were full of other rides, decisions had to made as to what to do with the rest of the rides. As Bill Howard had winter business in the Southern states, he would take the remaining rides with him on the road. (Both, courtesy Kathy Savard.)

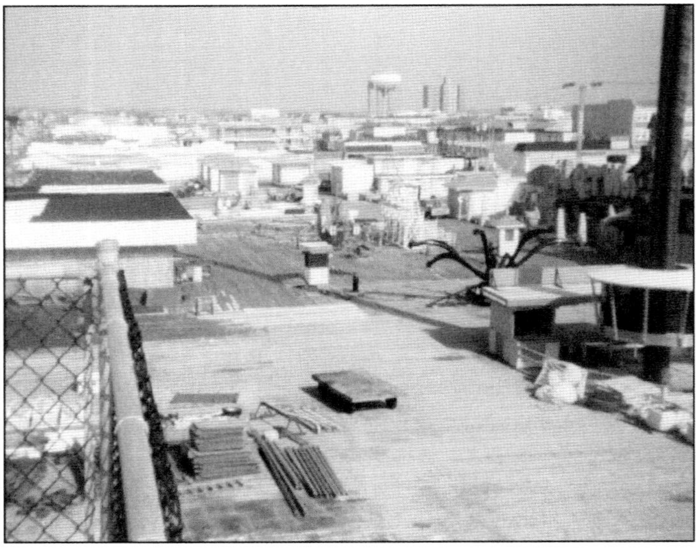

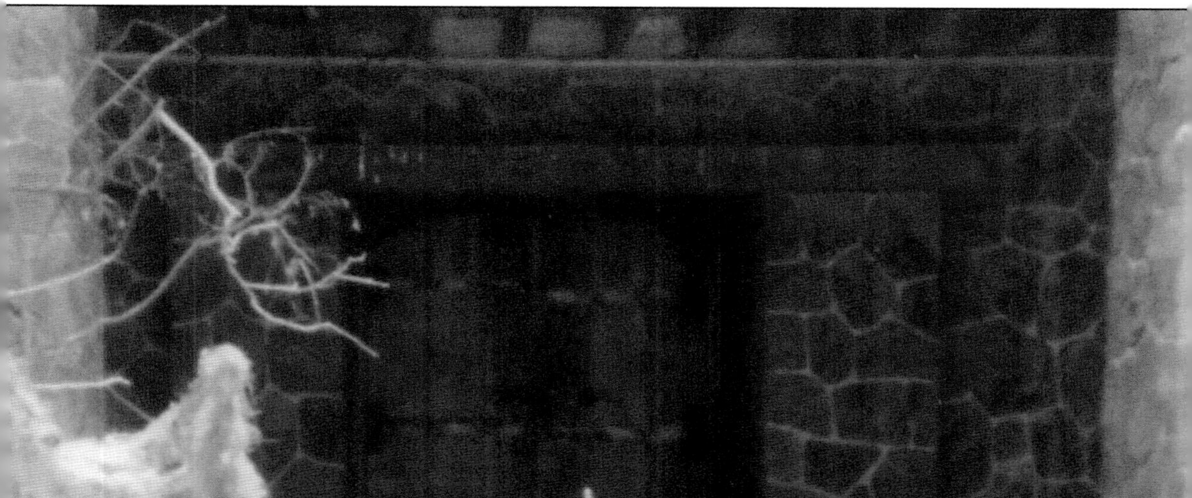

While Dennis Easy and Sheila Rubin made many of the ghoulish creations inside Castle Frankenstein, others also helped out with the front. Peter Savard built these large doors to look like those from an old castle. As Rubin explained, upon entering the doors, a coffin was laid between two human-size hands. The actor or actress in the coffin would lie still until hearing the front doors slam, at which point he or she would come to life and explain the rules of the castle; Rubin herself played this part many times. After the speech, the patrons would pass through another door and into the elaborate set of Frankenstein's laboratory. (Courtesy Kathy Savard.)

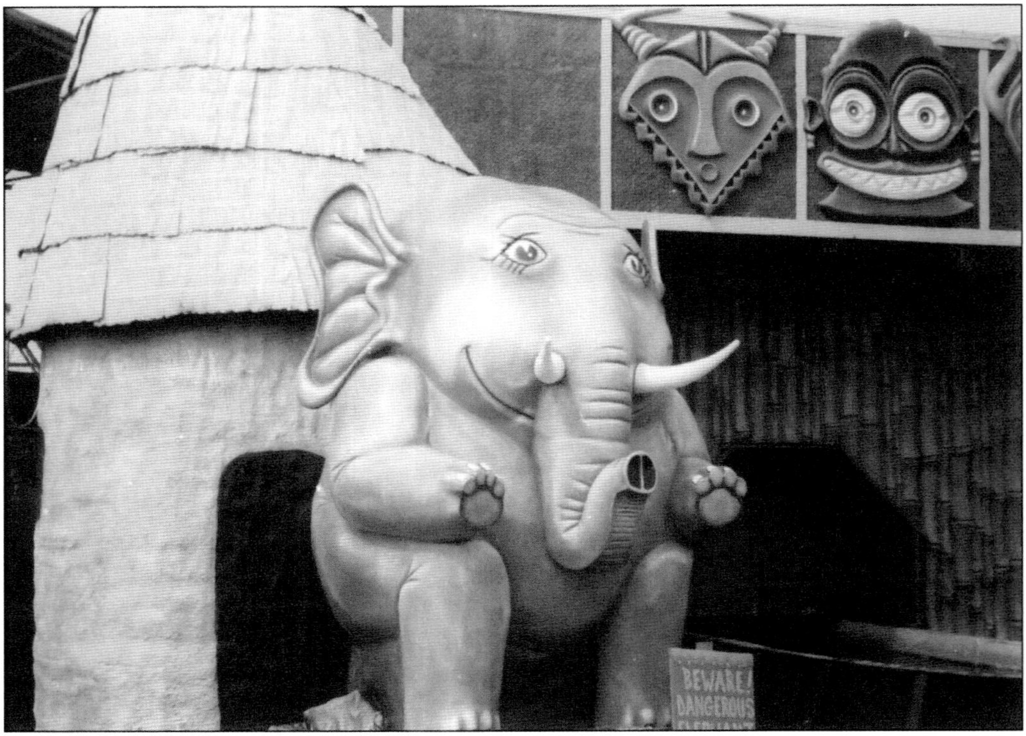

Jungleland, not to be confused the Hunt's Pier Jungleland, was designed and built Jack and Wayne Seddon. The elephant was made by the American Young Blood Company and could also work as a vacuum. Wayne Seddon said that the elephant arrived with no ears or tusks. Seddon added these parts, as seen in the photograph, along with the rocks that he is sitting on. (Courtesy Jack and Wayne Seddon.)

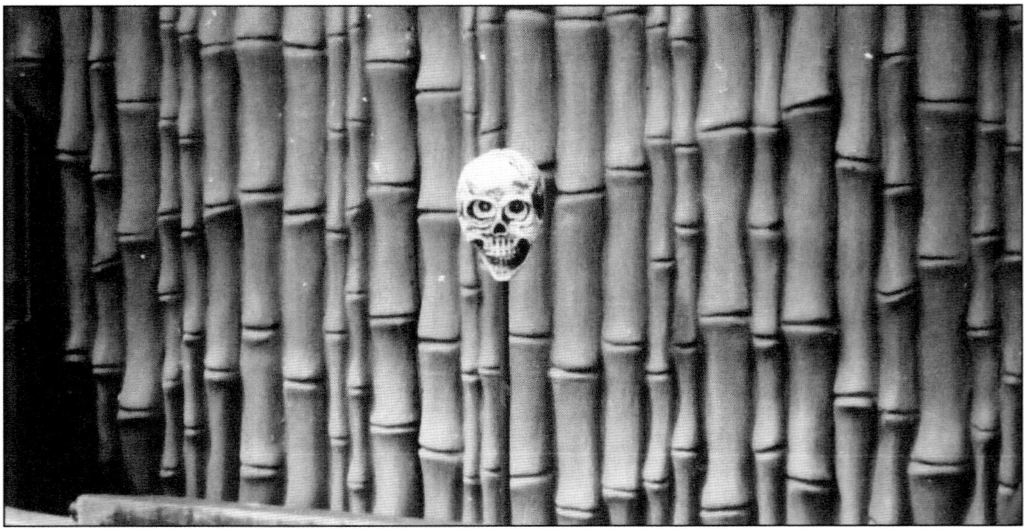

This is one of the many skulls made for Jungleland. The Seddon brothers made the eyes look as if they were trained on the customers. The "bamboo" walls on the outskirts of the ride were fiberglass. When Vince Kostek, the Hunt's Pier manager, came to see the new ride, he asked, "How did you get it so smooth?" At that point, Kostek cut his finger on the fiberglass. (Courtesy Wayne Seddon.)

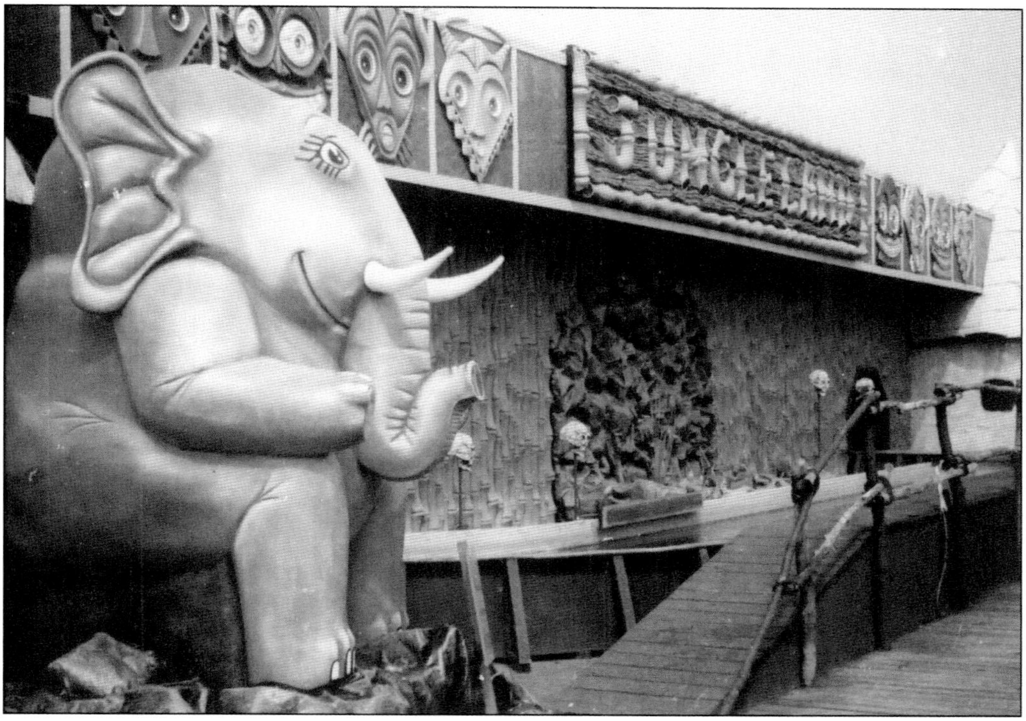

The rock quarry in the center of the front was nothing more than crushed cardboard boxes that were painted and covered in fiberglass. At one point, this was a waterfall. Note the break in the ride, the panel at the bottom of the rock quarry. When the ride operator would need to stop a boat, he would pull a lever that would bring the panel out. Also note the skulls on sticks. At night, the ride was lit up with yellow, green, and red spotlights, which gave the ride a very tropical look. (Courtesy Jack and Wayne Seddon.)

This is the loading station at Jungleland. Though the title was the same as the one on Hunt's Pier, Fun Pier's Jungleland was very different. The designs for tiki masks on the top were taken out of books. Once the design was decided upon, the Seddon brothers carved, painted, and placed them on the top of the ride next to the sign. The sign itself was hand carved and then covered in fiberglass as well. Peter Savard made the small brown boats for Jungleland. (Courtesy Jack and Wayne Seddon.)

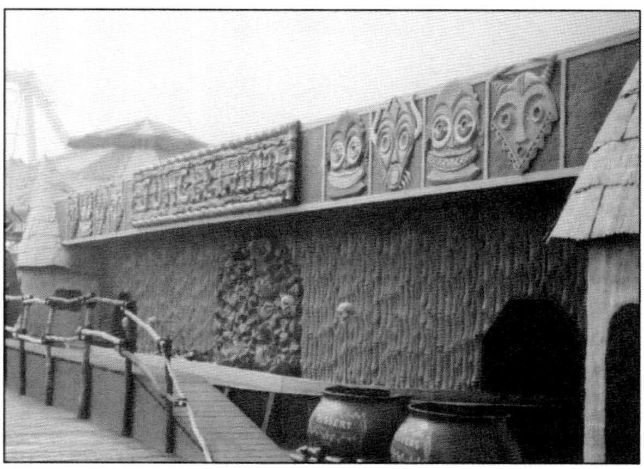

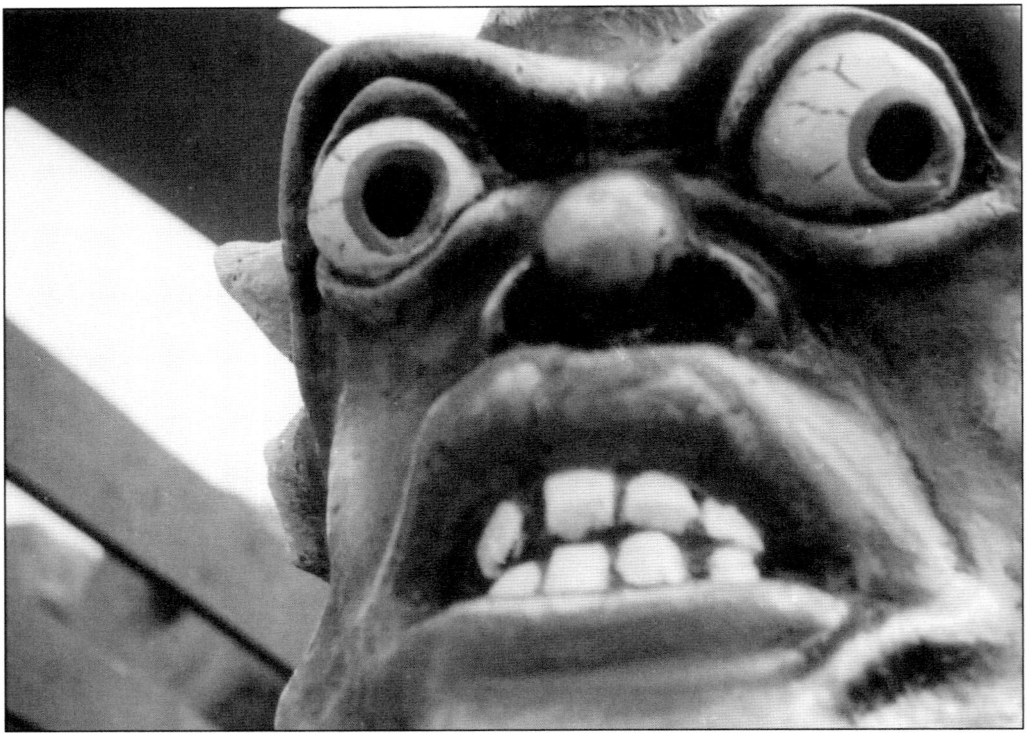

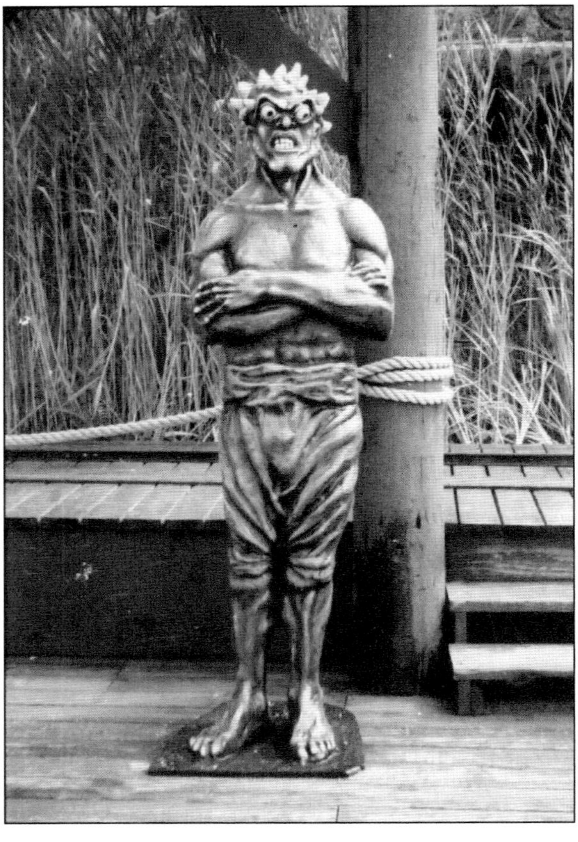

Wayne Seddon redesigned this eerie prop, which started out as a benign genie-type figure. As he recalled, this prop was taken from the inside of Lost World. He then sculpted clay over the original to make a menacing face. After it was dry, Wayne covered the clay with fiberglass and painted it. This prop was positioned next to the steps of the loading station for Lost World. Jack Seddon is no longer in the amusement-display business, but Wayne Seddon continues his amusement-display work at Gillian's Wonderland Pier, which is located on the boardwalk in Ocean City, New Jersey. The Seddon brothers worked on Fun Pier until September 1985. (Both, courtesy Wayne Seddon.)

Three

INTO OBLIVION

Although the 1970s were solid seasons for Fun Pier, Bill Howard could only make interest payments to Joe Barnes. The trademark rides of Fun Pier continued to disappear. The Sky Tower had been suffering from hydraulic problems and would occasionally get stuck. This presented a huge maintenance problem, as the motors were at the top of the ride and repairing it was treacherous work, since it involved climbing out onto the top of the capsule. Only the hydraulic pumps were on ground level. Sky Tower was finally closed to customers and sat idle until the ride capsule was removed in the spring of 1985. The tower pole would not be removed until 2009. The Ski Ride was also falling into disrepair due to exposure to the elements. Lost World, which was known for its ride-through/walk-through combo, failed the ride inspector's exam. The walk-through portion of Lost World was shut down to the public due to one too many tight corners and poor lighting in the caverns below. Electrical wires were also starting to become exposed and presented a hazard, so Lost World became a ride-through only attraction. Castle Frankenstein was the next victim of increasingly tougher safety requirements because there was no sprinkler system inside, so by July 1982, it too was shut down—never again to open its doors.

On August 13, 1984, the Castle Frankenstein attraction burned to the ground, along with Beach Grill, which was located directly behind the castle. The fire caused an estimated loss of $200,000. On November 24, 1984, the pier's other dark ride, Lost World, caught fire. The blaze claimed other mainstay attractions on Fun Pier, including Crazy House, the Jet 400 roller coaster, and the former Mirror Maze structure. In fact, the whole northern half of the pier underwent a radical change and permanently altered what many remembered as the classic Fun Pier.

To get the pier up and running in time for Memorial Day weekend in 1985, Bill Howard partnered with Don Deggeller of Deggeller's Attractions to provide rides to fill out the pier, but it was not enough, and an unsuccessful 1985 season led Bill Howard to sell Fun Pier.

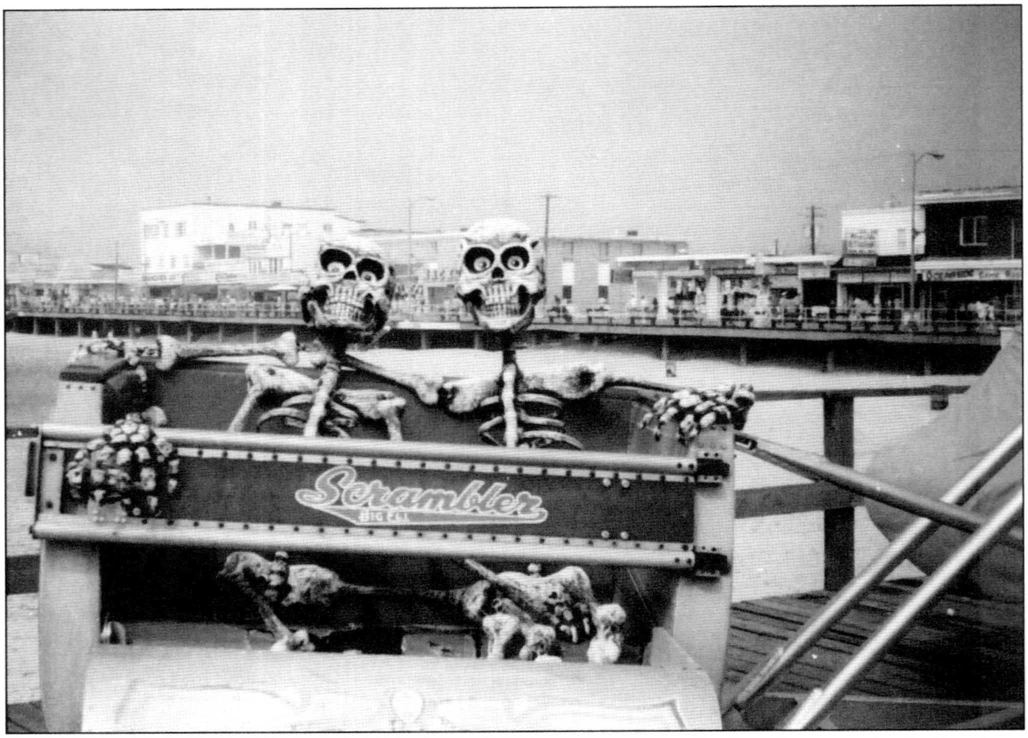

Jack and Wayne Seddon were known as practical jokers on the pier. In this photograph, the brothers positioned two of their prop skeletons from Jungleland inside the ride cars of the Scrambler. This scene caught the attention of many patrons—some laughed to no end, and others were horrified. The Scrambler was a product of the Eli Bridge Company. Note the Roberts Avenue Mack's Pizza in the background. (Courtesy Wayne Seddon.)

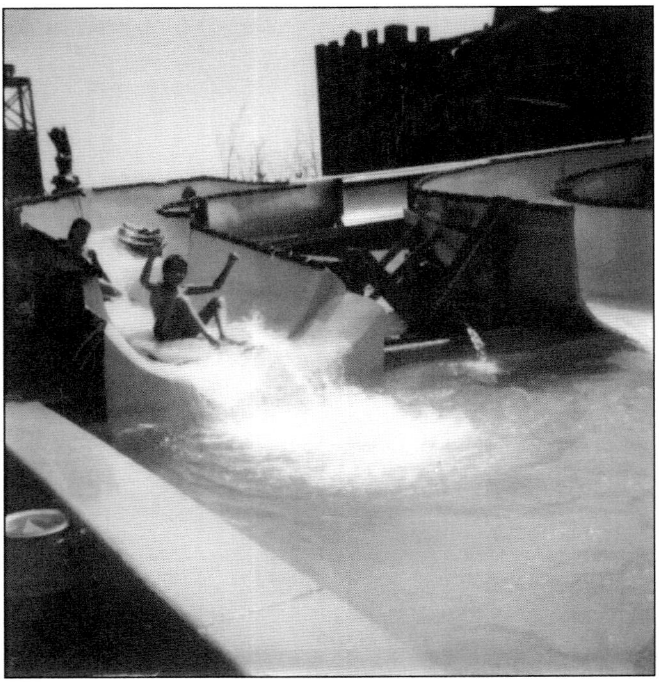

Customers cool off on a hot summer day on the Fun Pier waterslide with Castle Frankenstein eerily looking over them. The waterslide, or Fun Slide as it was called when on Fun Pier, continued to be a star attraction. An unfortunate accident occurred on August 6, 1980, as seven people crashed through a section of Plexiglas while sliding on the waterslide. (Courtesy Marc Scarvalli.)

Whether it was Tiki Train, Devil's Inn, or Lost World (as in this photograph), the infamous King Kong stood guard. At one point in Lost World's early years, patrons would exit the walk-through section of the ride between the gorilla's legs. The gorilla stood 20 feet tall. (Courtesy Mike Bukowski.)

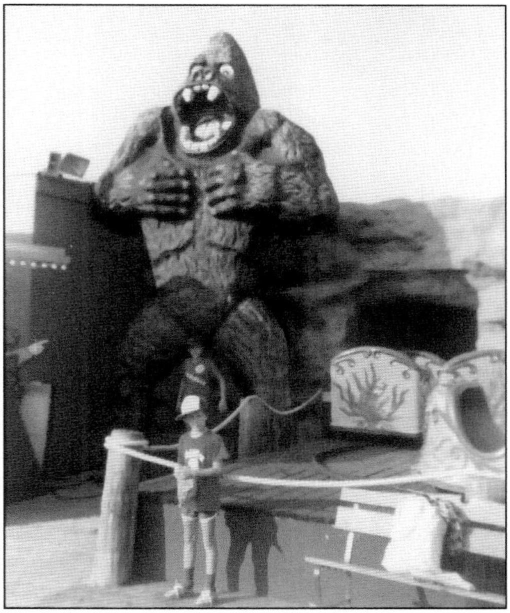

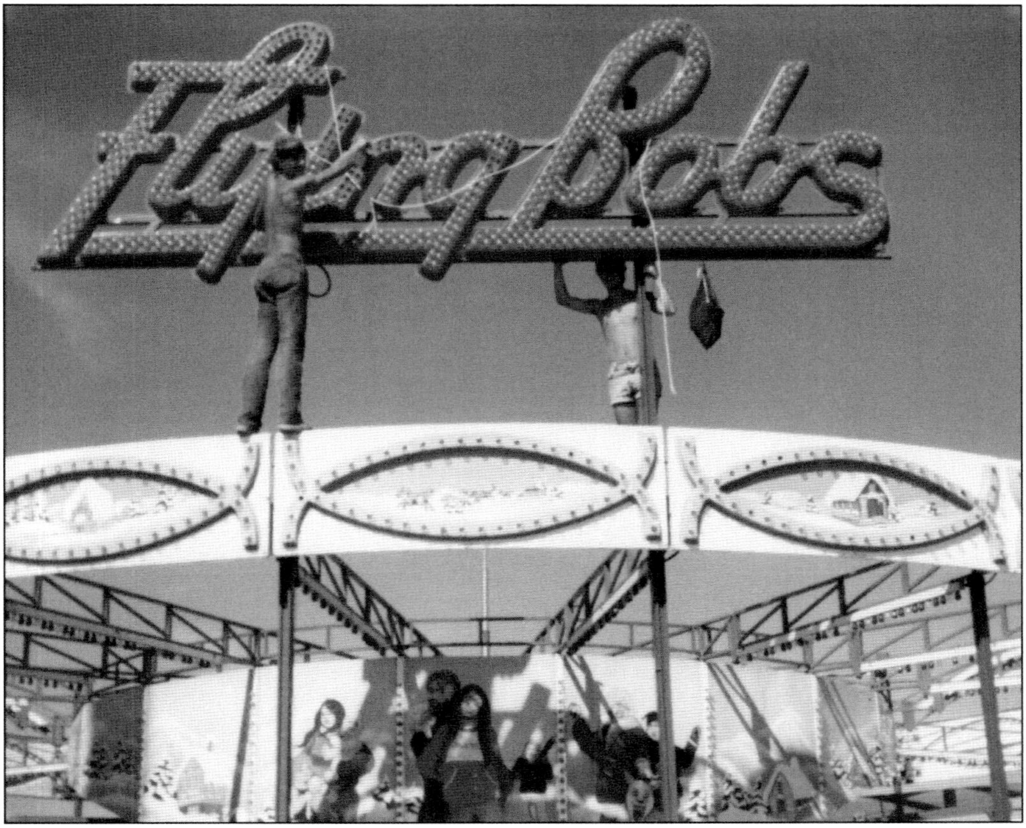

The Flying Bobs are being put together after they were acquired from Hunt's Pier. The crew said the hardest part was getting all the light bulbs in, because there were hundreds of them. This was only one of many portable rides that Bill Howard owned during his ownership of Fun Pier. (Courtesy Lee Durland.)

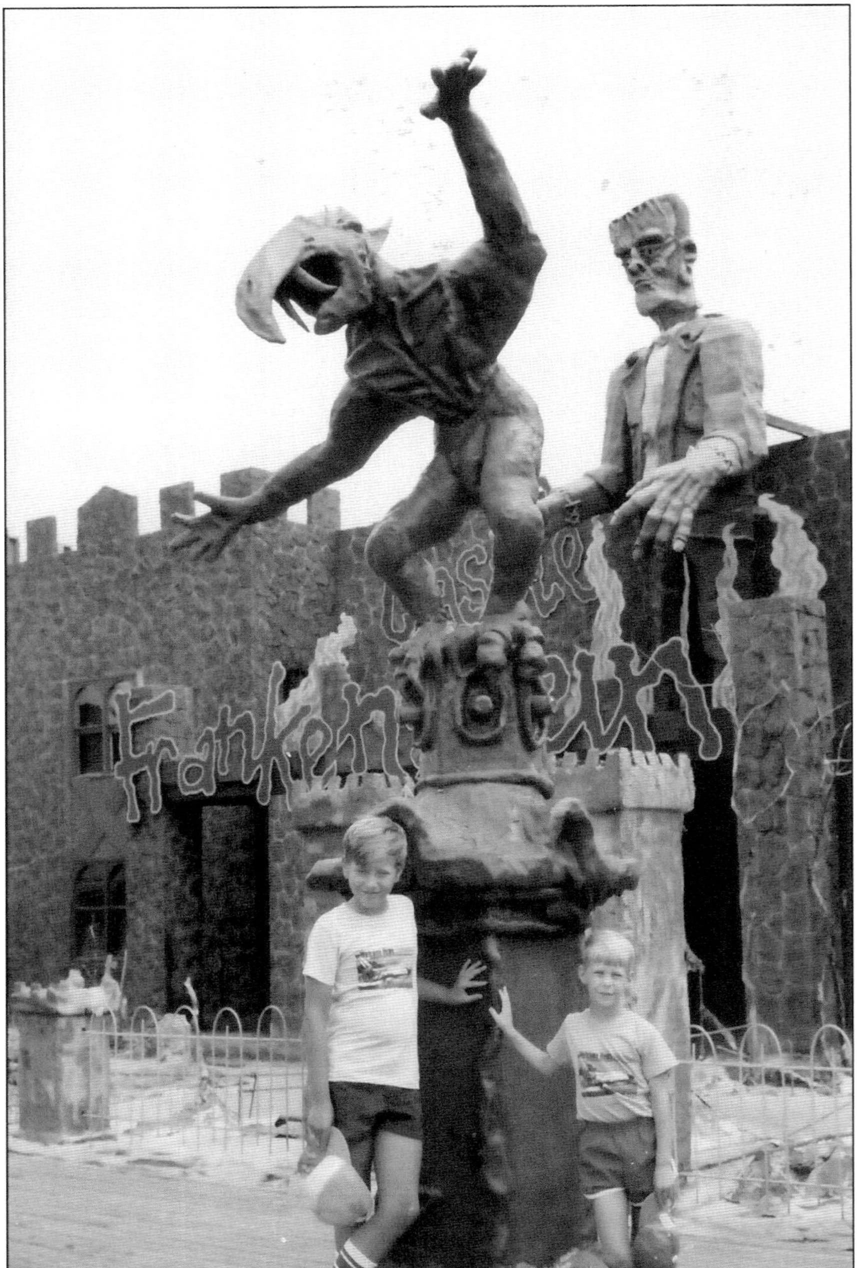

Mike Bukowski (right) stands with his brother, Chris, by the gargoyle in front of the graveyard scene of the castle. The graveyard also served as part of the attraction. Customers would have to walk through the graveyard maze before crossing the entrance doors. Actors would also be in position to hide in sections of the graveyard, pop out, and scare people. In this photograph, the castle has been closed and the graveyard has already been ruined. Note that even the windows have been broken. The castle looked most eerie at night with flashing strobe lights in the windows. Dennis Easy would stand looking out of the upper window and use a microphone to talk directly to people walking past the castle as a way of trying to make them believe Frankenstein's monster was doing the talking. (Courtesy Charles and Mike Bukowski.)

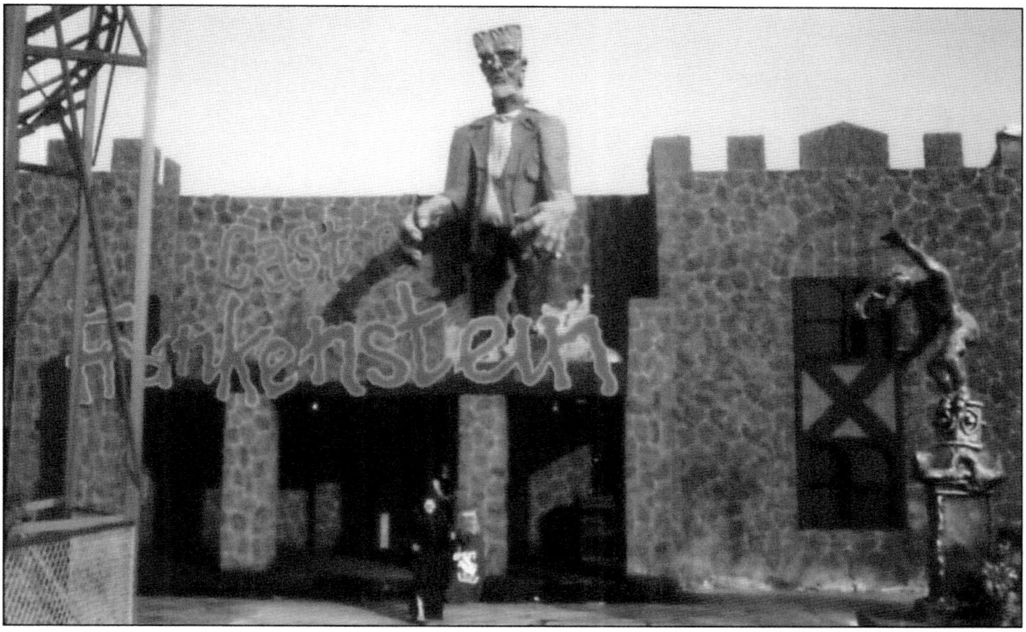

This photograph shows the elaborate detail of the castle. Note that the graveyard scene is missing. The graveyard was not present the first season of the castle, which is said to have been 1978. Castle Frankenstein was short-lived on Fun Pier. During this era, Wildwood also had an elaborate Dracula's Castle on Nickels Midway Pier. (Courtesy Jim Abbate, National Amusement Park Historical Association.)

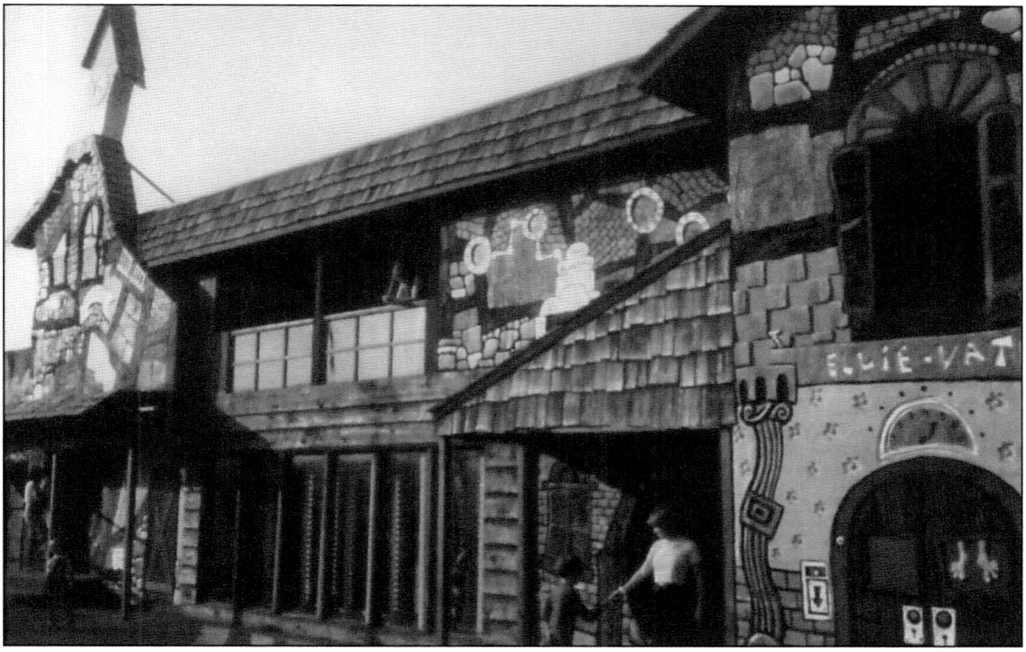

The facade of Crazy House appears here after a makeover by Jack and Wayne Seddon. By the early 1980s, the original paint job was in need of a touch-up. The Seddon brothers came to work on the pier in 1979, and one of their first assignments was to highlight the facade of Crazy House. (Courtesy Jim Abbate, National Amusement Park Historical Association.)

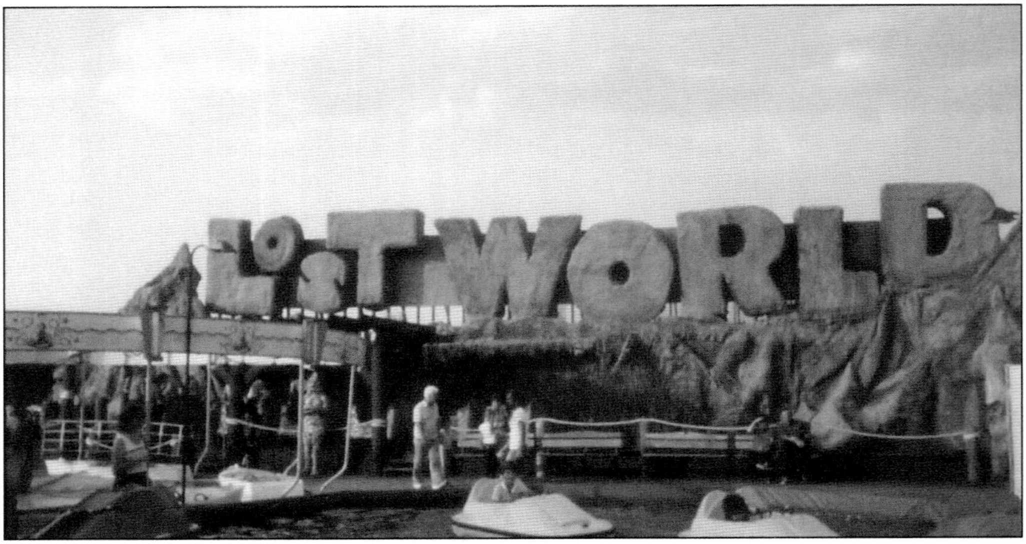

Lost World would also receive a makeover by the Seddon brothers. Originally, the pools on the loading station were for props during the ride's earlier incarnations. When Jim DeMusz rethemed this ride, less was more, with only small tree branches placed in the pools. Jack Seddon felt that the ride should be covered in grass and thus placed reeds into the pools. This worked all too well, as the reeds grew up and over the ride. They had to be maintained, but many felt this was just the right look for a lost world. (Courtesy Jim Abbate, National Amusement Park Historical Association.)

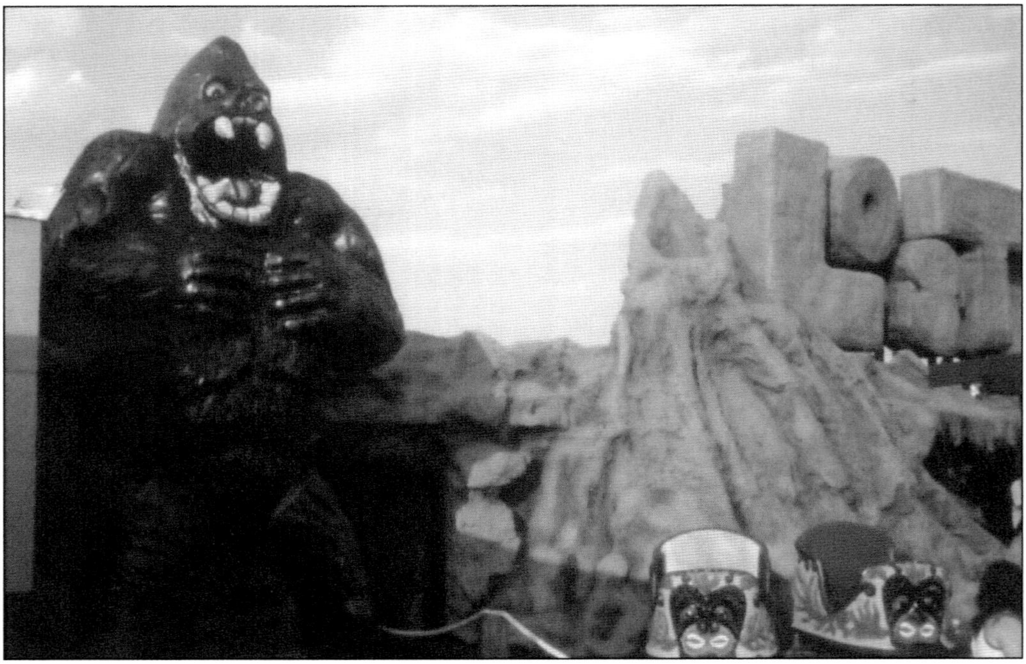

By 1983, Lost World was only a ride-through; the walk-through section had been closed due to fire-code restrictions. The opening between the gorilla's legs (which had been the walk-through part of the ride) was permanently sealed off, as it was no longer needed. Note the ride cars with the bizarre faces. The cars in this photograph are under repair. (Courtesy Jim Abbate, National Amusement Park Historical Association.)

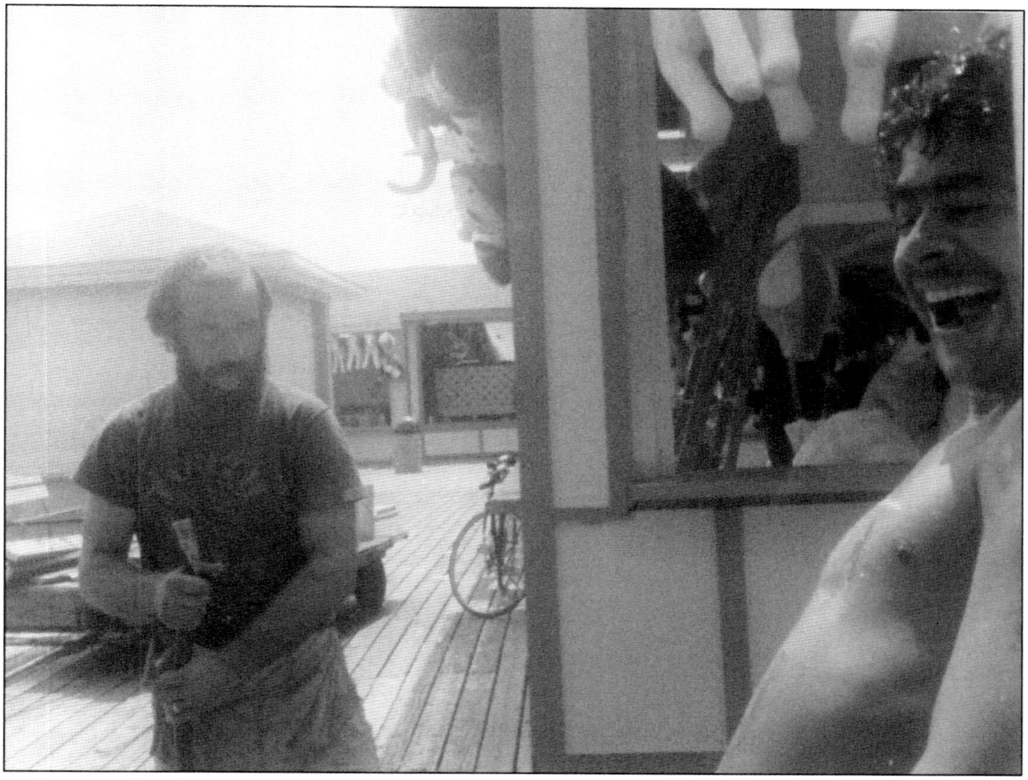

Peter Savard replaces the boards on the pier. The crowbar was used to lift the old, weak boards and also to set the new planks in place. He says this was a much better way of replacing the old boardwalk on the pier. Most of the time, he had to work replacing huge sections of the boardwalk after the Zoom Boom truck would crash through the weak boards to the beach. The Howards were still making payments to Joe Barnes while maintaining their other businesses down south. Each spring, Savard would be asked to test the boardwalk with the Zoom Boom. (Both, courtesy Albert Butler.)

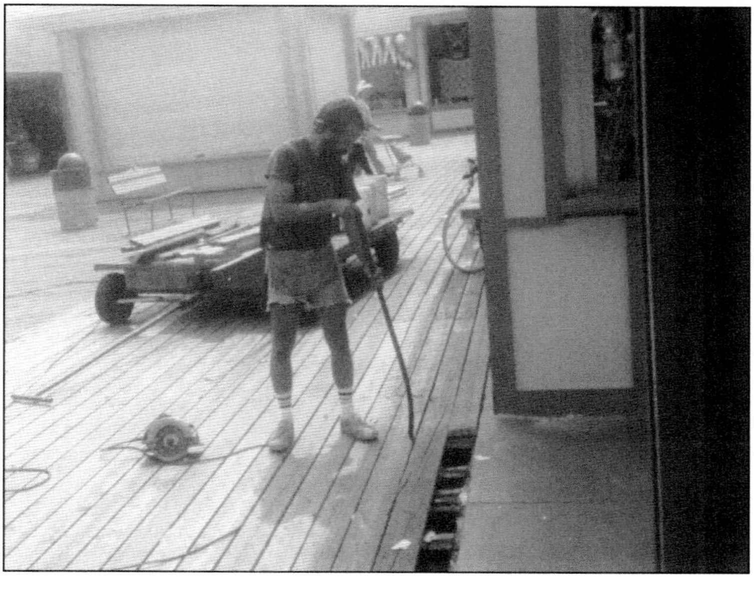

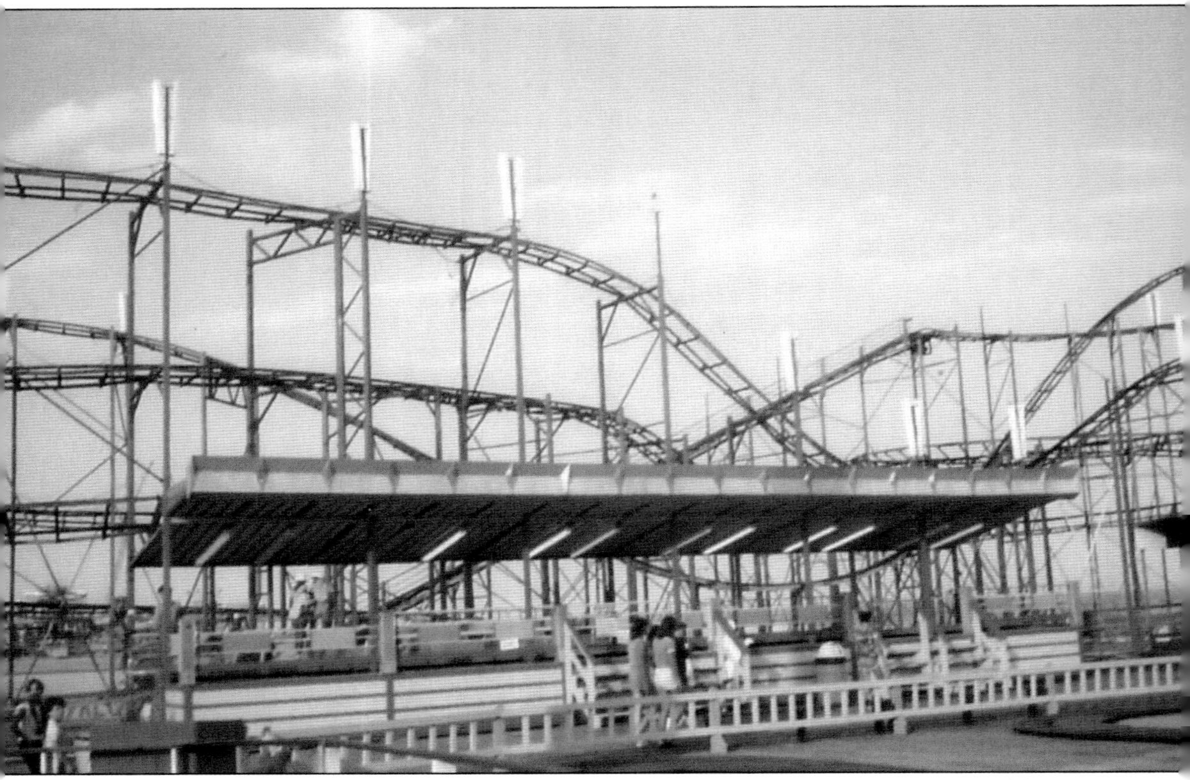

The Zyklon B, a steel roller coaster, only lasted a few summers on Fun Pier. The owner of the coaster had been forced to change the name, which it shared with the poisonous gas used in Nazi death camps. This roller coaster, named by the defunct Italian manufacturer Pinfari, was replaced by the Jet 400, another steel roller coaster. Zyklon B was set on the northern side of Fun Pier, in front of Castle Frankenstein. Pinfari was also the manufacturer that made the Supersonic roller coaster on Sportland Pier. (Courtesy Jim Abbate, National Amusement Park Historical Association.)

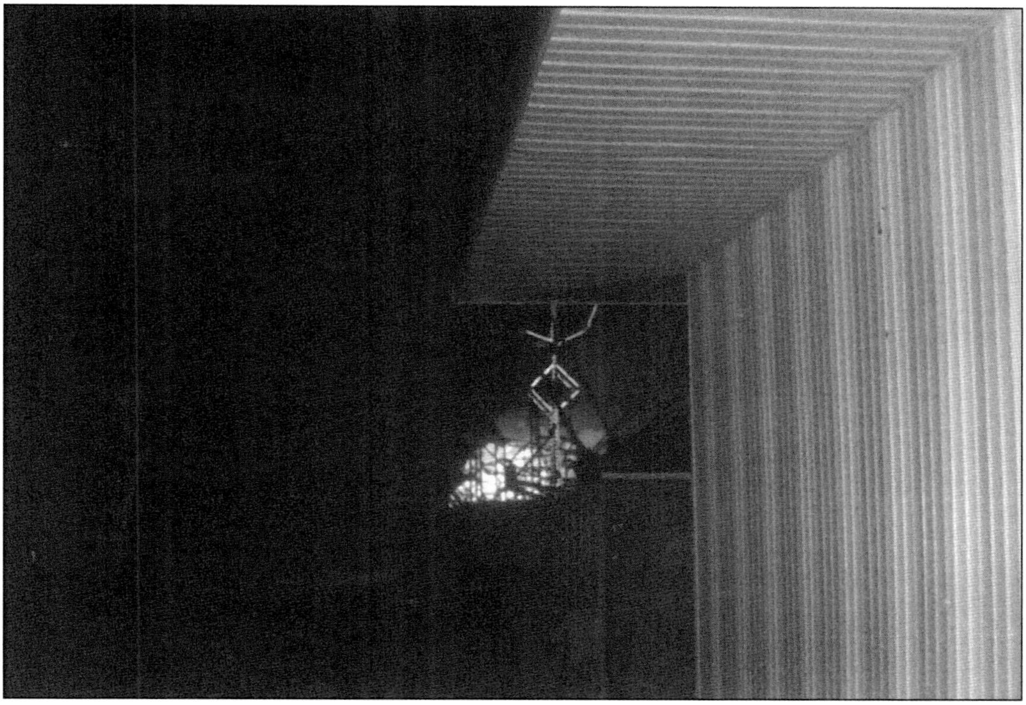

On August 13, 1984, Castle Frankenstein burned to the ground and caused an estimated $200,000 in damages. It has been reported that the fire started around 3:30 a.m. and may have originated from an electrical line that ran under the pier to a main fuse box in the Beach Grill snack bar. (Courtesy Gary Ross.)

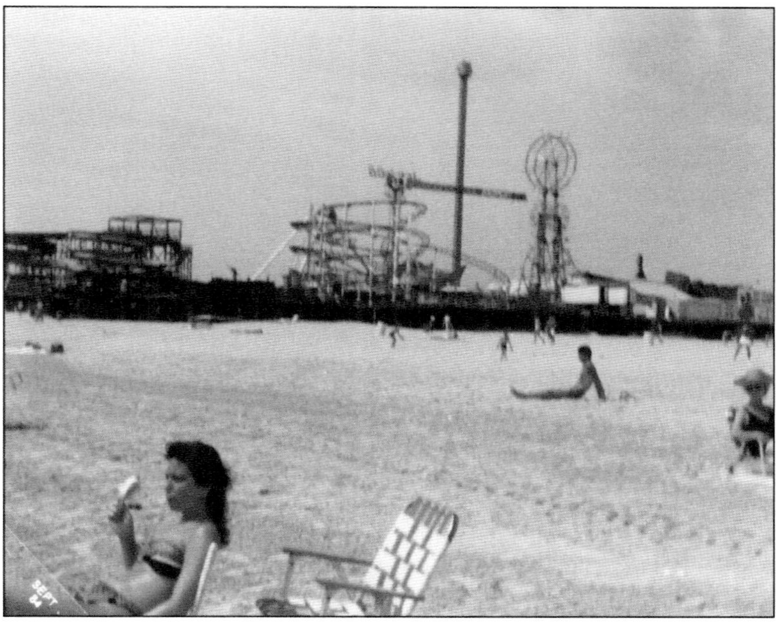

This photograph was taken within days of the Castle Frankenstein fire. The pier continued its daily operations with plans afoot to fill in the void where the castle stood. This was the beginning of the end for Fun Pier, though most did not realize it at the time. (Courtesy Marc Scarvalli.)

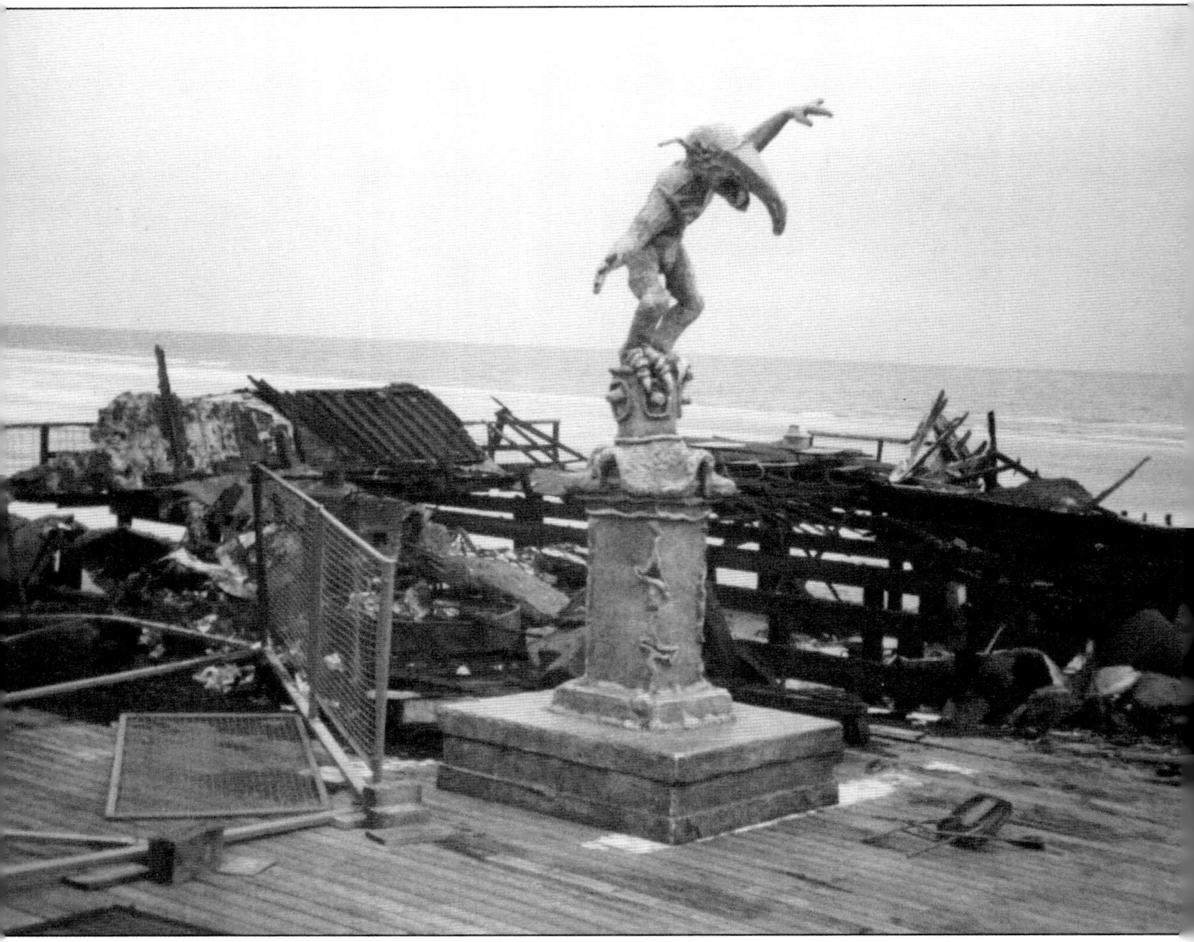

Ironically, this gargoyle from Castle Frankenstein survived the fires of 1984. This was one of at least three gargoyles handmade by Dennis Easy. The other gargoyles were lost to the fire of August 13, 1984. The gargoyles were one-of-a-kind, as no mold had been cast. Jack and Wayne Seddon would do refurbishing work for the castle after Dennis Easy and Sheila Rubin left Fun Pier in 1981. (Courtesy Stephen Armstrong.)

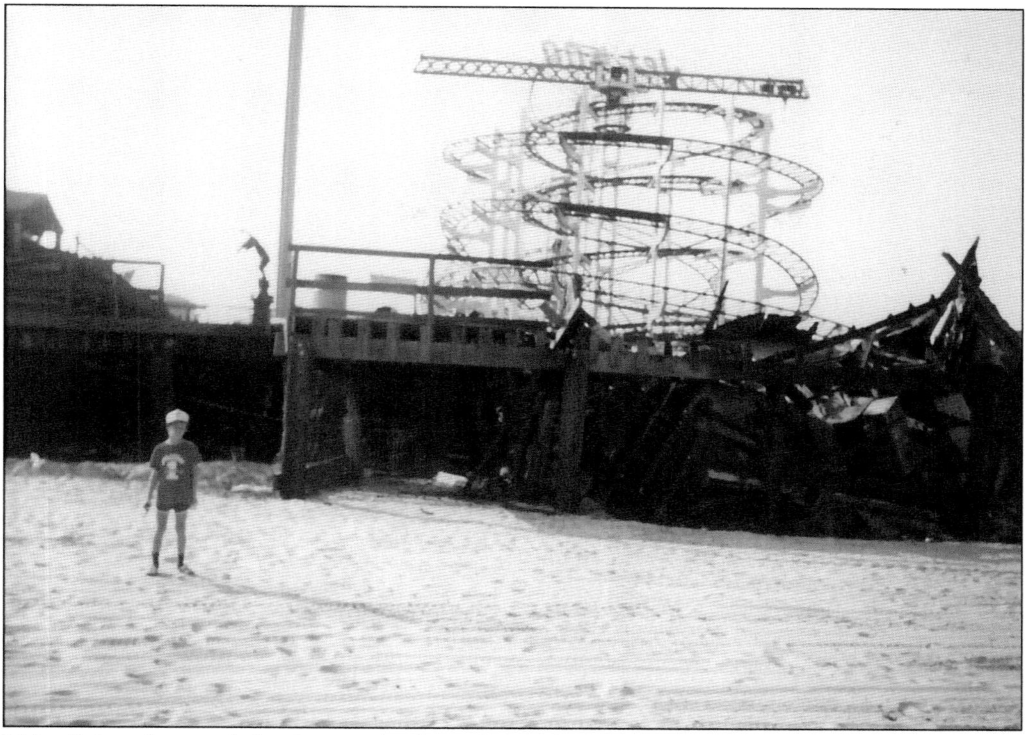

Mike Bukowski stands by the wreck of Castle Frankenstein. This was a most unusual fire that began in the early morning hours. The castle only saw operation for four full summers. Memories of what was inside are hazy to most with the exception of its creators. There was much conjecture about the cause of the fire, but nothing definitive was ever determined. (Courtesy Charles and Mike Bukowski.)

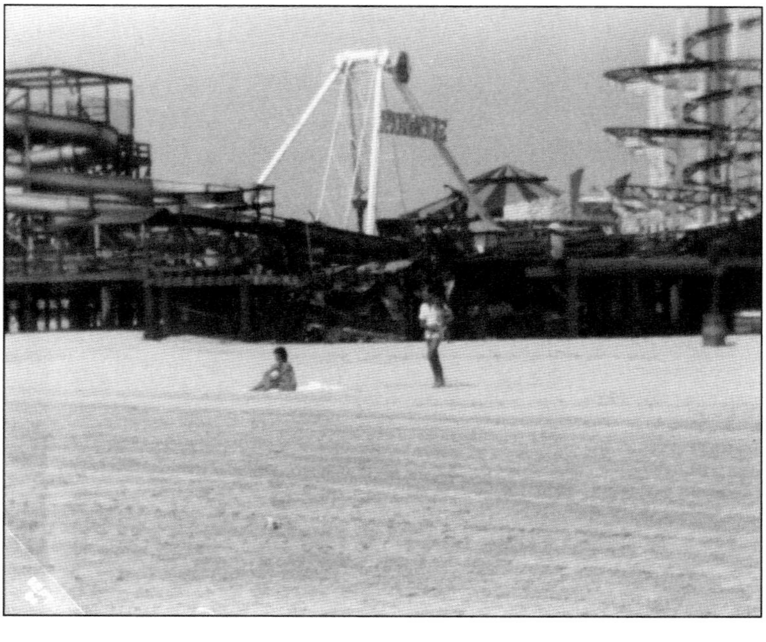

This is a closer look at the damage from the castle fire of August 1984. Himalaya was then on Fun Pier. Most teenagers and young adults hoped a new and improved castle would be built to replace the old one, but that never happened. (Courtesy Marc Scarvalli.)

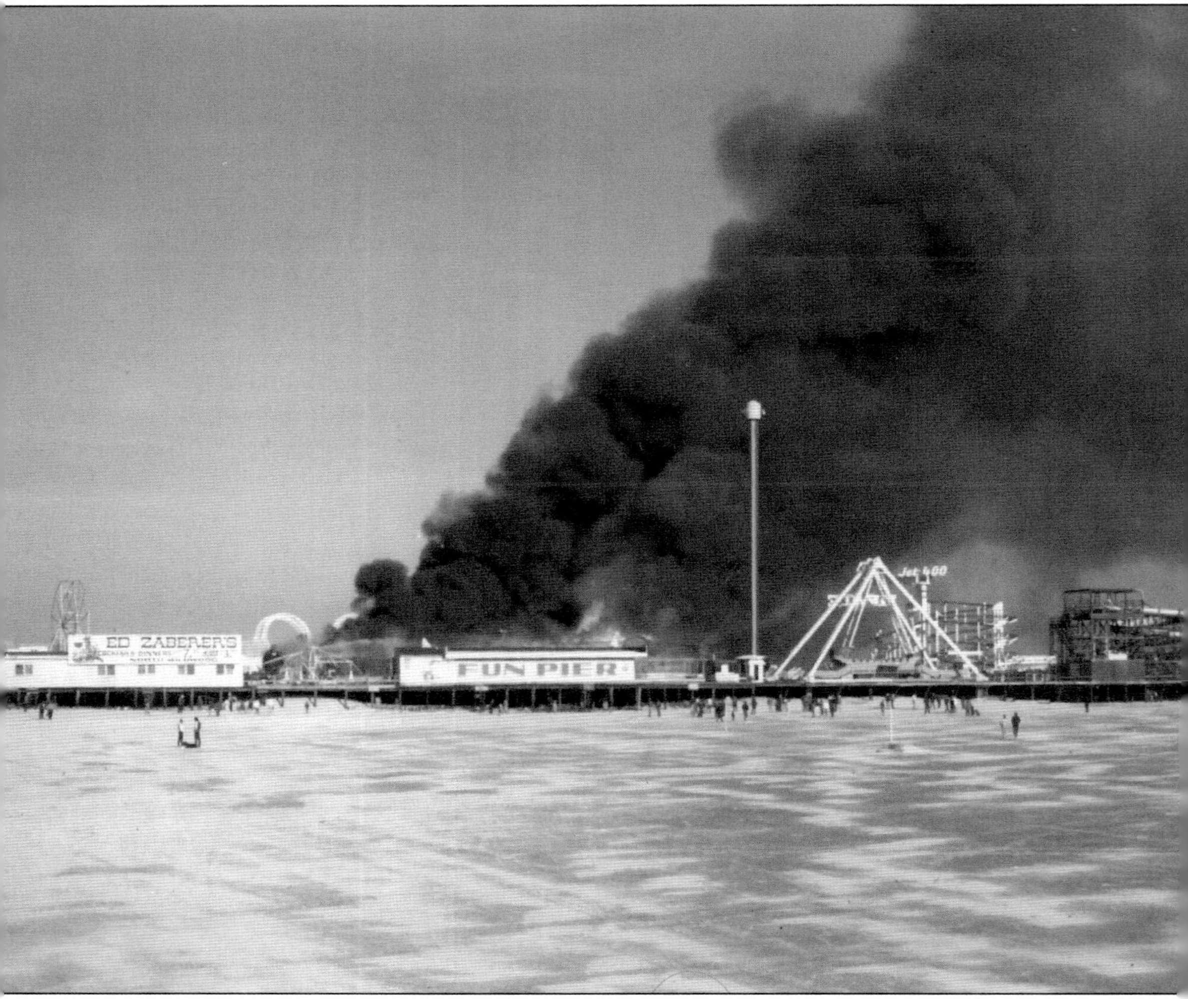

On Saturday, November 24, 1984, the Lost World fire is burning. Lost World was made up of large quantities of polyurethane foam; once the foam caught fire, it made the black clouds that are seen here coming off the top of the ride. This was a clear but brisk and windy day; the smoke could be seen from Wildwood Crest. Many locals quickly headed down to the beach to watch the fire. The blaze lasted a few hours with devastating effect to Fun Pier. (Courtesy David Williams.)

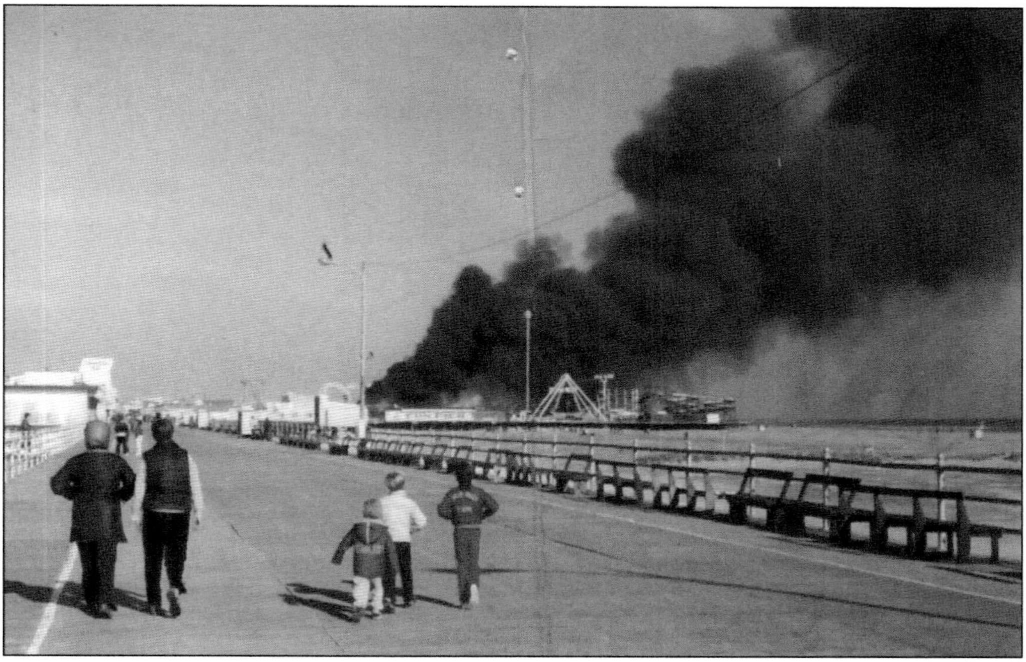

Dark clouds poured up into the sky above Fun Pier. The clouds created an eerie display that could be seen all over the island. The fire began on Saturday afternoon over the Thanksgiving holiday weekend. No official reason has been formally given as to the cause. (Courtesy Gary Ross.)

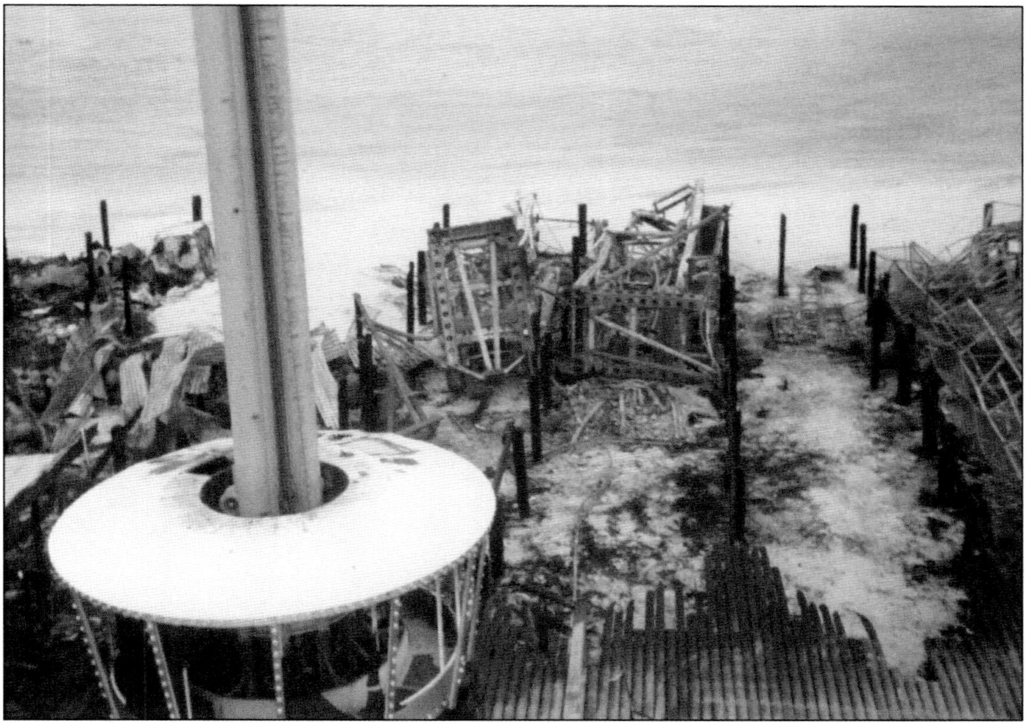

This is the spot where Crazy House once stood. This photograph was taken after the Lost World fire, which quickly spread to Crazy House and the former Mirror Maze building. The Sky Tower sustained some damage but was no longer in use in any case. (Courtesy Stephen Armstrong.)

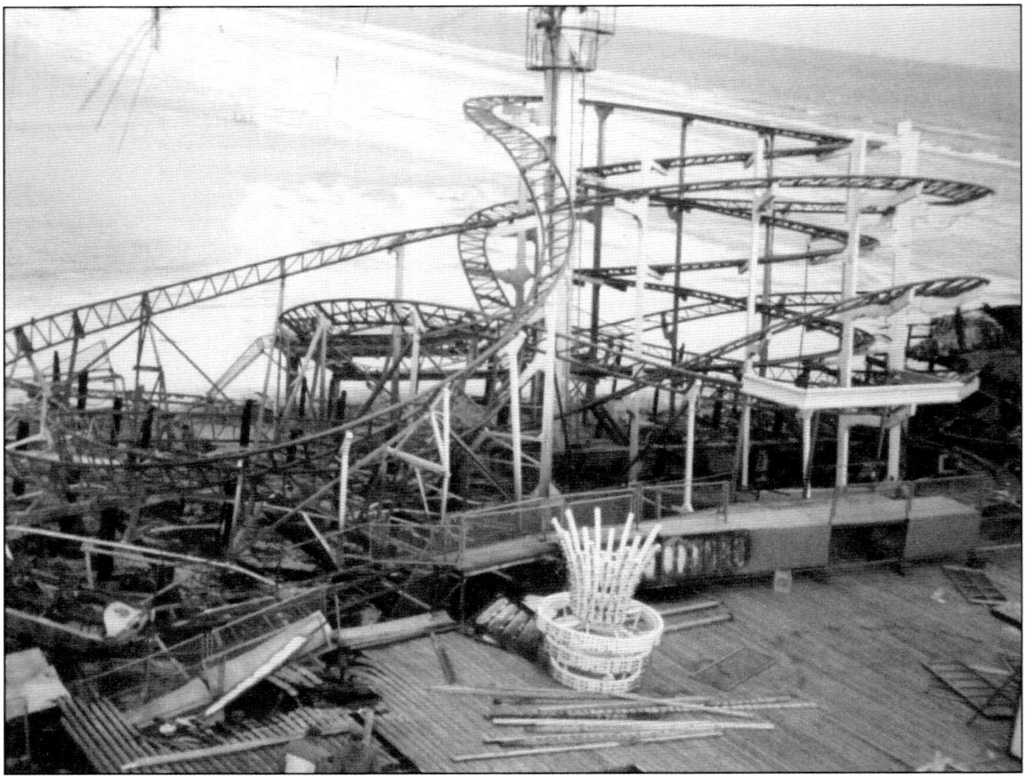

After the fire, the Jet 400 roller coaster sustained enough damage that it could not be repaired. The Jet 400 replaced the Zyklon B roller coaster, which had been in its place the previous summer. The northern side of Fun Pier had to be reconstructed after the severe damage sustained from the November 1984 fire. Note the crown for the Scrambler next to the loading station of the Jet 400. Fun Pier is not remembered for roller coasters. The pier is mostly remembered for its custom-made attractions and games. Joe Barnes had set out to create a unique experience on the Wildwood Boardwalk. Barnes succeeded, as Fun Pier is still fondly remembered over a half a century later. (Both, courtesy Stephen Armstrong.)

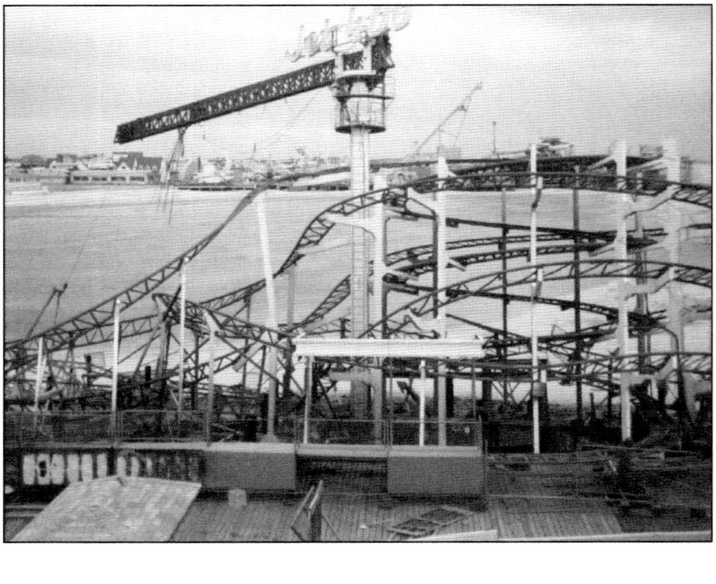

The Ferris wheel was unharmed by the fire. The second of two fires for Fun Pier during 1984 was a two-alarm fire that was battled by 60 firefighters from three companies, two of them volunteer. The fire was reported by a passerby who phoned it in from a pay phone. (Courtesy Stephen Armstrong.)

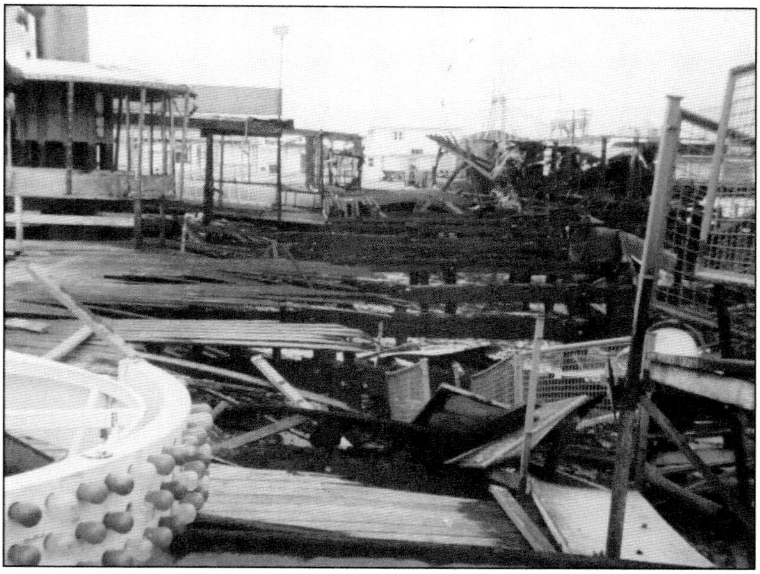

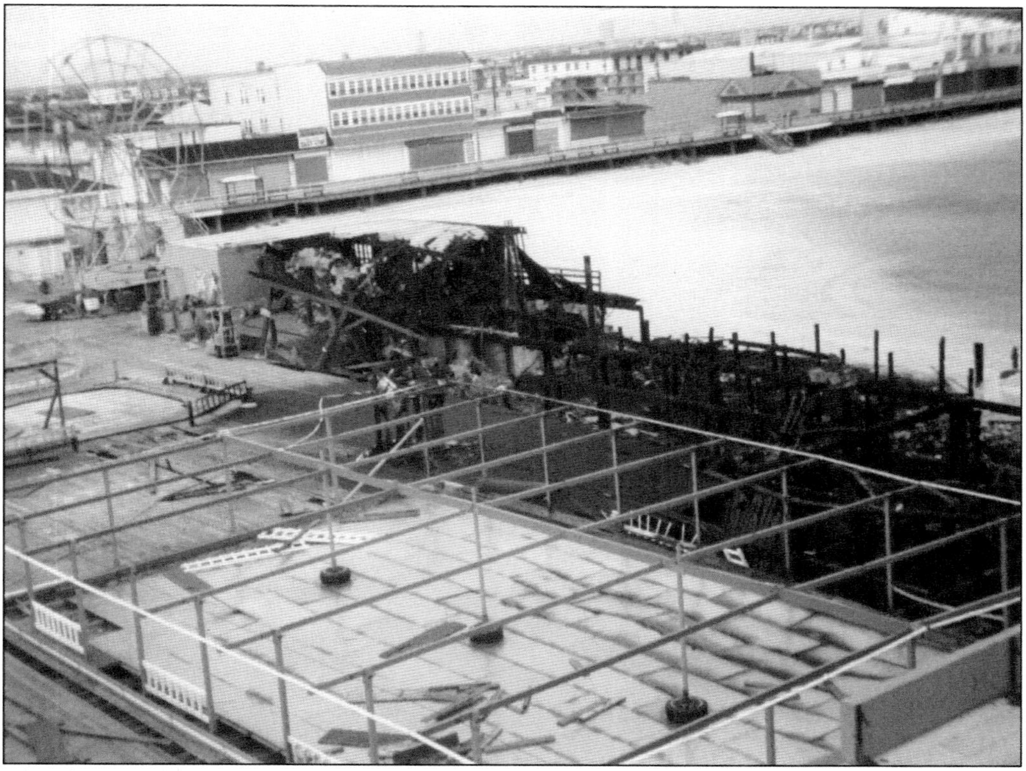

This photograph overlooks the spot where the Lost World once stood. While most people remember the ride as Lost World, there are still those who remember it best as either Devil's Inn or Tiki Train. Very few remember it under its original name, Batcave. (Courtesy Stephen Armstrong.)

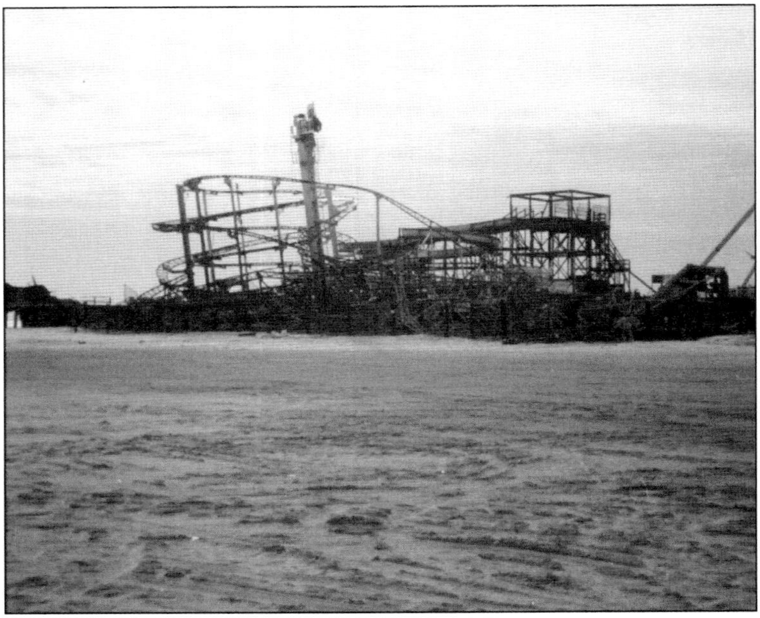

The catastrophic damage caused by the fire is pictured here. Even 27 years later, no official report as to its cause was ever revealed to the public. The rumors run rampant though, ranging from inside arson to the owners needing to collect on lost revenue to a homeless person living inside the ride with an electric heater. (Courtesy Stephen Armstrong.)

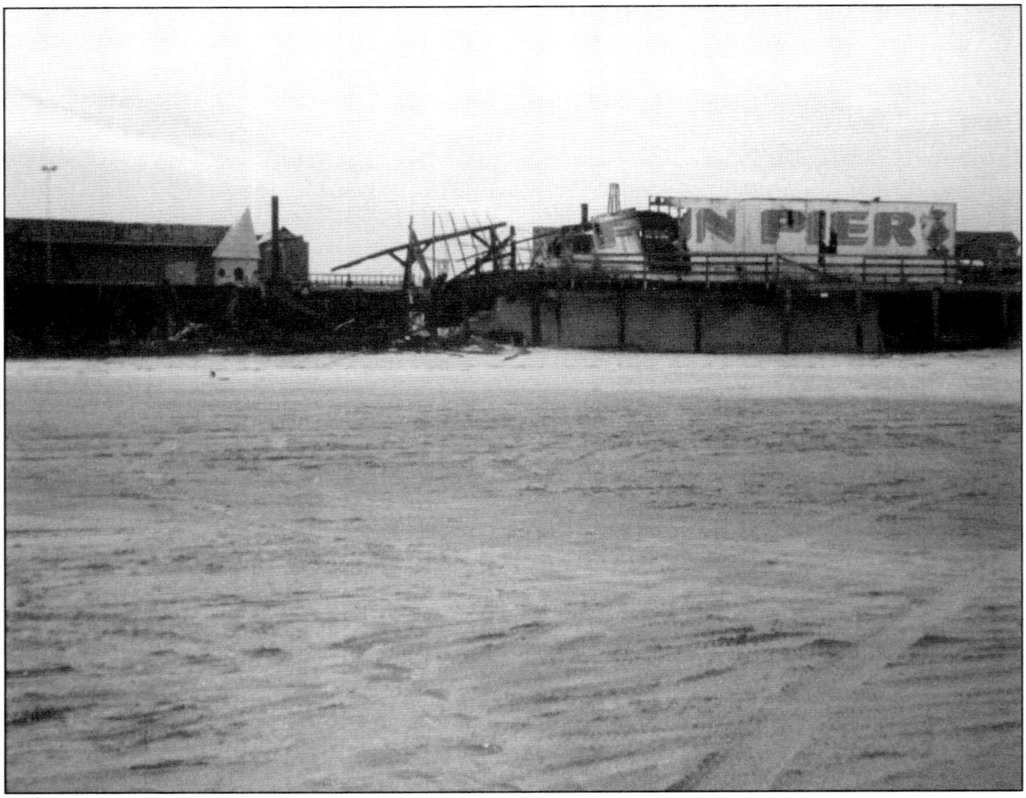

Fun Pier's Jungleland (left) was unharmed from the catastrophic fire that consumed the northern side of the pier. The Fun Pier sign was attached to back of Lost World. Note the cinder block shell under the sign—this was originally the walk-through section of Lost World. The walk-through section was made of foam and was a tight squeeze, according to most who remember it. (Courtesy Stephen Armstrong.)

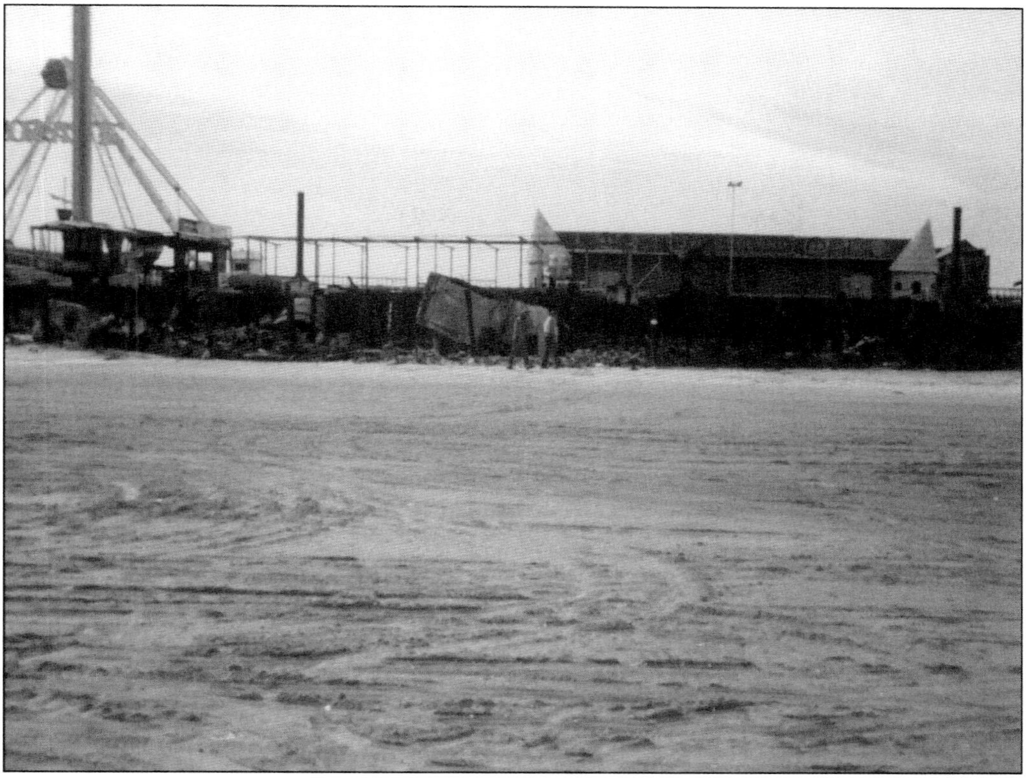

This photograph shows the spot where Crazy House once stood. Note the once-spinning barrel along with other wreckage. The fire sadly consumed mostly all of both Crazy House and Lost World, leaving no souvenirs. By this time, Sportland Pier, in North Wildwood on the boardwalk, was also in the process of sale. (Courtesy Stephen Armstrong.)

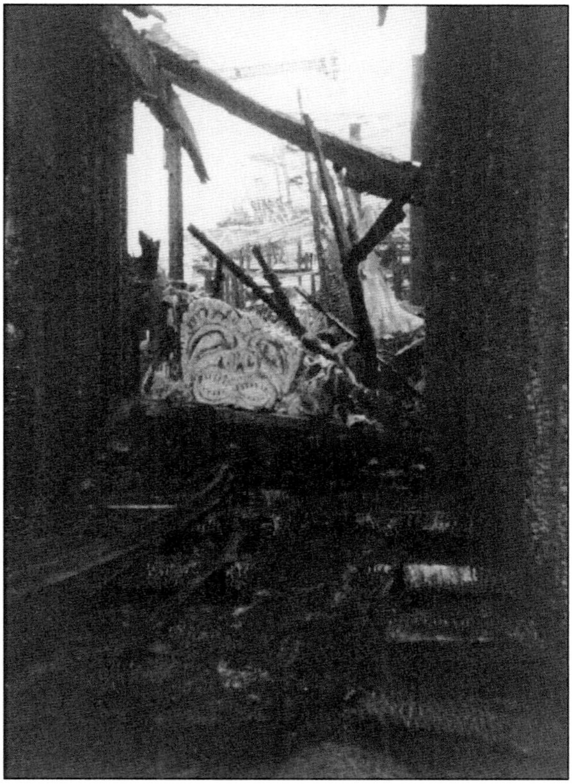

This is the interior of one of the tunnels of Lost World where the dark ride cars were stored during the winter months. The faces, which were on both the fronts and backs of the cars, have an eerie appearance. For many dark-ride enthusiasts who remember the ride, Lost World was the scariest on the pier, even though the walk-through section had been closed down. (Courtesy Stephen Armstrong.)

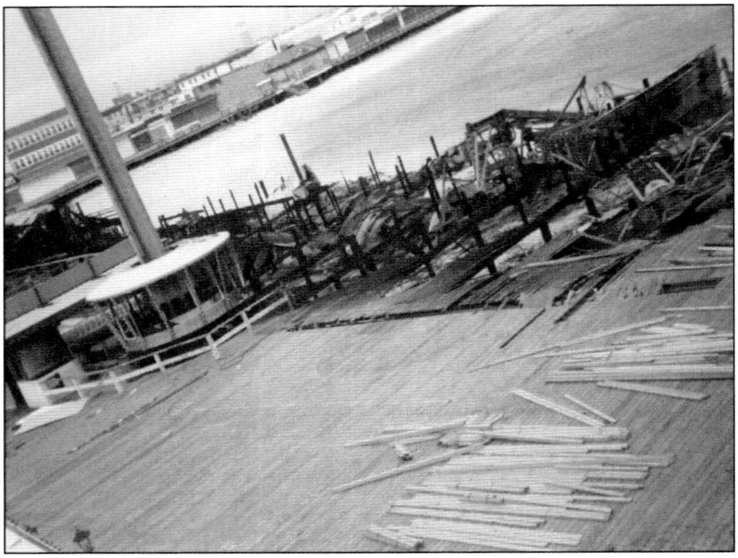

Repairs are underway in this photograph. This was such a mammoth task that Bill Howard had to partner with Don Deggeller of Deggeller Attractions. Note the new boards being prepared. According to most reports, King Kong was saved. While some were upset after the fire, fearing the worst, there were others that saw this as a new opportunity. (Courtesy Stephen Armstrong.)

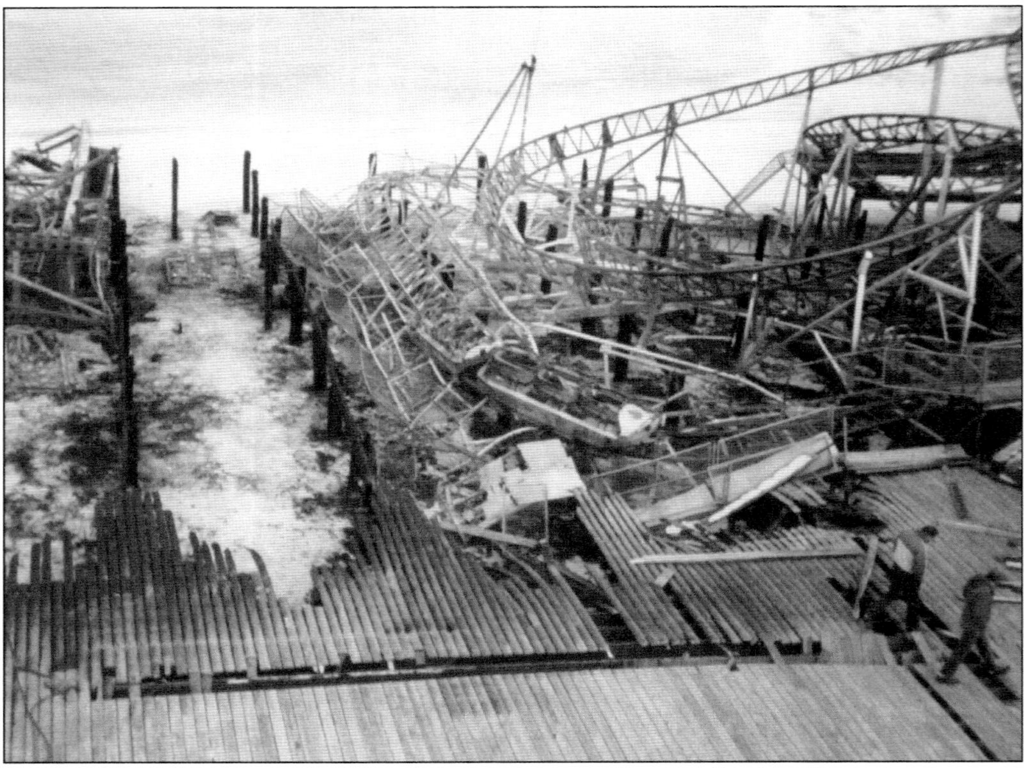

It is easy to see the fire damage to the Jet 400 roller coaster. Ironically, the roller coaster survived the Castle Frankenstein fire earlier in 1984 with only minor damage. This time, it would need to be scrapped. This was a sad time for Fun Pier; the future looked very uncertain. (Courtesy Stephen Armstrong.)

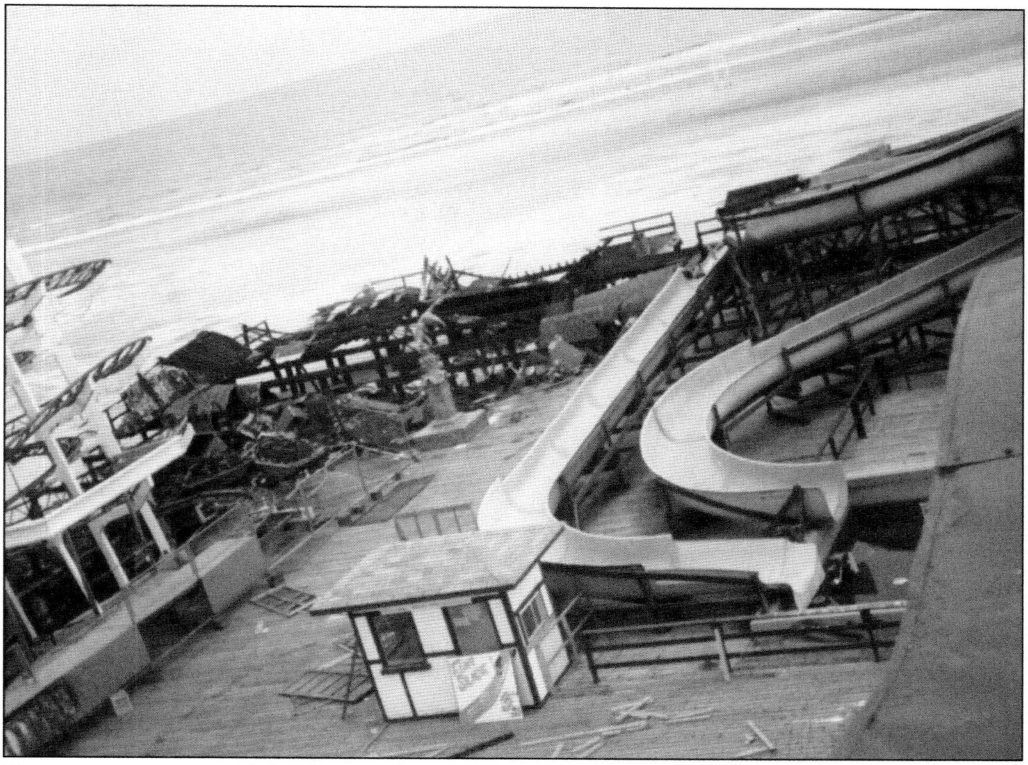

Here are more views of the damage from the fire. Even the bumper car building was destroyed. Though Fun Pier would be resurrected for another summer, many felt that without the mainstay attractions such as Lost World, Crazy House, and Castle Frankenstein, it just was not the same. Joe Barnes was still connected to Fun Pier during this time, as he had yet to be paid in full by Bill Howard. The two men had considered many options, and finally, Bill Howard partnered up with Don Deggeller to try to bring Fun Pier back to life. (Both, courtesy Stephen Armstrong.)

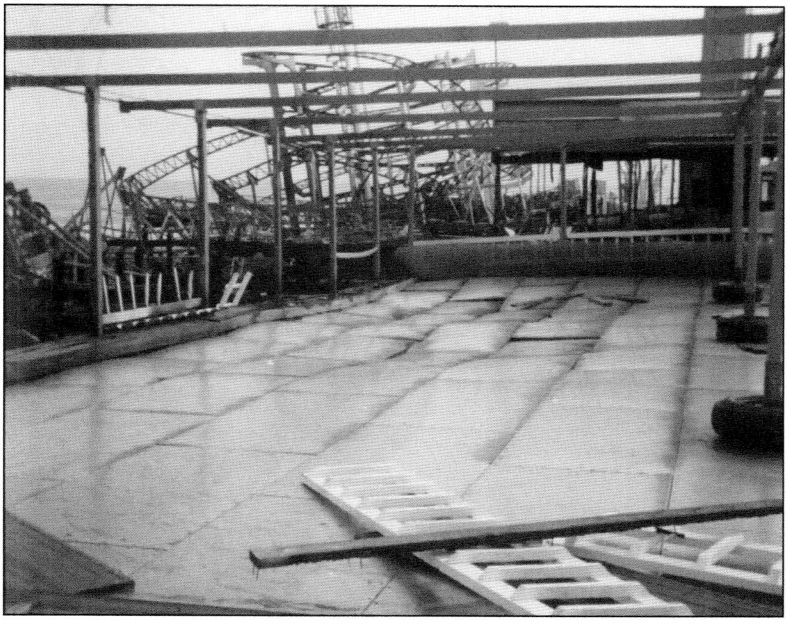

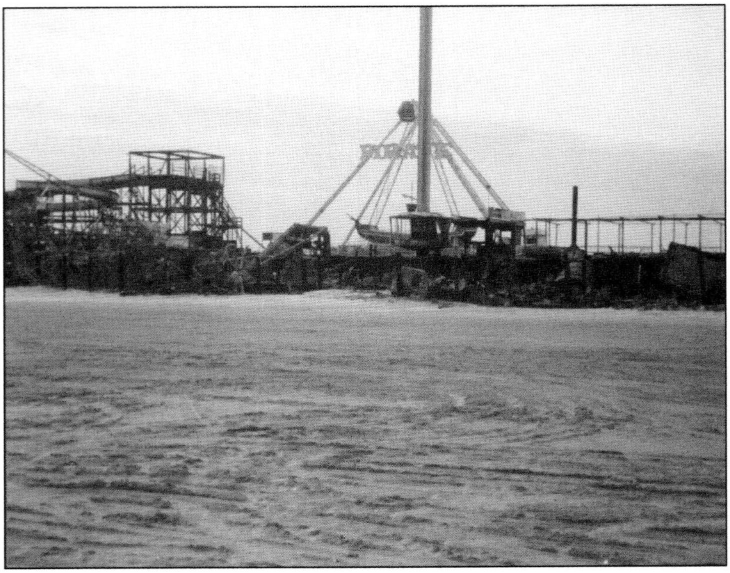

The Pirate survived the fire and would be part of the newly renovated Fun Pier in 1985. After the fateful season of 1985, the Pirate was sold to Don Deggeller. During the remainder of the 1980s, Fun Pier was used as an attraction for the Hanneford Circus before being redeveloped by Morey Development. (Courtesy Stephen Armstrong.)

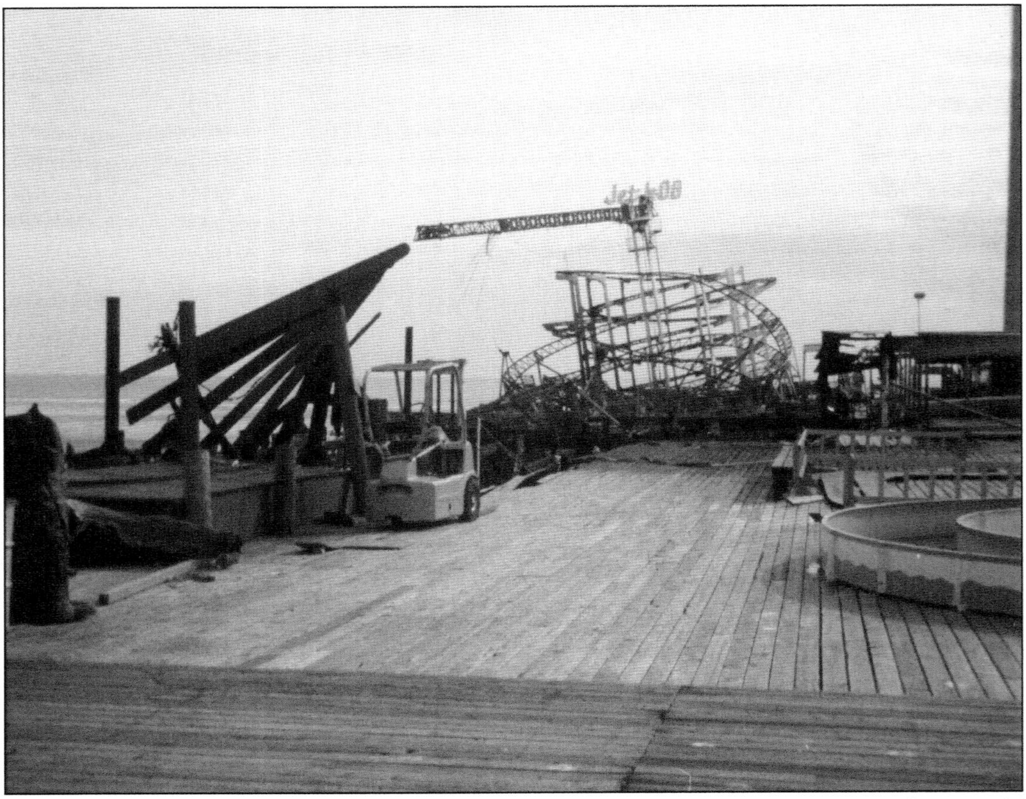

The loading station for Lost World appears in this photograph. As apparent here, nothing could be salvaged from the fire. The final summer saw only carnival-type rides where the classic rides had been the year before. (Courtesy Stephen Armstrong.)

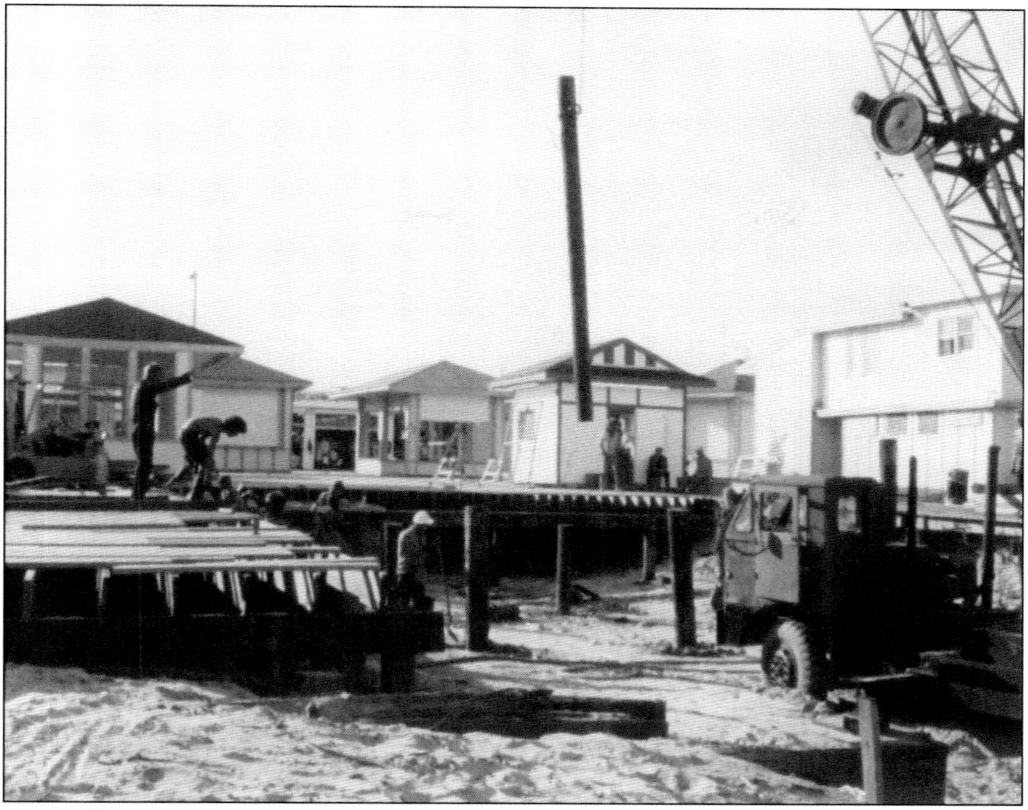

Pictured here during the spring of 1985, massive renovations are underway. All new planks and even some pilings replaced the charred remains of the pier that was. For many enthusiasts, the new short-lived incarnation of Fun Pier was forgettable. (Courtesy Albert Butler.)

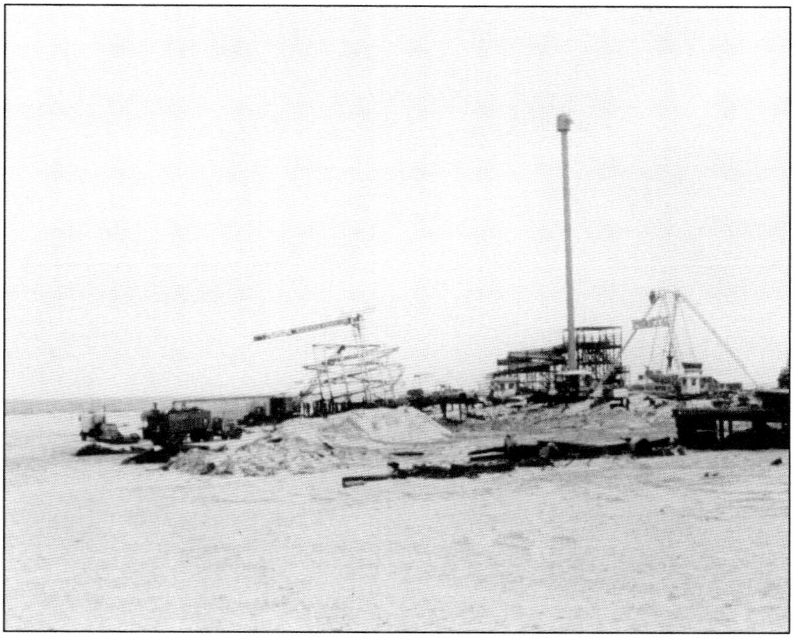

The Lost World fire from November 1984 was so massive that work had to begin as soon as the insurance adjuster's report was complete. This could not come soon enough for Bill Howard if he wanted to reopen by Memorial Day weekend in 1985. (Courtesy Albert Butler.)

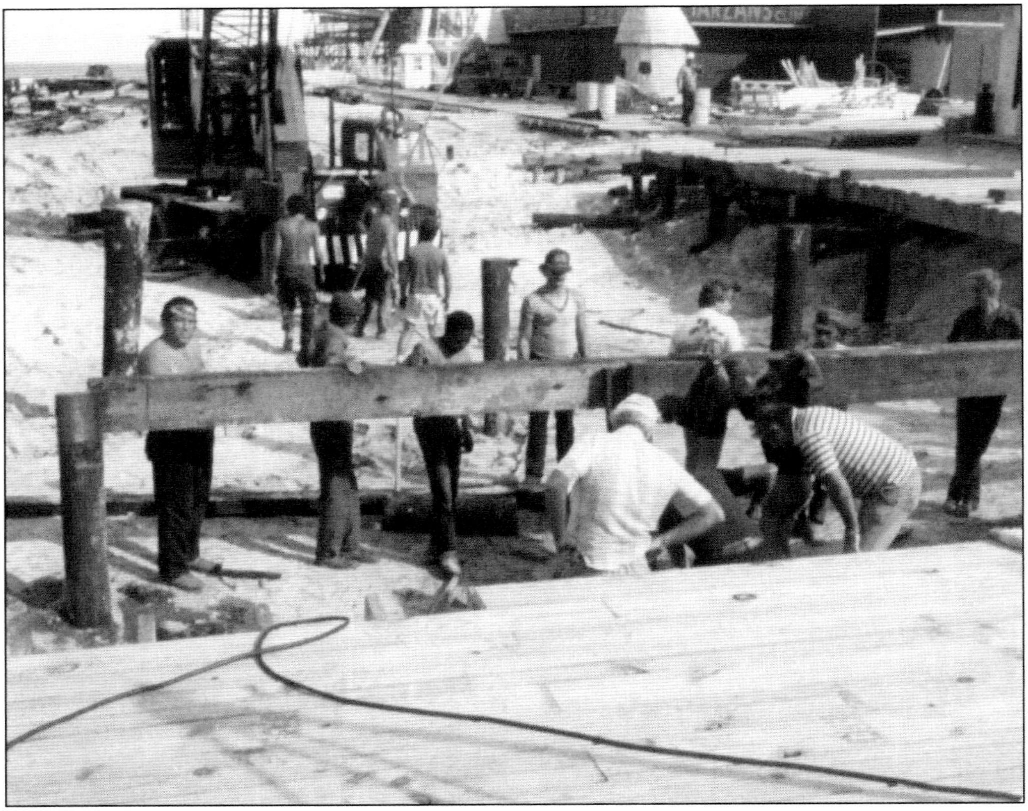

The entire northern side of Fun Pier was completely rebuilt for the 1985 summer season. Note that Jungleland was unharmed by the fire. Jack and Wayne Seddon had been working on a theme for Fun Pier. As both Lost World and Jungleland lent themselves to a more prehistoric theme, the Seddon brothers decided to continue with that theme. This led to the creation of Tarzan's Vine Climb. The stretch ladders pulled tight with no handrails, and the customer had to climb to the bell at the top to get the prize. Most of the time, the ladder would flip the customers off, and they would land on an air mat. (Courtesy Albert Butler.)

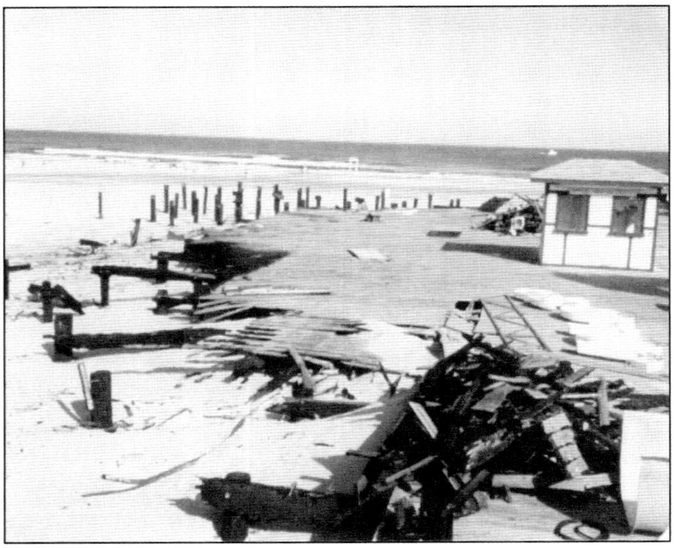

For the reconstruction of the pier, Don Deggeller employed his own crew. Bill Howard had a few of his own, such as Peter Savard and Art Fiala. As seen in the photograph, the project was massive. Savard and Fiala worked together so often that they had their own system worked out. (Courtesy Albert Butler.)

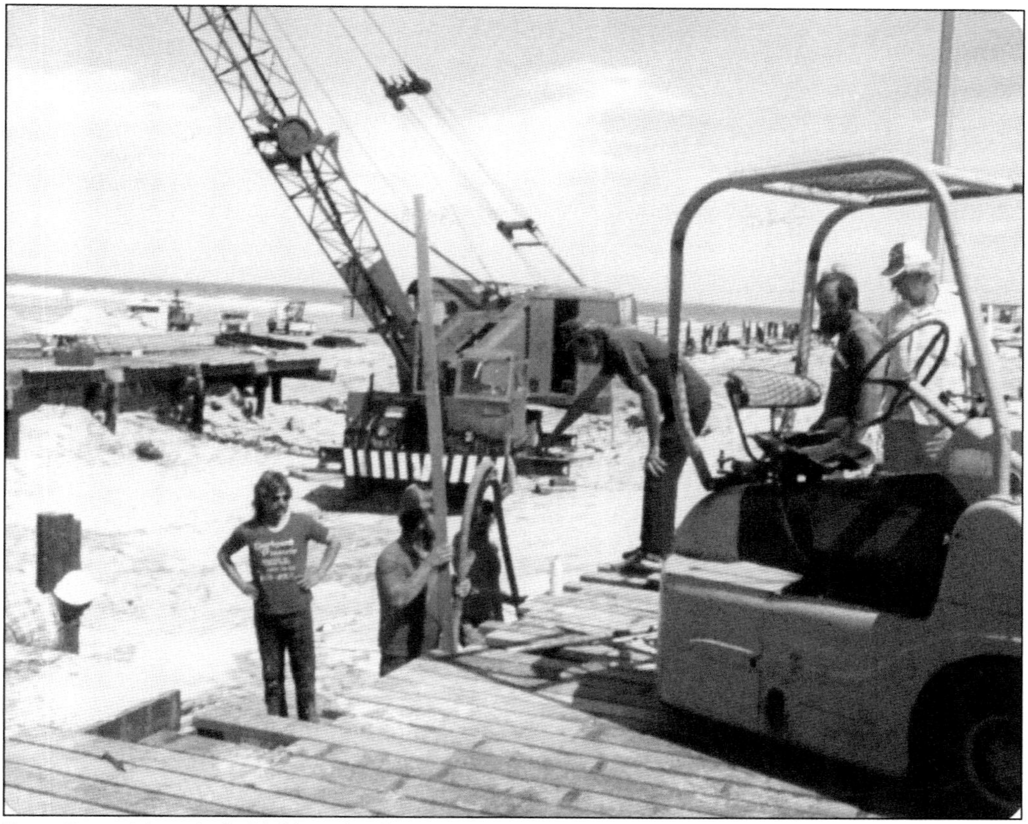

Peter Savard (inside forklift) and Bill Howard are pictured here during the reconstruction period in 1985. The deck was not only reconstructed, it was slightly expanded as well. Bill Howard was wise enough to realize who the most valuable players on the pier were, and Bill would make offers to those players to travel with him to other attractions during the winter months. (Courtesy Albert Butler.)

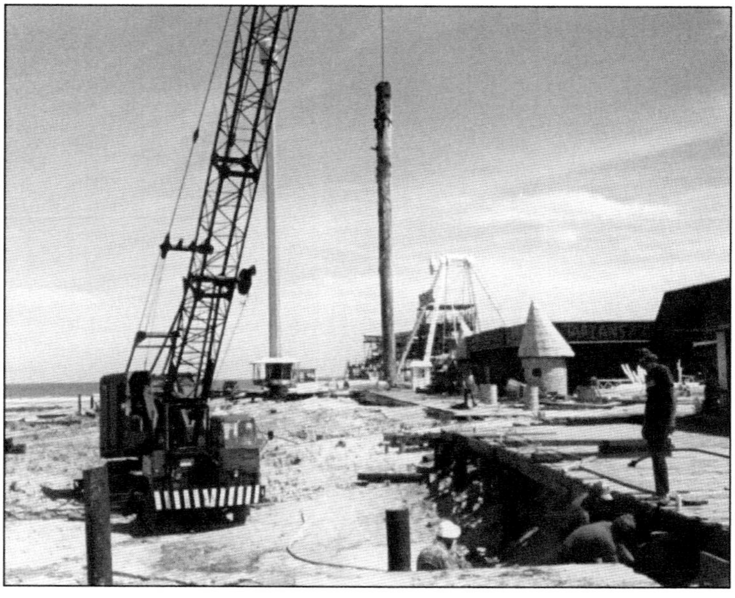

Construction continues on Fun Pier. The Jungleland dark ride is on the right, with the Tarzan's Vine Climb game attached on its right side, facing the front of the pier. (Courtesy Albert Butler.)

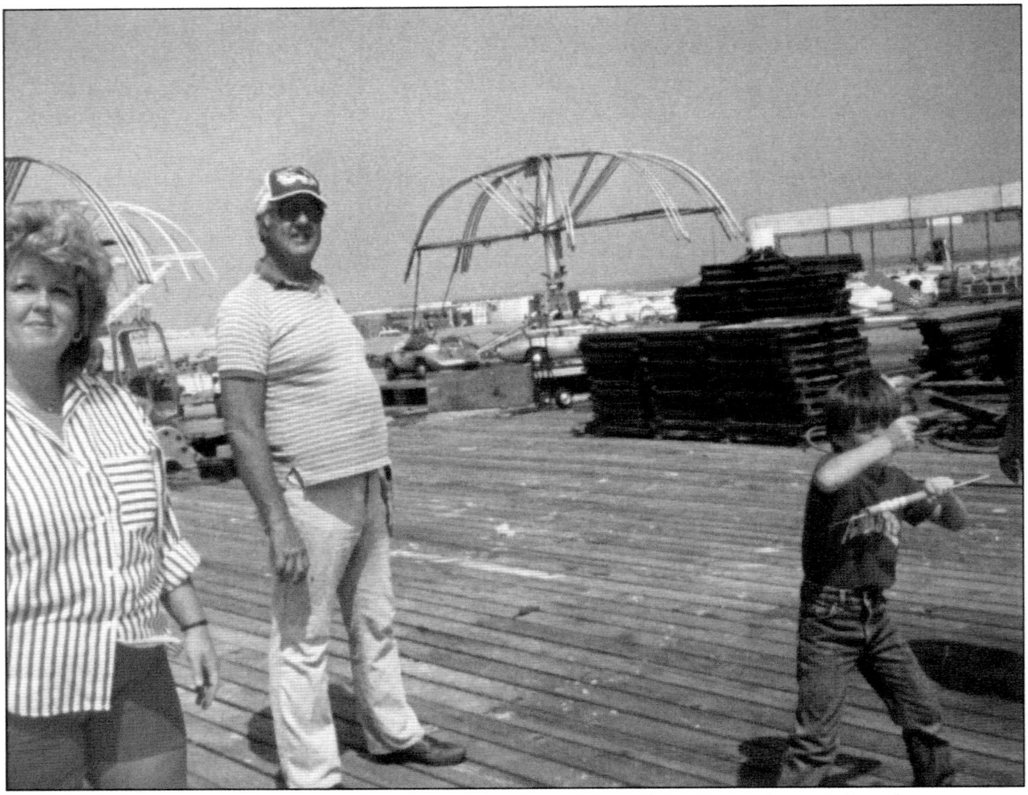

Bill Howard oversees the installation of new amusement rides. Howard was a hands-on owner. No job was too small or too big, not even the massive task of rebuilding half of Fun Pier. The common joke on the pier during the reconstruction of the deck was "no more Zoom Boom." (Courtesy Albert Butler.)

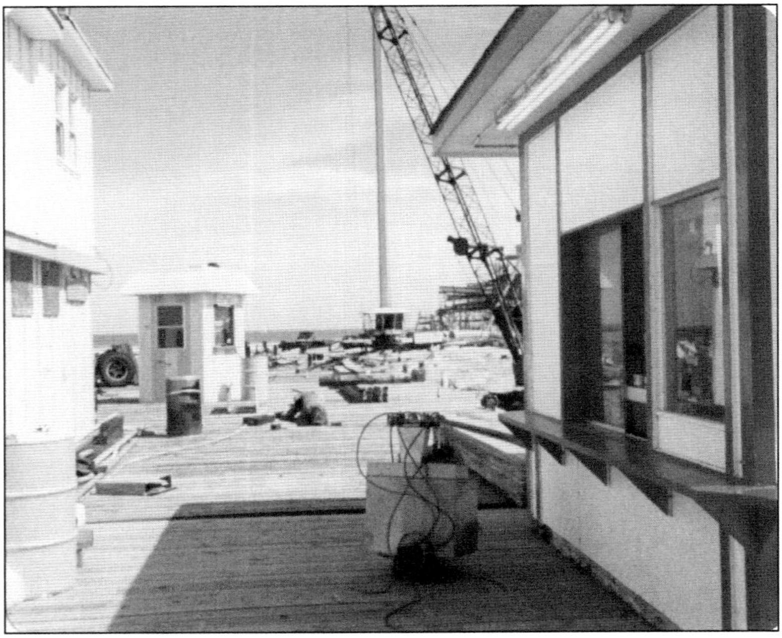

The classic rides are nothing more than a memory in this photograph. Hopes were high and expectations were grand for the next season, which was being touted as the beginning of a new era for Fun Pier. Sadly, this era would last only a few months. (Courtesy Albert Butler.)

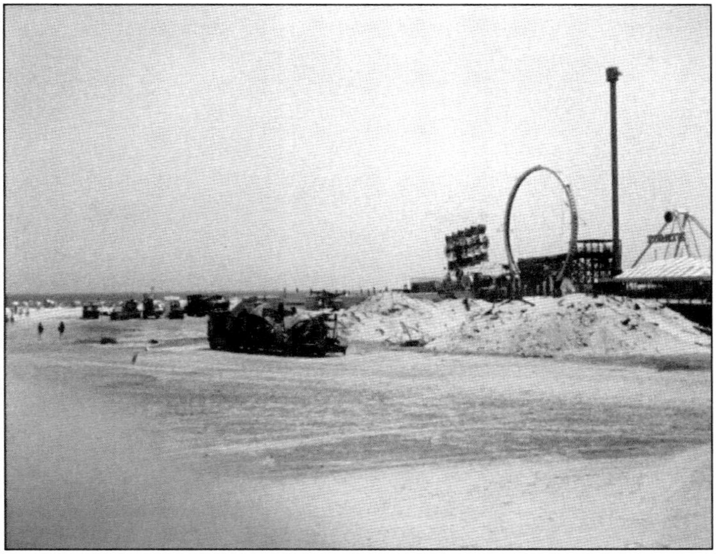

The Zipper and the Catapult were installed for the final season of fun. They were not necessarily new rides, but they were new rides for Fun Pier. While this was considered a valiant effort at the time, Wildwood vacationers were looking for newer thrills. Beginning in 1985, many of the nostalgia seekers felt that it was no longer the classic Fun Pier that they had grown up with. (Courtesy Albert Butler.)

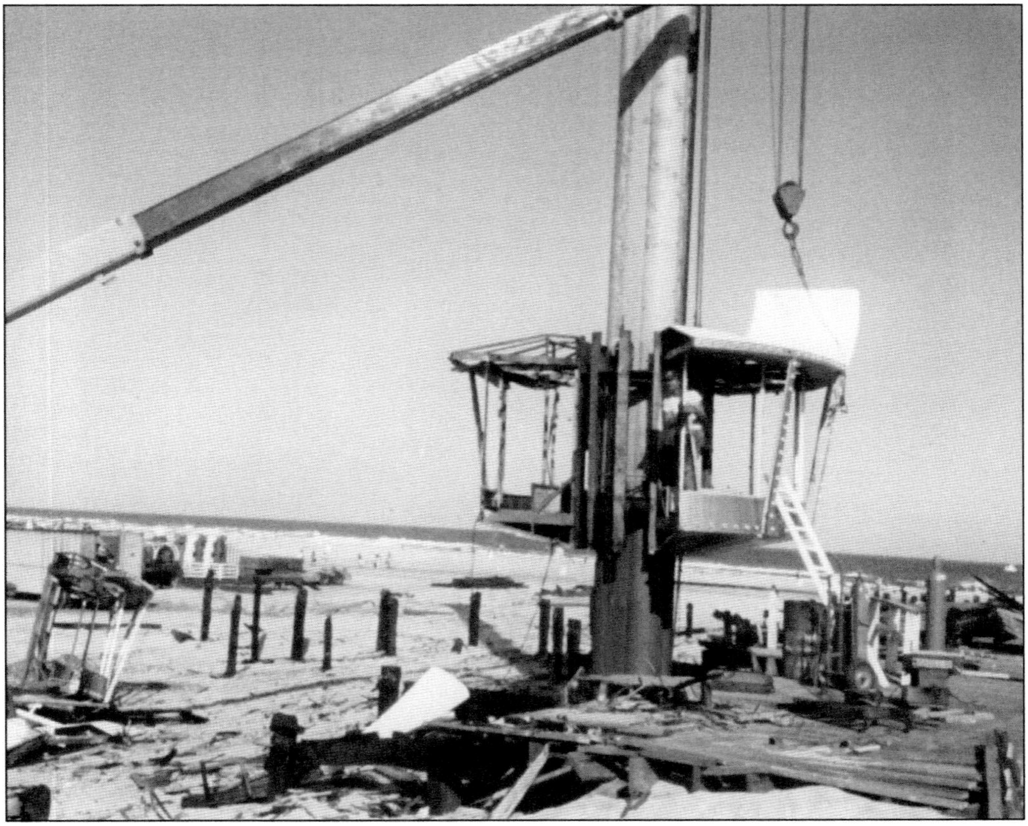

The Sky Tower is removed in April 1985. The tower pole would remain on the pier until May 6, 2009. According to Peter Savard, the Sky Tower sat on a concrete base about 12 feet thick, and its pilings went down 30 to 40 feet under the sand. Though younger boardwalk fans did not know what the pole was from or for, many still remember the Sky Tower. Even though its operation was short-lived, the Sky Tower was a sight to behold when it was operating on the Wildwood Boardwalk. (Courtesy Albert Butler.)

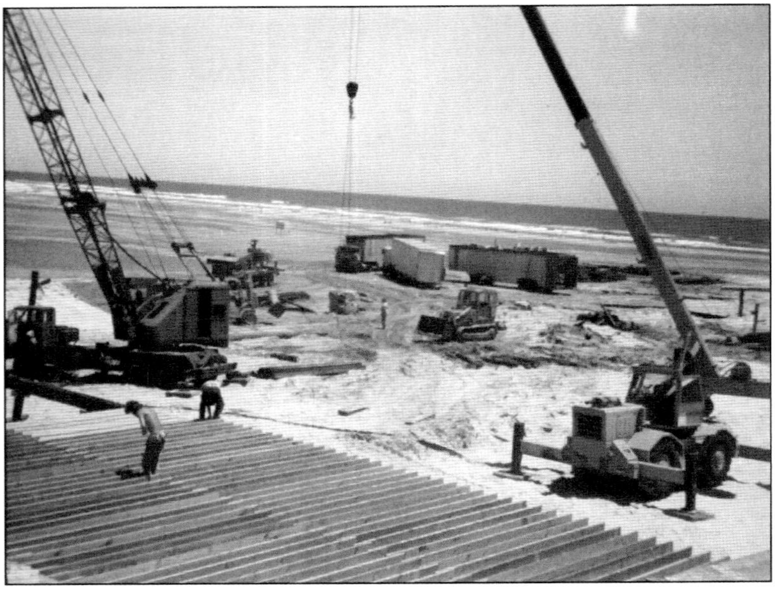

Blood, sweat, and tears went into the restructuring of the northern half of Fun Pier. The Lost World destroyed even the original pilings. The reconstruction took several months to complete. (Courtesy Albert Butler.)

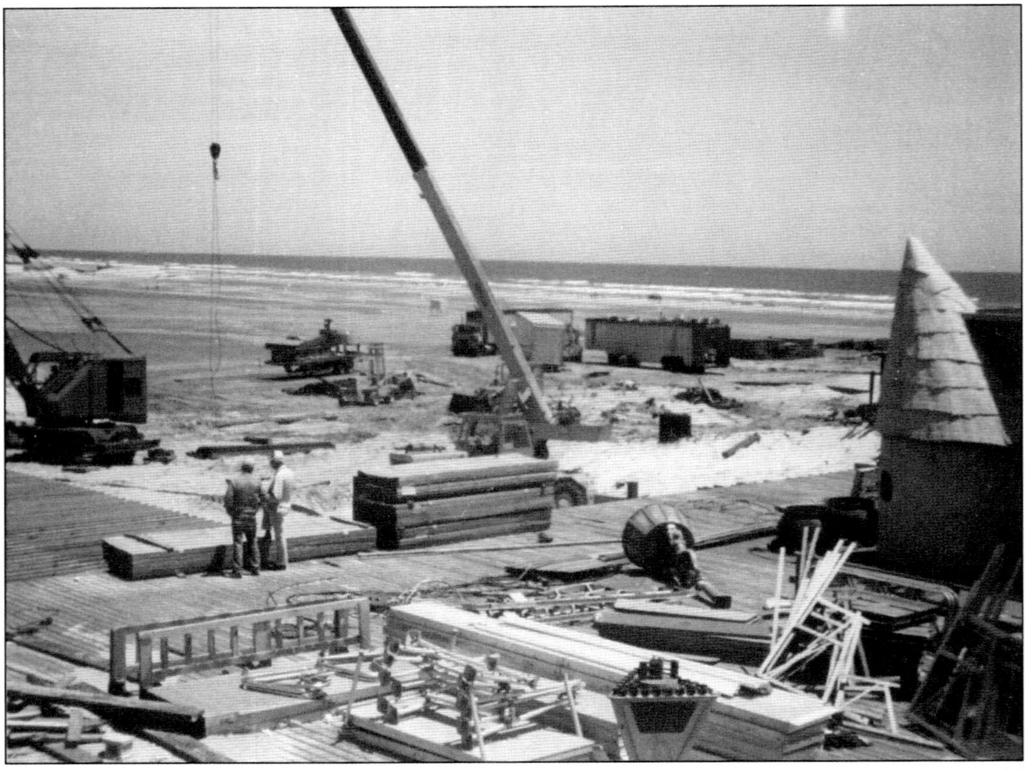

Bill Howard (to the left in a baseball hat) was confident that the reconstruction of the pier would make for more positive and profitable summer seasons ahead. Sadly, he was wrong, as Fun Pier would begin its final season. Bill Howard did continue to manage his other operations down South for many years. (Courtesy Albert Butler.)

This photograph shows the old section of the pier and the new construction. Note the Jungleland dark ride on the left side with the elephant sitting out front. There are very few relics left of what was Fun Pier; the elephant is one of the only ones, and it is owned by a private collector. (Courtesy Albert Butler.)

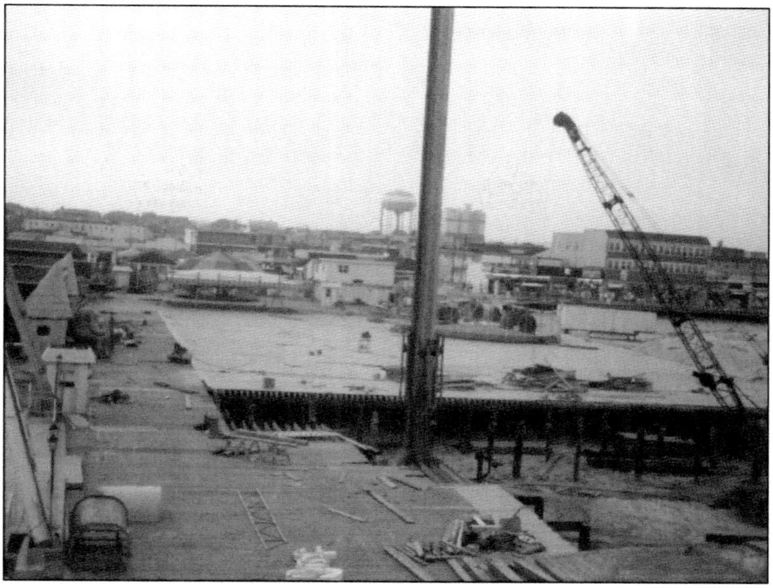

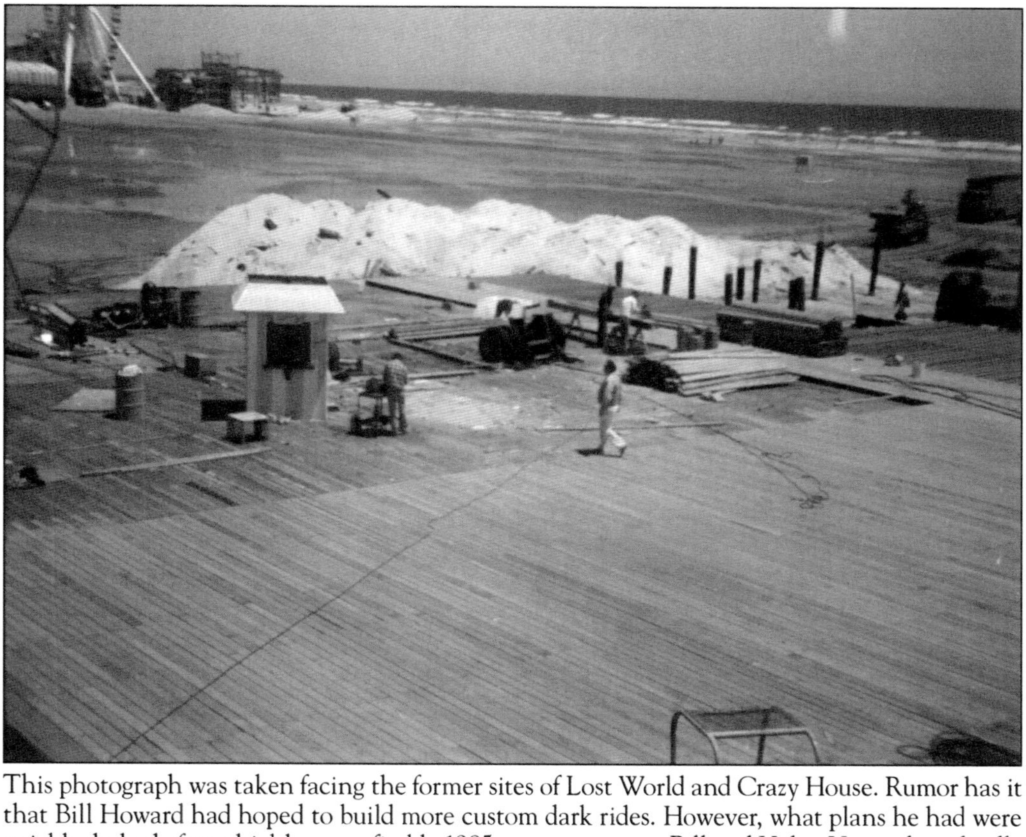

This photograph was taken facing the former sites of Lost World and Crazy House. Rumor has it that Bill Howard had hoped to build more custom dark rides. However, what plans he had were quickly dashed after a highly unprofitable 1985 summer season. Bill and Helen Howard are fondly remembered by those who worked for them on Fun Pier. (Courtesy Albert Butler.)

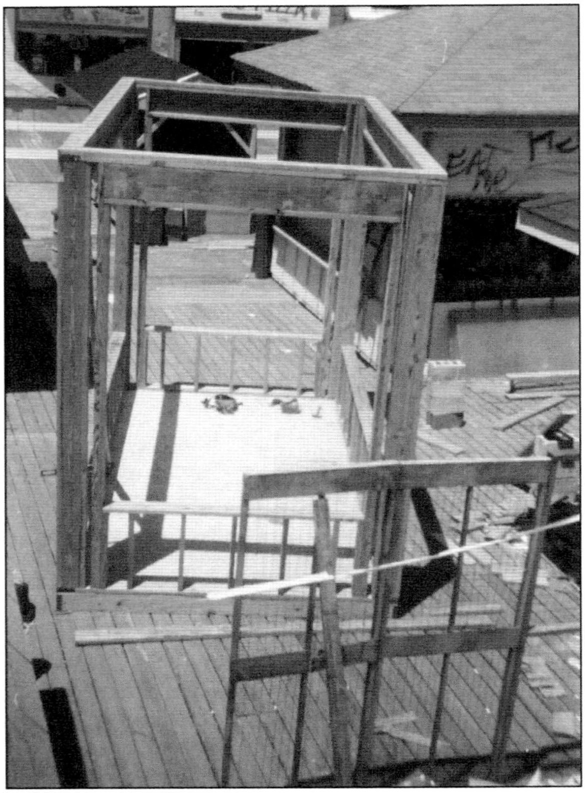

Construction was in high gear, but as Memorial Day weekend approached, there was a mad rush to get things finished. As always, optimistic pier employees felt "there is always next season." The pier was purchased by Morey Development in 1987. Since then, the pier has been redeveloped and renamed twice. It is currently known as Morey's Adventure Pier and is located between East Spencer and East Youngs Avenues in Wildwood. (Courtesy Albert Butler.)

There were many new faces on Fun Pier in its final season in 1985, but the feeling was the same. In the early years of Fun Pier, carnies like Bill Howard and J.D. Floyd put up rides on Fun Pier; in 1985, Don Deggeller, owner of many carnival attractions, was the new carnie on the pier. Deggeller brought along most of his usual crew to assist with the reconstruction and placed new rides on the pier for what would be its final summer. (Courtesy Albert Butler.)

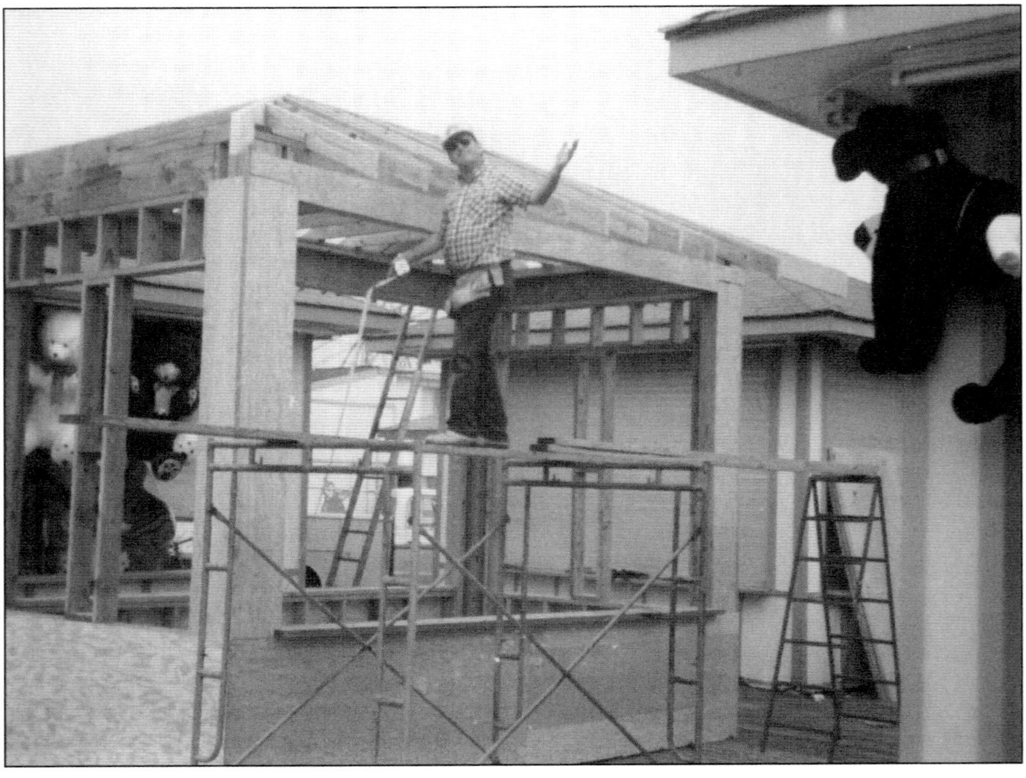

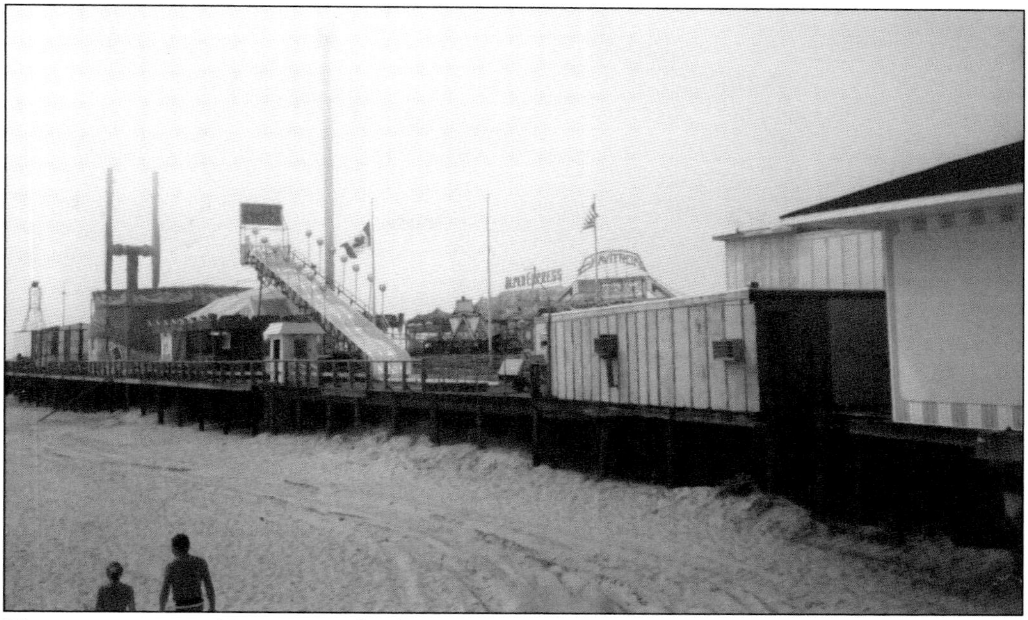

The pier is pictured here in its final summer in 1985. Deggeller Attractions gave Fun Pier a somewhat different look and feel. However, for most of those who remembered the early years of Fun Pier, this look harkened back to its original form. (Courtesy Marc Scarvalli.)

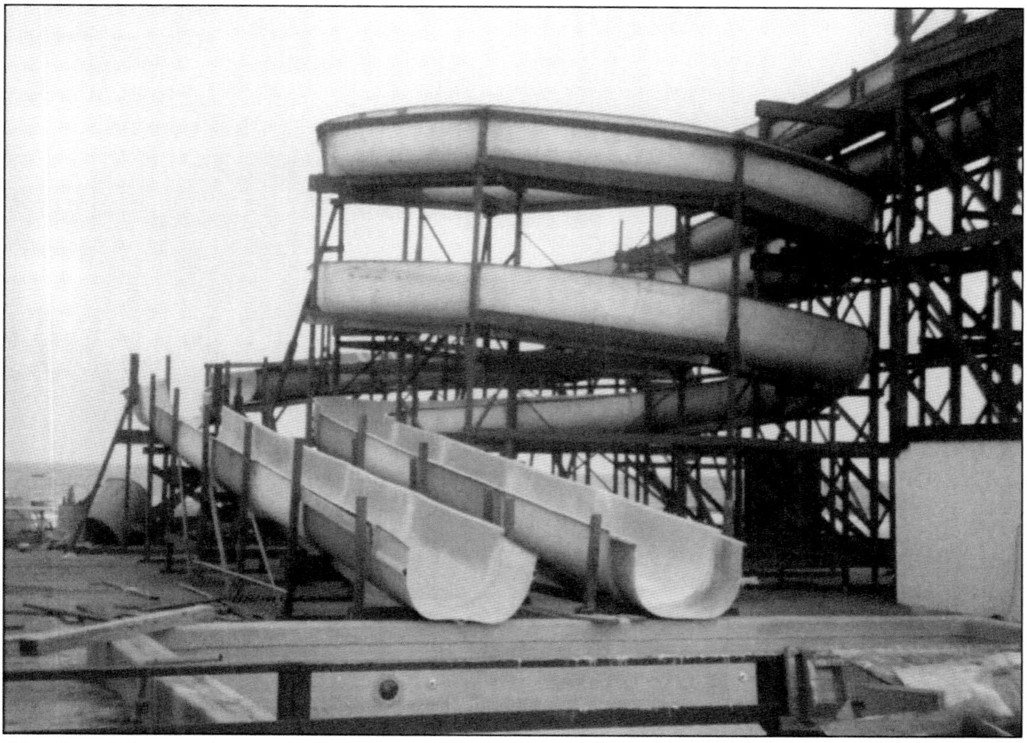

The Funslide was dismantled and removed for the 1985 season. Despite the popularity of the slide, the decision was made that as the pier was rebuilt, it was a time for change. Different rides and new partners were to make a difference for what would be the final summer for Fun Pier. (Courtesy Stephen Armstrong.)

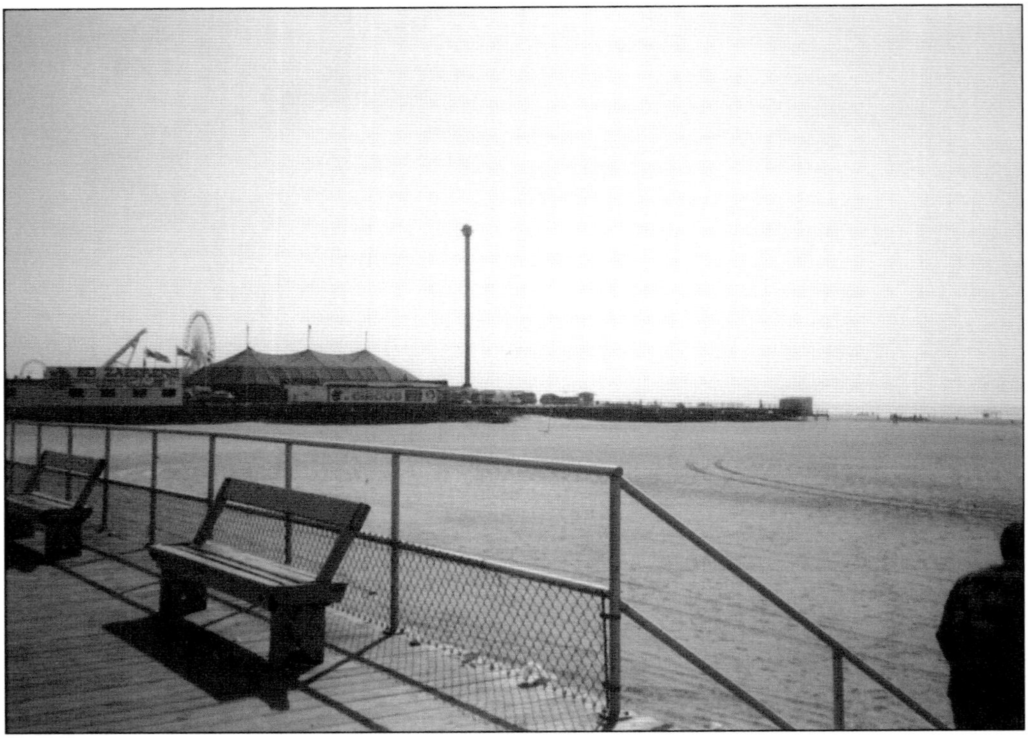

Morey Development purchased Fun Pier on April 1, 1987. This 1989 photograph shows the Hanneford Family Circus, which had leased the pier before the Moreys redeveloped the pier into Wild Wheels. The Hanneford Family Circus, based in America, dates back to 1690. It has been called the oldest circus in the world. The circus is now known as the Royal Hanneford Circus, one of the largest and most respected circuses in America. Fun Pier was renamed Morey's Adventure Pier. (Both, courtesy Marc Scarvalli.)

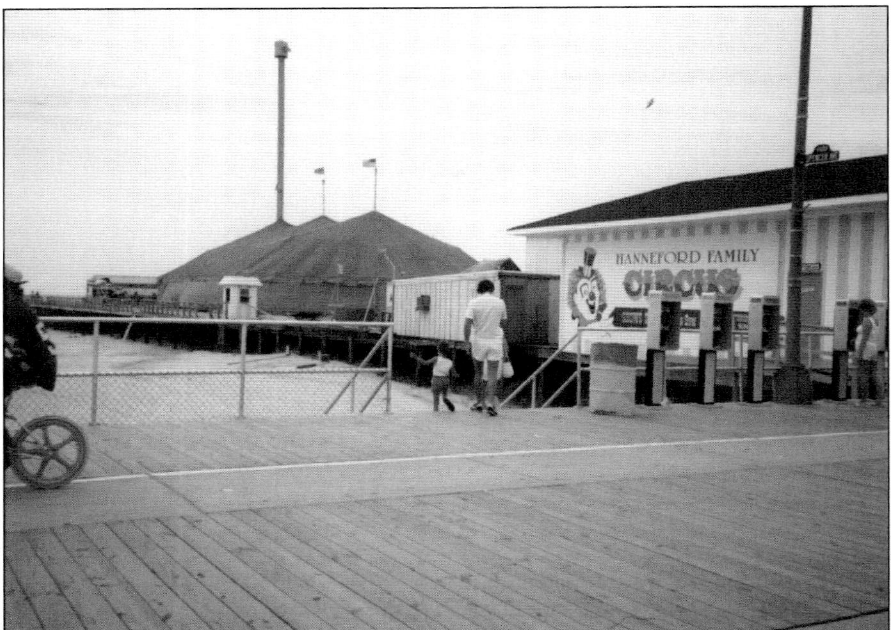

Four

Wheeling in the Future

Although there had been rumors of a possible merger between Fun Pier and Sportland Pier, these were squashed on April 1, 1987, when a settlement was reached. Fun Pier was sold to Morey Development for approximately $3 million. While many were excited by Morey's acquisition of a third pier in Wildwood, people wondered when the pier would open. After sitting idle for a few summers with only the game operations going on, plans were afoot to redevelop the pier into Wild Wheels. To its credit, Morey's entered into a series of development plans. During this time, word came out that the pier would be an interactive amusement. This meant that the emphasis would be on active customer participation.

Wild Wheels had a NASCAR-style raceway, a wall-climbing experience, and a variation on the bungee jump called the Ejection Seat. The star attraction would be a new wooden roller coaster known as the Great White, which stills thrills patrons to this day.

In 2006, the pier was renamed Morey's Adventure Pier, and it boasts such additional attractions as the Skycoaster, Screamin' Swing, Highflyer, and Inverter. The Grand Prix raceway is also a high-interest ride on the pier. The Mummy 3D was a walk-through attraction and the only dark ride since Morey Development purchased the pier.

Morey's Piers are currently at work on more designs and plans for what was once known as Fun Pier. As development of new rides and attractions are set to take place over the next few years, some will look back with nostalgic fondness at the pier's past, while Fun Pier lives on in its latest incarnation, waiting to thrill customers again.

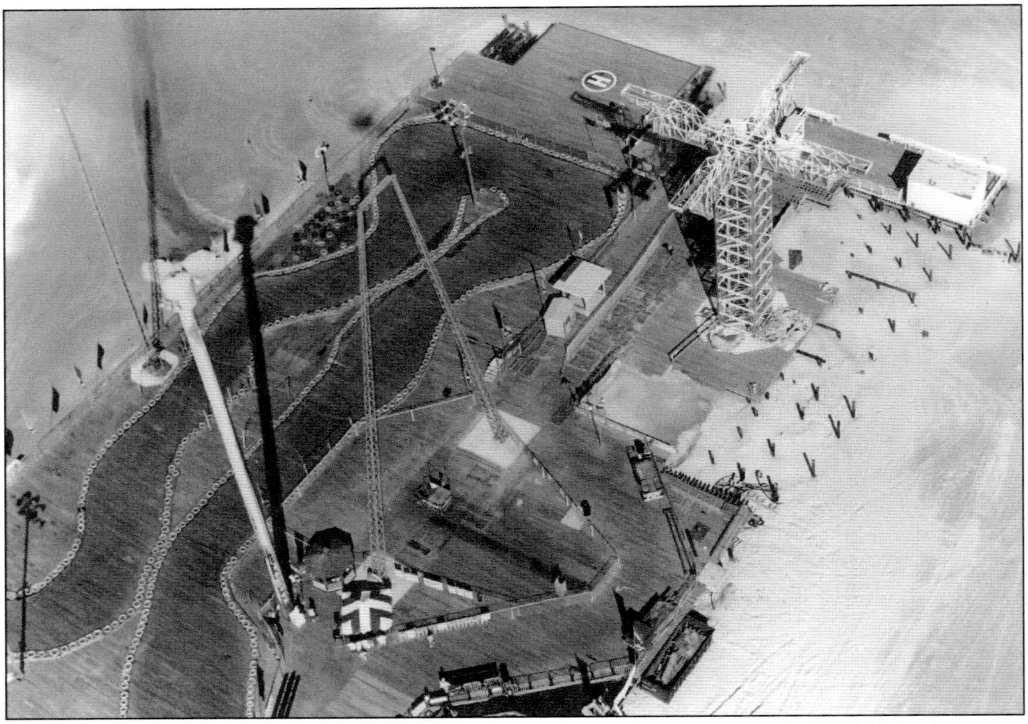

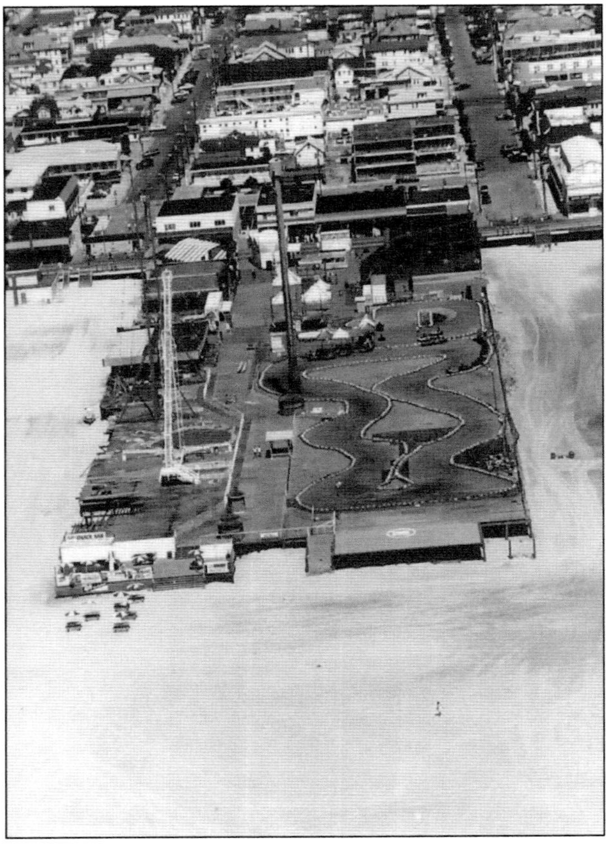

Here is Morey's Wild Wheels as it appeared in the early 1990s. Note the pilings—this is where the waterslide used to be. The spot where the pool used to be is also visible upon closer inspection. The Skycoaster, which is still on the pier, is also visible in this photograph. The helicopter launch pad is on the back left of the pier. (Courtesy Anthony Canzano.)

This is Wild Wheels as it appeared in its early years before the Great White was built. The Beach Grill is on the left, while the Sky Tower pole looms over the pier. The former Jungleland building is also visible in this photograph. Dark River is located on the left. (Courtesy Anthony Canzano.)

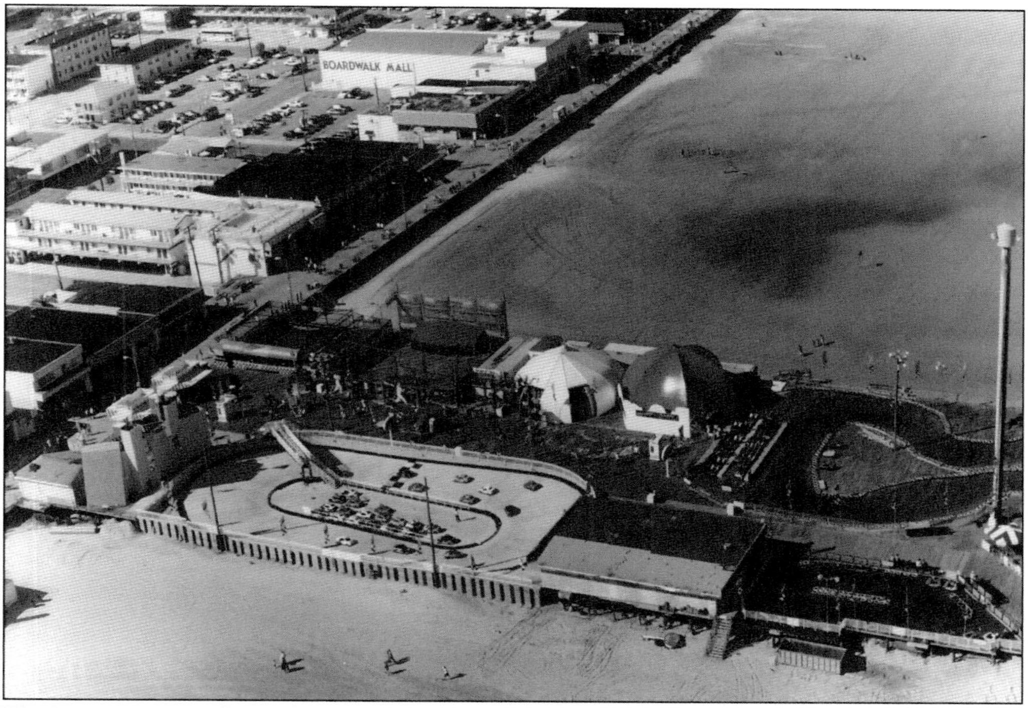

The boat tag game is located to the front right of the pier in this photograph, with the batting cages behind it. The Grand Prix raceway is clearly visible next to the former Jungleland building. The Cinema 180 would eventually become the Mummy 3D walk-through on Adventure Pier. The go-karts were in full use on the back of the pier during these years. (Courtesy Anthony Canzano.)

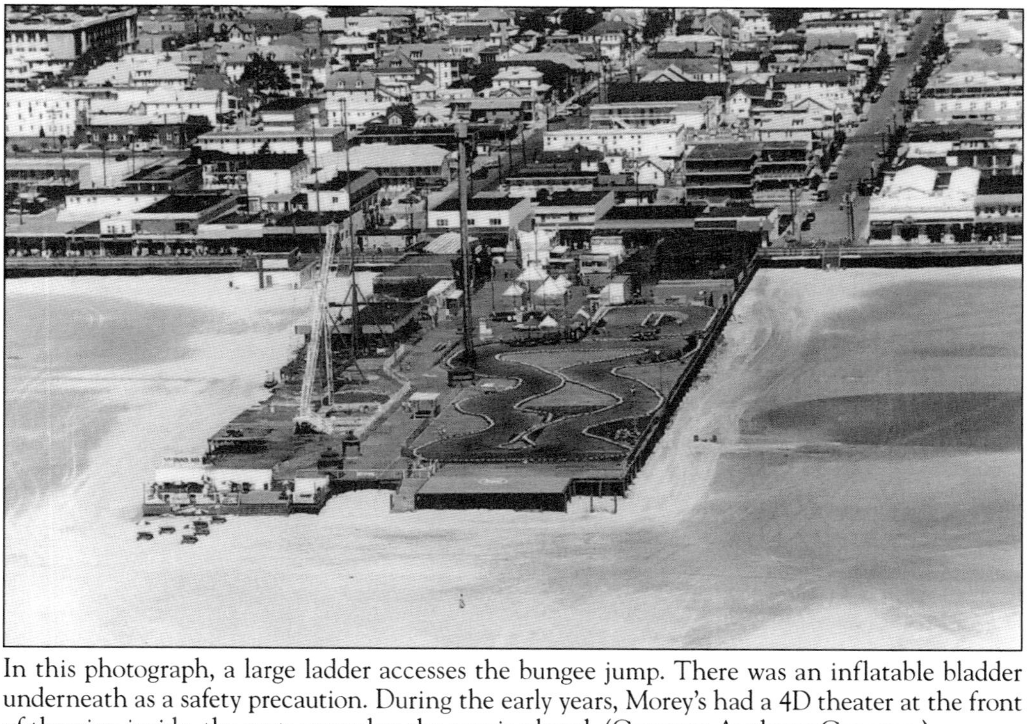

In this photograph, a large ladder accesses the bungee jump. There was an inflatable bladder underneath as a safety precaution. During the early years, Morey's had a 4D theater at the front of the pier; inside, the seats moved as the movie played. (Courtesy Anthony Canzano.)

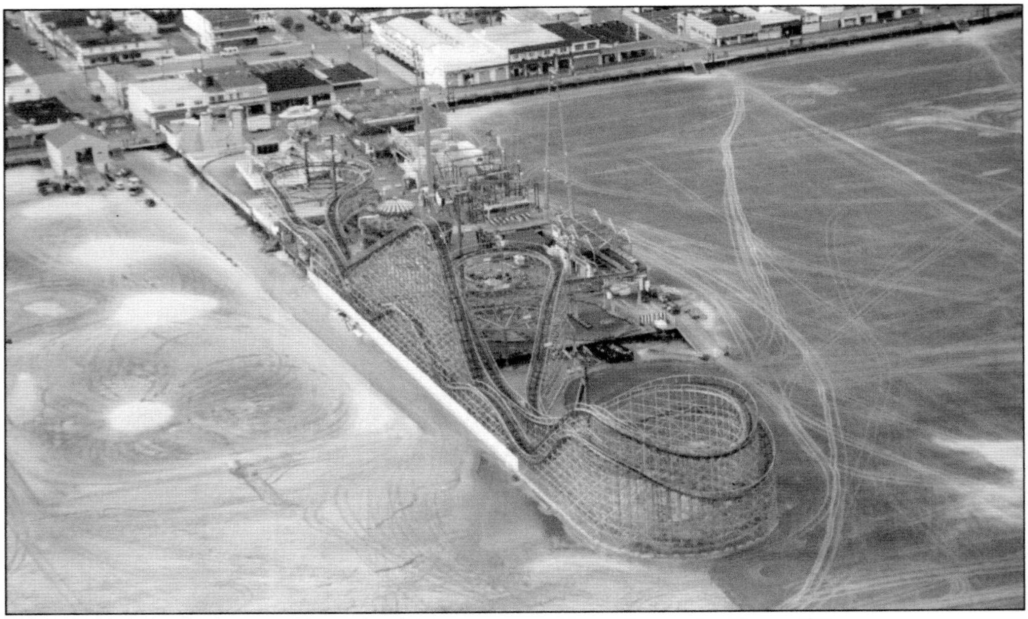

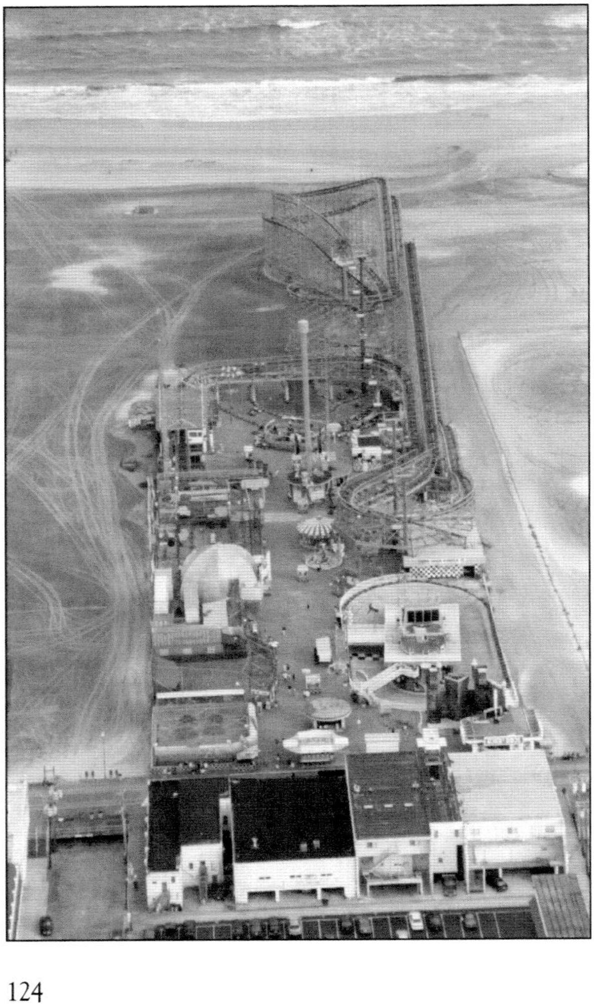

Once the Great White was constructed, the pier began to take on a new life. Jersey Junkyard was an Allan Herschell ride that remained on the pier for many years. It will be removed for the 2012 season to make way for more adventurous rides. The Mummy is also set to be removed. (Courtesy Anthony Canzano.)

This aerial photograph shows the rock-climbing adventure at the front right on Morey's Adventure Pier. The current plan is to redevelop Adventure Pier with more thrilling rides and attractions. Many dark-ride enthusiasts were upset by the removal of the Mummy, but perhaps more dark rides will be built in the near future. (Courtesy Anthony Canzano.)

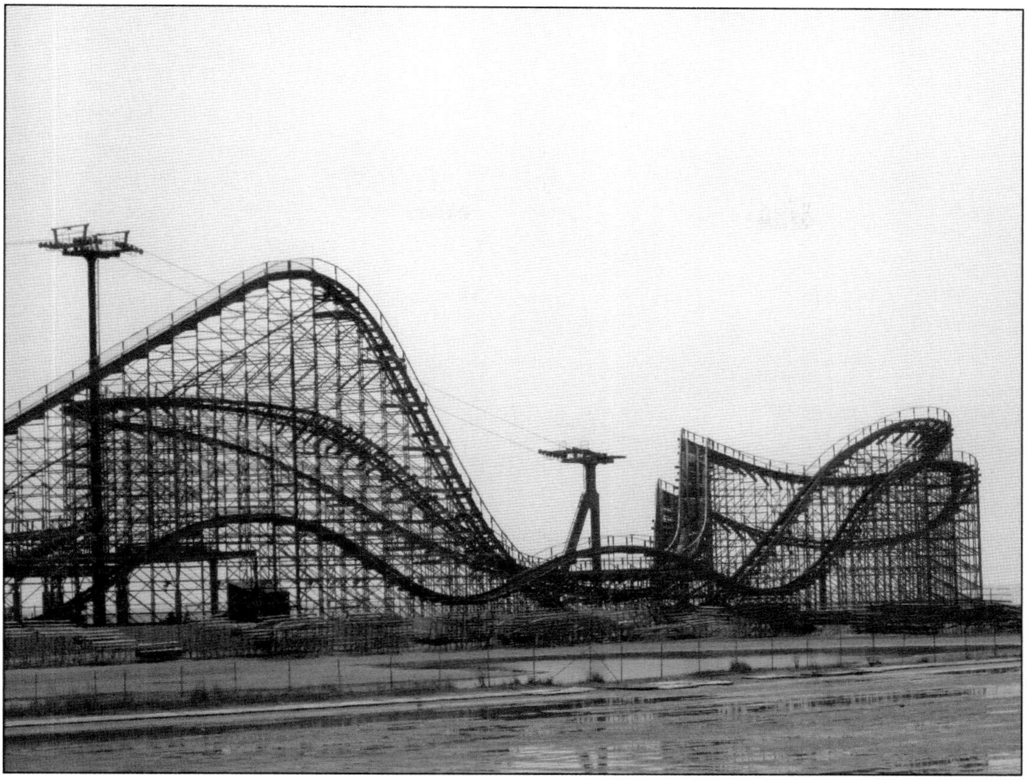

This is the eye-catching Great White on Morey's Adventure Pier. This wooden work of art was built in 1996. It is categorized as a hybrid roller coaster (it has a steel structure). The Great White has the capacity to accommodate up to 1,200 riders per hour and reaches speeds of up to 50 miles per hour. The maximum height of this roller coaster is listed as 110 feet, with a drop of 100 feet. The ride lasts two minutes. Riders must be 48 inches tall to ride this amazing wooden coaster. The Great White has been dazzling coaster enthusiasts for years and is the star attraction on Morey's Adventure Pier. (Both, courtesy Steve Oxenrider.)

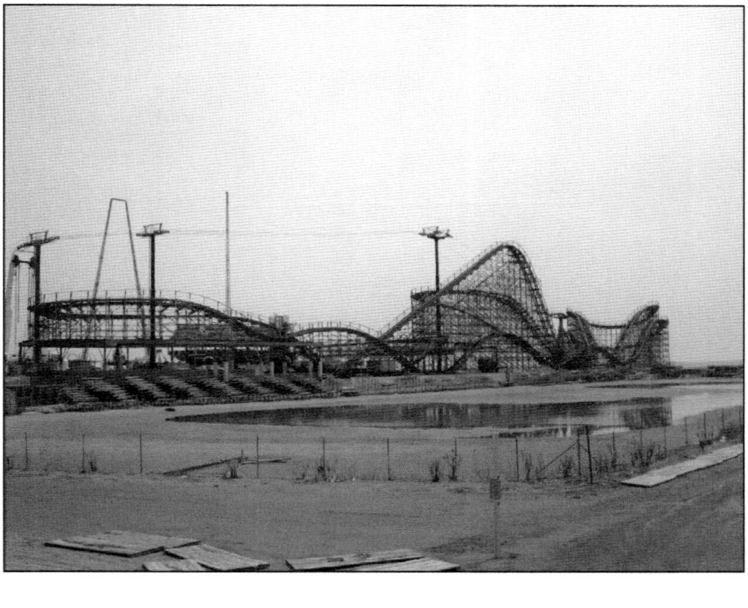

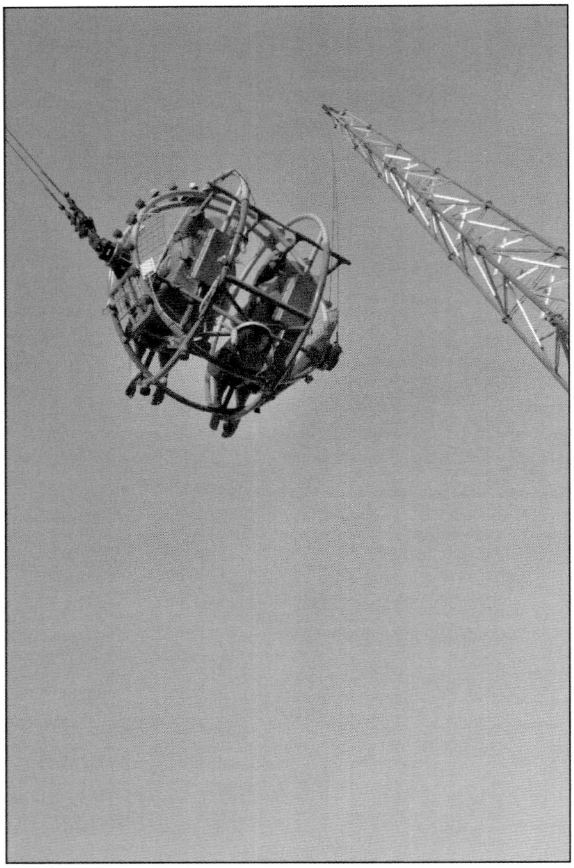

The Spring Shot was originally owned by the Catanosas. This is a real thrill ride that catapults the riders into the atmosphere. A video recorder is built into the car so that passengers can relive their reactions time and time again. The Spring Shot is manufactured by Funtime Industries. The height at the top of the launch is 320 feet with a speed of more than 75 miles per hour. This ride was installed on the pier for the 2002 season. The required height to ride the Spring Shot is 44 inches. This ultimate thrill ride is still going strong on the pier. (Both, courtesy Morey's Piers.)

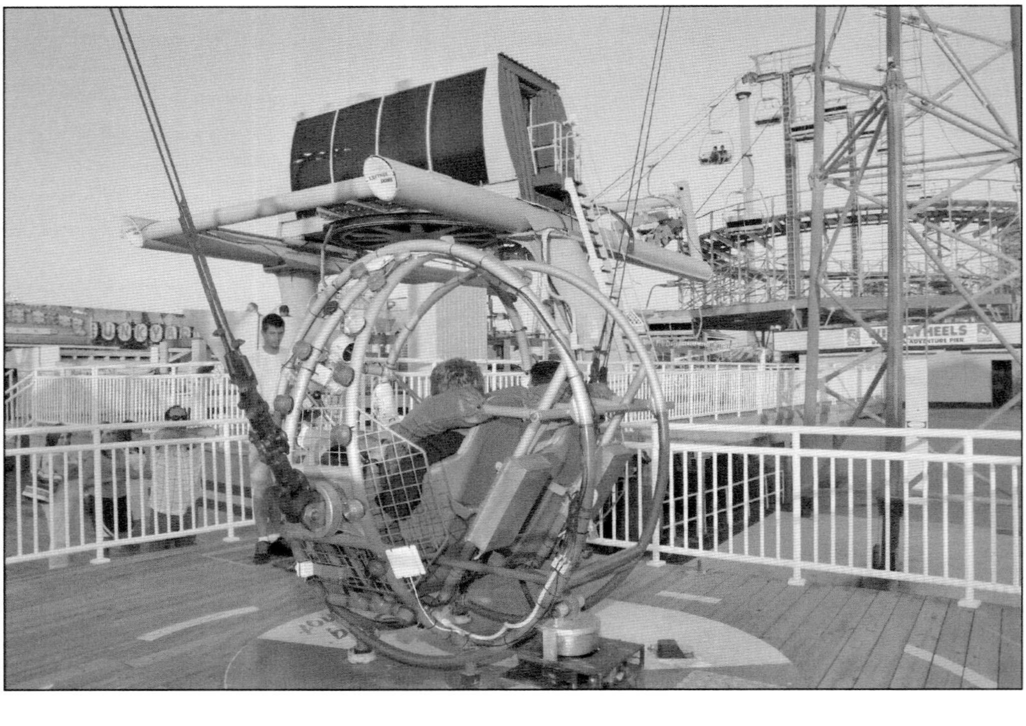

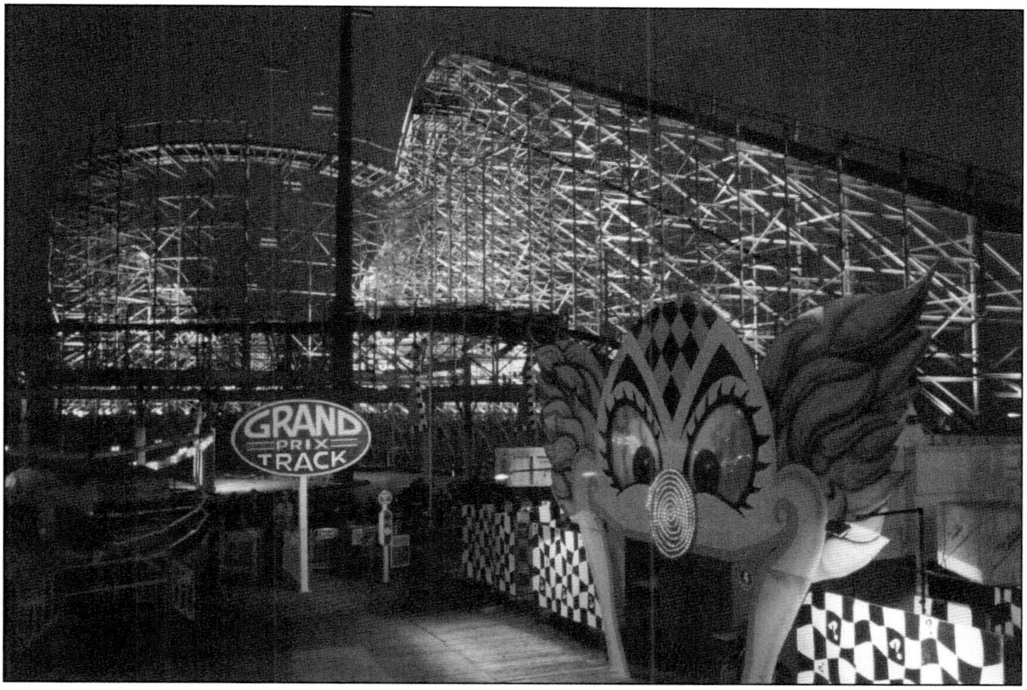

The large clown face serves as the entrance to the Chamber of Checkers on the pier. This maze has been on Morey's Adventure Pier for many years and continues to be a top family attraction today. This ride has no height restrictions and is considered a mild experience. (Courtesy Morey's Piers.)

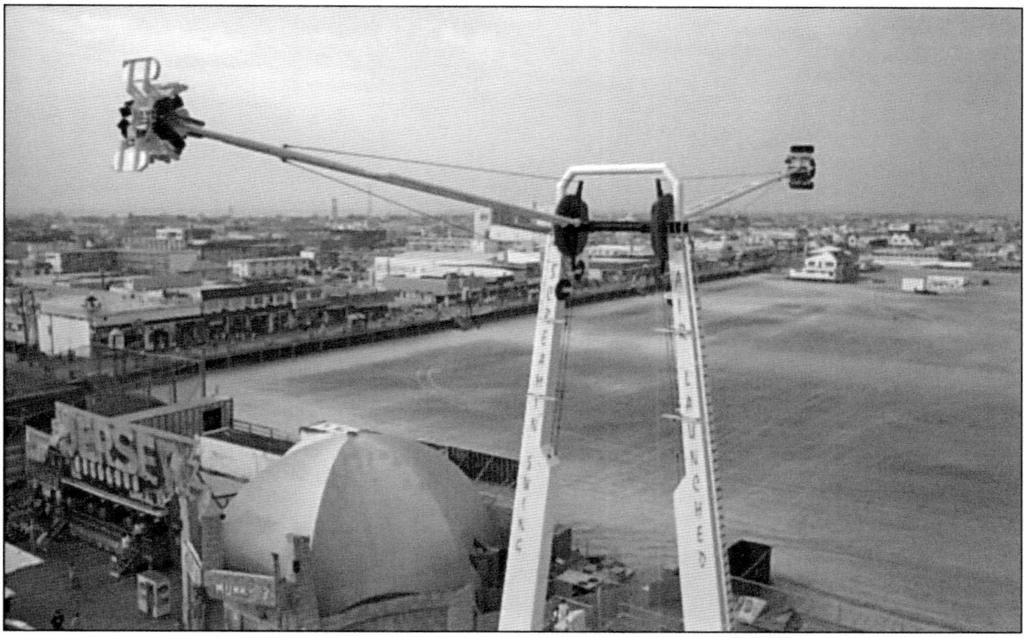

The Screamin' Swing is manufactured by S&S Power, Inc. This swing is over 60 feet tall and can seat up to eight. Customers experience g-forces of more than 4.0 as a state-of-the-art launch system propels them high into the sky. All customers must be 48 inches tall to ride the Screamin' Swing. The Screamin' Swing goes as fast as 60 miles per hour. (Courtesy Morey's Piers.)